Dirty Secret

*A Daughter Comes Clean About
Her Mother's Compulsive Hoarding*

Jessie Sholl

G

Gallery Books
New York London Toronto Sydney

Some names and identifying details have been changed.

Gallery Books
A Division of Simon & Schuster, Inc.
1230 Avenue of the Americas
New York, NY 10020

First Gallery Books trade paperback edition January 2011

GALLERY BOOKS and colophon are trademarks of Simon & Schuster, Inc.

For information about special discounts for bulk purchases,
please contact Simon & Schuster Special Sales at 1-866-506-1949 or
business@simonandschuster.com.

The Simon & Schuster Speakers Bureau can bring authors to your live event.
For more information or to book an event contact the Simon & Schuster
Speakers Bureau at 1-866-248-3049 or visit our website at
www.simonspeakers.com.

Designed by ATTIC

Manufactured in the United States of America

10   9   8   7   6   5   4   3   2   1

Library of Congress Cataloging-in-Publication Data

Sholl, Jessie.
    Dirty secret : a daughter comes clean about her mother's compulsive
hoarding / by Jessie Sholl.
        p. cm.
    1. Compulsive hoarding—United States—Case studies. 2. Sholl, Jessie.
3. Sholl, Jessie—Family. 4. Compulsive hoarding—United States—Patients—
Family relationships—Case studies. 5. Mothers and daughters—United
States—Case studies. 6. Mothers—Minnesota—Minneapolis—Biography.
7. Minneapolis (Minn.)—Biography. I. Title.
    RC569.5.H63S4 2011
    362.2'5—dc22

                                                        2010042872

ISBN 978-1-4391-9252-8
ISBN 978-1-4391-9253-5 (ebook)

Family members of compulsive hoarders can often, though not always, point to a particular trauma that occurred right before the hoarding began. It's as if there's a pattern in their brains, awaiting the right trigger to set the hoarding behavior in motion. My mother's trauma that triggered the true hoarding was Roger dying.

Throughout the rest of the day I come across photographs of her and Roger together, as well as (unopened) Mother's Day and birthday cards from me, on the floor under or among the junk piles. For a second I wonder how she could be so careless with these things.

But it isn't carelessness. It's the mental illness of compulsive hoarding. That's why she insists on keeping broken sewing machines and broken coffeemakers and a broken dishwasher hogging the last of the free space in her kitchen; that's what compels her to leave her possessions out in the open rather than on a shelf or in a drawer; and that's what leaves her frozen in place whenever she needs to make a decision—in the bank, in the grocery store, in the middle of her cluttered staircase— while she mumbles to herself, weighing the consequences of choosing X, Y, or Z. It's all because of a mystifying mental illness that happens to have a depressingly low rate of recovery.

I wish there were a magic pill or surgery or something instantaneous to fix her, but there isn't. I wish I could convince her to stop, but I can't. Not that that's going to keep me from trying.

This title is also available as an eBook

For my mother, whose only request when I asked her permission to write this book was that I employ "radical honesty."

In that spirit, here goes.

PROLOGUE

D ON'T KICK ME OUT!" MY MOTHER SAYS WHEN I PICK UP the phone. It's a little hard to understand her, though, because she's laughing so hard.

"What are you talking about?"

She can't be considering inflicting a visit on me. That is not going to happen.

"I'm putting my house in your name," my mother says. "You have to promise not to kick me out after it's yours."

"I don't want your house," I say. "You couldn't pay me to take your house."

"You have to take it." She stops laughing. "I have cancer."

My first thought: My mother is going to die.

My second thought: I can finally clean her house. She hasn't let me inside in more than three years, not since the last time I cleaned—or, rather, gutted, it.

David, my husband, is standing in the doorway between the living room and the kitchen, watching me. I mouth the words *Cancer, my mom has cancer,* but he doesn't understand. And why would he? I don't understand what's happening myself.

"Mom, please. Just tell me what's going on."

"Okay," she says, sounding suddenly drained of all energy. "I had a colonoscopy and they found a polyp and it's malignant. I have colon cancer. I want the house in your name in case the bills are higher than my insurance—that way they can't take it away."

"What did your doctor say? Tell me exactly what he said."

At this, my husband comes over and sits down next to me on the couch. He lifts our dog, Abraham Lincoln, onto my lap, thinking his presence will comfort me, but I shake my head and allow the dog to squirm off. I already feel myself floating away from here, already mentally searching for a way to fix my mother, like always.

"They won't really have a prognosis until the surgery," she says. "But with the house in your name, it'll be yours no matter what."

She says it as if she'd be bestowing the most spectacular palace upon me, rather than what her house really is: the source of so many years of frustration, embarrassment, and grief. I can't imagine anything worse than being legally responsible for that house. Except my mother having cancer.

"Jessie, will you do it?" She pleads. "Will you let me put my house in your name?"

"Will you let me clean?"

"Yes." Her lack of hesitation makes me even more worried. She must not think her chances are good.

"Okay."

* * *

MY MOTHER IS a compulsive hoarder. She's one of those people who dies because the firemen couldn't get through the piles of newspapers and clothes and books and shoes and garbage, whose junglelike lawn makes the whole block look shoddier, whose friends and neighbors are shocked when they finally see the house's interior: They had no idea their friend/daughter/nurse/teacher lived that way. They had no idea anyone could live that way. Yet an estimated six million Americans do.

I've long searched for the perfect concoction of begging, conniving, and bribing that would finally make my mother throw out the trash and keep her house clean. Because I know that if I could get her to unclutter her house, her cluttered mind would follow: Somewhere under all the filth is a reliable mother, a consistent and compassionate mother; somewhere under the heaps of moth-eaten sweaters and secondhand winter coats, the cardboard boxes kept because they're "just such good quality," the jar after jar of unopened jumbo-sized facial scrubs and green clay masks and aloe vera skin creams, the plastic forks and dirty paper plates and gum wrappers and dried-out pens and orphaned Popsicle sticks. Every surface covered, crowded with layer upon layer of *stuff*. I know she's in there; I just have to find her.

I make the preparations to fly to my hometown of Minneapolis from New York City, where I've lived for most of the last decade. I tell no one that while I'm in Minneapolis for my mother's surgery the majority of my time will be spent filling up garbage bags and hauling trash from her house, that my muscles will ache so badly I'll barely be able to lift a coffee mug to my lips, that only an hour-long soak in a scalding-hot bath at my dad and stepmom's house at the end of each day will erase the layers of filth and grime from my skin. Only my husband knows that part. I tell no one else because it's my secret. And I tell no one at all that in spite of our complicated relationship, the thought of her dying is absolutely unbearable and that if that happened I would be shattered into a million pieces and there would be no way, no one, to put me back together.

1

I TAKE AN EARLY FLIGHT AND ARRIVE IN MINNEAPOLIS IN the late morning. That afternoon my stepmom Sandy and I are meeting my mother at the lawyer's office so I can sign the papers about the house. My dad and Sandy normally have limited contact with my mother, but before I left New York, Sandy called me and offered to help in any way she could; she even agreed to let my mother sign power of attorney over to her, since I live so far away. I wish I could call my brother so he could help, but that's not an option.

When my mom arrives, Sandy and I are waiting for her in the parking lot in front of the lawyer's office. My mom gets out of her giant rusty car and I try to ignore the fact that the back-seat is piled to the ceiling with garbage bags, clothes, shoes, and God only knows what else. It's April, and warm for a Minneapolis spring. My mother's in one of her signature knee-length sweater-coats, the baggy black leggings she's taken to wearing in the last few years, and a roomy pale blue T-shirt, or as she says in her lingering Boston accent, "a jersey." Her keys hang on an orange plastic coil around her neck. Her curly hair is completely gray now—sometimes she dyes it brown or auburn—and cut in a chin-length bob, with bangs. It looks pretty decent for cutting it herself.

"You look good, Mom," I say, leaning down to hug her. At under five feet, she's the only adult I know that I have to lean down to hug. "How are you feeling?"

"Not too bad," my mom says and takes a sip of what I'm sure is coffee from her ever-present travel mug. Right after she called me with the news about her cancer I went online and found out that the statistics for colon cancer are good. Really good. And now, seeing how plump and healthy she looks, I'm even less worried. Then again, both of her parents died of cancer. So I'm worried, but not panicked.

"Thanks for coming, Sandy," my mother says, sounding shy.

"Of course," Sandy says and squeezes my mom's shoulder.

Inside the small office, the lawyer: blond, pretty, and hugely pregnant, is waiting for us at the reception desk.

"Right this way," she says, her Minnesotan vowels elongated as she adds, "How're you guys doing?"

"Good, okay, fine," we say, and take our seats around a conference table in a windowless room. A small stack of papers sits in front of each of us.

"Does anyone want coffee?" the lawyer asks, and my mother accepts, topping off the contents of her travel mug. My mom drinks two or three pots of coffee a day and nothing else. She hates water, which I've been trying to get her to drink for years. She won't touch it. Just like the vitamins I've bought her, just like the leafy green vegetables I nag her about. And she's the one who's a nurse. She picks up her travel mug by wrapping both her tiny hands around it and takes a big sip.

I wonder what the lawyer thinks of us. She seems like the most normal of creatures; it's hard to imagine that she's encountered such a strange repackaging of a family. A daughter owning her mother's house? The ex-husband's wife holding power of attorney? Then again, maybe it doesn't seem so strange. At thirty-seven, I have friends my age who are beginning to make choices for their aging parents. Because my mother's and my roles were reversed early on, I probably shouldn't be rattled by this new, official responsibility. But when I glance down at the stack of papers in front of me, it takes all my self-control to keep from jumping up and pacing.

My mother, on the other hand, appears as relaxed as I've ever seen her. She's smacking her gum and sipping her coffee as happily as if she's just found a treasure trove of misshapen wool sweaters or a bundle of dog-eared twenty-five-cent detective novels at her favorite thrift store, Savers. I know she likes the idea of not having to be responsible for herself anymore. Like the time she called me at my dad's when I was nine, demanding that I come up with the money to pay her outrageous water bill, since I was the one who must've left the hose on the last time I was there. I laughed, thinking she was joking, and she hung up on me. It turned out the bill was so high because my mother hadn't paid it in months. But what stayed with me afterward was the relief in her voice at having come up with a "solution" before she bothered to call the water company and work out the problem herself. It was the same relief I heard in her voice the following year, when I told her I didn't want to live with her every other week anymore and that from then on I'd be living with my dad and Sandy full-time.

The lawyer tells Sandy which papers to sign and explains that she should keep them in a safe if she has one.

And then it's my turn. In one sense, it might be good for me to have the house in my name—that way I could force my mom to finally sell it and move into a condo. But the idea of that house in my name is too repellant. My hands won't move toward the papers.

"I can't do it," I say, and at that moment I recognize a way out. "David and I have low-income health insurance. With a house in my name we wouldn't qualify anymore."

I have no idea if we'd actually be disqualified—I just know I don't want that house. I really, really, really do not want that house.

"You have to," my mother whisper-orders, her hazel eyes opened wide.

"No I don't. I can't."

The lawyer looks unfazed. Maybe it's the pregnancy hormones. "How about this," she says and suggests we sign the papers and leave them in her office without filing them. We can file them later if it becomes necessary.

"Okay," I say and sign them.

And just like that, my mother goes back to smacking her gum and sipping her coffee, a pleased half smile across her face.

After the lawyer's office, we go to a coffee shop to discuss my mother's postsurgery plans. For about the hundredth time in the last few years, I suggest that my mother sell her house and buy a condo. Partly it's for selfish reasons: The smaller the space, the easier it'll be for me to clean during visits. Plus, in a condo the yardwork and repairs would be taken care of.

"Helen, I think that's a great idea," Sandy says. "I can help you find something."

Sandy and my dad are Realtors, with their own company and a few agents who work for them; they occasionally buy a house, fix it up, and try to sell it for a profit, with my dad doing all the carpenter-type duties.

"No," my mom says. "I'm happy in the house. I'm staying."

"That house is way too big for you," I say. It's got four bedrooms and a large backyard that as far as I know hasn't encountered a lawn mower in years. Besides, the only bathroom is on the second floor and it's not clear if my mother will be able to climb stairs after the surgery.

"How much could I get for it?" my mother asks Sandy. As soon as she hears the answer she starts shaking her head. "I know it's worth more! A house two blocks away sold for twice that last week!"

"I know that house, Helen—it was sold by one of my agents. No offense, but your house just isn't in that kind of condition."

"Should we go to Savers next?" my mom asks. "It's ninety-nine-cent day. Everything with a yellow tag."

"Mom, are you listening? What are we going to do about your house?"

"Maybe I'll go look at the cakes," my mom says. "I'm in the mood for something sweet."

She scrambles to get out of the chair, her movements clumsy and deliberate. She has the gait of someone just released from an iron lung, someone with equilibrium problems. At sixty-three, she moves with the grace, agility, and speed of a ninety-three-year-old. Or, to be fair to ninety-three-year-olds, maybe a 103-year-old. Sandy and I watch her hobble up to the counter. She's wearing sneakers, as always, and her already giant feet (I've got them, too) have spread even wider after years of back-to-back nursing shifts. I try to take some deep breaths, but the frustration over my mom's reluctance to even consider selling her house roils inside me. Not to mention the dread I feel about having to clean it. Again. I have to admit, though, there's another part of me that's excited—maybe this time it'll work. Maybe this time it'll stay clean.

"Are you okay?" Sandy asks me. "You must be worried about her."

"I am." I look down at my hands; I'm tearing my napkin into strips. "And I just wish I could get her to be serious for a second."

Right then my mom returns to the table, empty-handed.

"Oh, Jessie," she says, "I know what I'll do. I'll buy a van, one of those step vans!"

"What's a step van?" I ask.

"One of those vans that you step into! I'll buy one and I'll drive it to Florida."

"And then?" I ask. My mother is a terrifyingly slow driver. I've walked a mile in a Minnesota winter rather than drive somewhere with her. And even in a normal car she requires two phone books to see over the dash. There's no way she can drive across the country in a van by herself.

"And then I'll live in the van," she says.

"Mom, come on. I need to make sure you're going to be okay. You do have some kind of retirement fund, right?"

I've never been able to get a straight answer out of my mother regarding her money situation. For years my dad and I have speculated about her savings. Her expenses are so minimal—the house is paid off, she drives a used car, never takes vacations—that she must have something saved from all the years of overtime at the nursing home. She must, we say, have hundreds of thousands of dollars stashed away in a mattress. It was what her father did, after all.

Just before her cancer diagnosis she was fired from the nursing home for being too slow. It wasn't fair, she said, the people she worked with were so much younger, mostly in their twenties and thirties; they could just fly down the hallways while she struggled, and often didn't succeed, to finish her duties before she had to punch out. So she began punching out and then continuing to work, hoping no one would notice. But they did notice. She was warned, more than once, that she had to finish her work *during* her shift. But she couldn't keep up.

It was only because she was unemployed that she had time for the checkup that led to the colonoscopy that revealed the colon cancer. And since I'm the one who insisted she get health insurance a few years back, she says I've saved her life. Assuming she survives the surgery, and I'm definitely assuming she's going to survive the surgery. So I need to know how she's planning to live. She won't qualify for social security for two more years.

"The house *is* my retirement," she says now, taking a sip of her coffee. "Jessie, this is cold. Will you ask them to heat this up?"

"Just answer me. Do you have a 401k?"

"Oh, yeah, yeah, don't worry." She waves away my ridiculous concern. "I've got a plan."

"Good. What's the plan, Helen?" Sandy says.

My mother leans forward, her eyes glistening with excitement. "Cat beds!"

I drop my head into my hands, groaning, as my mother continues.

"These beds are like wicker baskets with pillows in them . . . and then the cats lie down and sleep in them!"

"Mom, be serious! This is about your future."

"These cat beds *are* my future. They're going to be so gorgeous, you just wouldn't believe!"

"Do you realize that beds for cats already exist?" I ask.

She shakes her head. "I've never seen them anywhere."

"Where did you get this idea, then?"

She leans back in her chair and is silent for a few seconds. "Okay. I do have another plan. I'm suing those motherfuckers who fired me! That was ageism and they can't get away with it."

"But you've been getting complaints at work for years," I say. "The work was too much."

"I don't care. What they did was illegal and those motherfuckers are going to pay. Just wait!"

EARLY THE NEXT morning my dad drives me to my mom's house on his way to check out one of Sandy's listings. Today is supposed to be the one day my mother and I will both be in the house while I'm cleaning, which will give me a chance to ask her before I throw out anything I'm uncertain about. Tomorrow she's going into the hospital for one last quick test and then the surgery—we'll learn her prognosis a day or two after that. I intend to finish as much of the cleaning as I can while my mom is in the hospital recovering; then I'll stay in Minneapolis for a few days after she's out, so I can help when she first goes home.

We pull up to the curb. The exterior of the house is the worst I've seen it—the paint peeling, some parts of the enclosed front porch piled to the ceiling with furniture, boxes, and giant empty picture frames. And that's just what I can see from here. But I'm going to do this, no matter what. This is my chance. I say goodbye to my dad and climb out of the car. The lawn is a foot high and the unruly bush plopped right in the middle of it at least six feet across. I quicken my pace as I walk up the narrow sidewalk and then the front steps. I open the creaky glass door and duck inside the porch, hoping no one has seen me. I don't want to be associated with the junk house.

A neglected heap of mail, who knows how many days' worth,

lies scattered under the slot. The red carpeting, in the few places I can actually see it, appears to have been splattered Pollock-style with motor oil. Two beat-up, three-speed bicycles lean precariously against one of the windows. In the corner stands a vintage washing tub, the kind where clothes are squeezed through a wringer. And in another corner there's something black and twisted, no, *coiled*—ohmygod, ohmyfuckinggod—

—it's a snake.

I'm out the door, down the steps, and to the sidewalk in a millisecond. At the curb, I lean over at the waist, taking shallow hiccuppy breaths. I don't even care who drives past—if it's a choice between being associated with the junk house or facing one of those hellish creatures, I'd happily tattoo across my forehead that I belong to the junk house. On the other hand, I don't want to give my mother the satisfaction of seeing me like this. I pull my cell phone from my purse and dial my husband. He'll know what I should do. He'll understand.

But he doesn't answer.

And I really can't put this off. I only have five cleaning days here and if the house is anywhere near as bad as last time, that may not be enough.

I force myself up the steps. Getting my eyes to look at the snake is another challenge. But somehow I manage. And maybe I'm at a better angle, but now I can see that what I thought was a snake is actually a pile of oil-black rags. A twisted pile of rags. Thank God. I feel the dizziness leave my head, as if clearing out a room's stale air by opening windows; my lungs expand, drawing deeper breaths.

I open the door and once again step inside the porch. Two crumbling armoires take up half of one wall. Boxes and paper bags are stacked all around and on top of them. This mess looks somehow familiar. And then I recognize it: Like stumbling upon the remains of a village buried by lava, the evidence of my last cleanup attempt lives on underneath. She was supposed to arrange for the Salvation Army to get the armoires. Ditto for the bags of old sweaters and the sets of inflatable furniture.

The glass part of the house's heavy front door is covered with a bamboo shade, so I can't see inside. I press the doorbell. My mother opens the door and steps forward onto the porch, pulling the door closed behind her so I won't come in.

"Oh, Jessie, let's go to Perkins before you start cleaning. I want some of their pancakes."

"Let me see the house," I say.

She freezes. I push the door open a few inches and steal a look behind her: The hallway is packed with stacks of even more ignored mail—her phone gets shut off on a semiregular basis because she can't find the bills—two ironing boards, a mound of ratty looking sweaters, winter boots and coats and snow pants heaped directly underneath an empty metal coatrack, at least one box of marshmallow Peeps, milk-colored storage bins that I know without checking are empty, an oversized plastic pail containing ironic jugs of Lysol and Pine-Sol, and dozens of unopened white plastic Savers bags with the receipts still stapled to the top.

I push past her, to the narrow path in the center of the hallway. It reminds me of the winters here, when people are too lazy to shovel their whole sidewalk.

"Christ, where do I start?" I ask no one, already overwhelmed. The last time I cleaned, three years ago, my husband was here helping me.

During a visit to Minneapolis, my mom had asked us to help her move a dresser. I hadn't seen the inside of her house in a few years, not since before Roger, her boyfriend of a decade, died. When David and I went in, I almost couldn't believe what I was seeing—while her house had always been messy and crowded with things I considered useless, the clutter had entered the realm of the pathological: plates full of hard-as-a-rock spaghetti, smashed up takeout bags from Taco Bell and Burger King, coffee mugs with an inch of solidified *something* on the bottom, containers of motor oil, calculators and flashlights and key chains still in their packaging, knitting needles, magazines, bunches of brown bananas, and fast-food soda cups bleeding brown stickiness down the sides took up every inch of the kitchen table and the counter. The sink was piled high with dishes and an open garbage bag in the corner overflowed with paper plates. If she'd switched to paper plates, I thought, how long had those dishes been in the sink?

"What's going on?" I asked her. "Why does your house look this bad?"

"I'm busy. I don't have time to clean."

I knew that was true; she was working as many doubles as the nursing home would let her. But still. "You can't be so busy that you have to throw Popsicle sticks on the floor," I said, pointing at a cluster on the other side of the doorway, in the living room. "Why can't you put them in the trash? This place is an absolute disaster."

"Oh, it's fine," she said.

"Tell me the truth. You really don't see anything wrong here?"

She shook her head. "It's not perfect, but it's not too bad."

All four burners on the stove were stacked with dirty pans, and the stove itself was crusted with grease that was cracked in places like a topographical map of the continents before they split apart.

"When was the last time you cooked?" I asked. My husband hadn't said anything; he probably had no idea *what* to say.

"I don't know," my mother answered. "I only liked to cook for Roger."

Family members of hoarders can often point to a particular trauma that occurred right before the hoarding began (though most hoarders show signs of it from an earlier age, often in their teens). My mother had always been a compulsive thrift-store shopper, and untidy and disorganized, but when I saw her house that day for the first time since Roger died, I knew this was different. And it wasn't just the trash everywhere. Her kitchen seemed utterly unusable, for one thing, and it was hard to walk from one room to the next. I'd heard the word "hoarder" in association with the famous Collyer brothers, and I suppose it stayed in my mind because I subconsciously suspected my mother was on the road to being one too—after all, as soon as she and my dad split up when I was seven, I began doing the cleaning, and as a kid I'd spend my summers weeding her front garden and planting flowers so my fellow students at the school across the street wouldn't guess at the mess inside.

But what I saw that day was a whole new level of clutter. Clearly, Roger's death had triggered my mother's true hoarding. And what disturbed me most was that she couldn't even tell.

Over the next few months I kept picturing her in that house, alone. So my husband and I came up with a plan. We usually visited Minneapolis once in the winter and once for a long weekend each summer; we decided that the next summer we'd extend our long weekend by a few days and clean her house.

David and I arrived, full of purpose, determined. But my mother was uncooperative—I had to explain each and every item I wanted to get rid of and she fought me on almost everything. Still, we ended up driving seven loads of stuff to the Salvation Army in her car and leaving a mound of full trash bags out by her garbage bins in the alley. When we left, the house was better, but it wasn't done. Somehow I managed, though, to push her house to the bottom of my priority list. Until the cancer. Until now.

"Honey, come on, I'll make some coffee. We'll sit and visit," my mother says, excited again. "Just for a few minutes. Please."

I follow her into the kitchen. But none of her three coffee-makers work.

"I know you don't go a day without coffee," I say, "so how have you been making it?"

"That one just broke," she says, pointing to an industrial-sized machine that looks like it was once white. "Oh, Jessie, now we *have* to go to Perkins!"

"The problem is, I need to start. There's a lot to organize, and Joe's showing up at one o'clock." Joe does construction and lawn work for my dad and I've arranged for him to help me haul the heavier items outside. At the end of the day another guy is coming with a truck to take the stuff away.

"Do you think Joe would help cut down this tree in the back-yard?" my mom asks.

"Tree? What tree?"

"Wait a minute, Jessie, I've got something to tell you. You know how they say there are no atheists in foxholes?" she asks, a laugh already starting to crack her voice, "I'm proof that that's not true! I'm still an atheist!"

"Good for you, Mom. Now what about that tree? What tree are you talking about?" Good Lord, I'm a humorless bitch. But someone has to take care of business and it certainly isn't going to be her.

"It's just this branch that's been growing against the house. It's not a problem." She waves it off. How does a "branch" grow against a house? I walk past her, toward the back door, which is blocked by empty paper grocery bags, more plastic bins, dirty dish rags, rolls of paper towels, the skeletons of shelving units she never got around to properly installing, giant metal pots still in boxes, and full bags of garbage I don't even want to guess the ages of. She stands behind me, watching as I try to get through it all.

"Oh, Jessie, the lock on the back door is broken. Do you think your dad and Sandy know a good locksmith?"

"I'll ask them tonight. Although I can't see why anyone would want to break in," I add, rudely. I can't help it. Most people, I imagine anyway, whose mothers are about to undergo surgery for cancer have visits where they get to know each other better or discuss fond memories or whatever it is that normal families do. I, on the eve of my mother's surgery, get to begin cleaning out her junk-filled house because she can't. The one bright side to this is that I'm too busy to worry about the cancer.

She's not offended by my rudeness, anyway. "I know, you can think of all this stuff as a burglar deterrent! It's my own free version of home security!"

As she laughs hysterically, I finally make it through the pantry and open the back door. She follows me out.

It is indeed a tree and it's growing right against the house. To my untrained eye it looks big enough to crack the foundation if left untended. The whole yard looks like something out of *Wild Kingdom*: There should be lions and tigers prowling the lawn, hunting prey. It was once a beautiful backyard, with neatly cut emerald-green grass, two lilac trees that every spring and summer filled the air with their purple scent, and a long garden running the length of it. Someone has put planks of wood down where the garden once was, which is odd because it's right up against the metal fence that divides my mother's lawn from the neighbor's. What is the purpose of the wood? It's like a shabby catwalk to nowhere. And the two lilac trees look like something you'd see in a movie involving a haunted forest with evil foliage that comes to life and strangles passersby. At the back of it all, the rickety, paint-flaking garage looks about to tip over.

"And there're those, too," my mom says, pointing at the rain gutters running up the side of the house to the roof. "Could he do those?"

They're totally rusted through in places, hanging off the house like a trapeze artist flailing in the wind. Then I notice the trim around the windows: The wood is coming apart from the house—it's as if nothing wants to be part of this decaying landscape. And I don't blame any of it. I don't want to be here either.

"Jesus Christ," I say.

"Oh, Jessie—" my mom says. "I just remembered something. The dryer guy is coming tomorrow."

"What dryer guy? What's wrong with your dryer?"

"It hasn't worked in over a year."

"How have you been drying your clothes?"

"I've been going to the Laundromat," she says, shrugging. "But I don't think I'll be able to get there with my clothes while I'm recovering from the surgery. . . ."

"What's your basement like right now?" I doubt a stranger should go down there.

"It's fine," she says, a nervous smile on her face.

She's lying. She brought it up for a reason. I need to make sure it's in decent shape. Except there's a problem: I haven't been able to go down to her basement in well over a decade. Even imagining entering that musty jungle makes my skin crawl. I'm not sure I can do it.

But someone has to. What my mother refuses to believe is that her house is borderline condemnable. If she needs private nurses to come in and care for her after the surgery, they could report her to social services. She could be taken from her house;

her house could be taken from her. I've told her this many times, but she just laughs and tells me I'm being ridiculous. The cleaning charts, the suggestions about Clutterers Anonymous meetings, my nagging these last few years about getting a retirement fund: all ridiculous.

It's a miracle that she finally listened to me about getting health insurance.

"Let's get started so we can be ready for Joe when he gets here," I say, intending to put off the basement for as long as possible. My mother huffs up the back steps ahead of me.

Inside, she says she needs coffee and threatens to go to Perkins without me.

"That's fine—you go, and I'll stay here and get started," I say, and she waddles out the front door. It'll be easier for me to work without her here, anyway.

I decide to start in the living room. I pick up one of the white plastic Savers bags and tear the stapled receipt off the top so I can open it. Inside is a pair, no, two pairs, of those sneakers that have no back on them—the clog meets the sneaker. The white fabric is vaguely gray. I pick up another bag and the contents are identical, except this time it's three pairs. Then another bag, again with two pairs. I don't even know where to put anything; I just shove the sneaker-clogs into a garbage bag and hope that she won't find them. The room is crowded with paperback and hardcover books, five sewing machines with hundreds of sewing patterns heaped on top, two foot massagers still in their boxes, a water-jet-infused bath mat, three electric heating pads that look secondhand, old magazine clippings of restaurant and book reviews, two banged-up motorcycle helmets, at least eight pairs of moldy cowboy boots my mother's convinced she can sell for *a fortune,* two three-foot-tall antique radios—the wood scratched and warped—hulking in one corner like bullies.

Half-consumed boxes of Entenmann's donuts and empty soda bottles and flattened Lean Cuisine boxes and crinkled candy wrappers.

Toward the top of the wall, almost to the ceiling, the plate rail supports half a dozen of those round tin containers that butter cookies come in. There's a tin embossed with the image of two Scottie dogs facing each other, a red one with white stars circling the edge, a rusty one that was originally pink, one with a fat snowman and snowwoman surrounded by snowchildren, and two identical tins with a Rosie the Riveter–type character flexing her muscles. Scattered between the round tins are miniature perfume bottles, many of which I gave my mother when I was a kid, back when she was still a "collector." They're relics of a road veered wildly off.

Tears spring to my eyes and I wipe them away with the back of my hand. I'm suddenly so exhausted that if there were anywhere for me to sit down in this room, in this whole house, I'd collapse right there. But I can't. Because every surface, every potential spot to sit down, is covered with junk. There's just so much junk, so much worthless, heartbreaking junk.

THE GENERALLY ACCEPTED definition of hoarding comes from a 1996 article by doctors Randy Frost and Tamara Hartl: "The acquisition of and failure to discard possessions that are useless or of limited value, resulting in clutter that renders living spaces unusable and causes significant distress and impairment." Hoarding was once thought to mainly afflict people who'd grown up in deprived circumstances—the Great Depression, for example—but most hoarding experts no longer subscribe to that theory. Therapists have treated hoarders as young as three, and their problem didn't necessarily come from watching an afflicted parent. Studies have shown that genetics is more of a factor in the disorder than mimicking behavior—in fact 85 percent of hoarders have a first-degree relative they'd describe as a pack rat. Besides, if hoarding were caused by trying to make up for a previous lack, wouldn't hoarders keep only items they could use? Instead, they often keep things the rest of us find nonsensical, like newspapers from the past twenty years or my mother's many sneaker-clogs.

Initially hoarding was considered a symptom of obsessive-compulsive disorder, like counting or frequent hand washing—since up to 30 percent of people with OCD have hoarding issues. But brain scans of hoarders reveal decreased activity in areas related to memory, decision making, spatial orientation, and emotions. As a result of those brain scan studies, and the fact that medications effective for OCD provide no benefit for hoarders, many specialists in the field are beginning to look at compulsive hoarding as its own discrete syndrome, most likely caused by brain abnormalities.

My mother clearly has problems with spatial orientation and memory: That's why all of her possessions have to be kept out in the open, while most of her shelves and drawers remain empty. That's why rather than an address book for phone numbers, my mother has scraps of paper taped to the door between the hallway and the kitchen. She's got three of my last phone numbers and addresses taped there, yet still, when she has to call me back for some reason or send me something in the mail, she asks each and every time for my information all over again.

BY THE TIME she comes home from Perkins, I've made some piles and cleared a patch of the hardwood floor. I've filled two garbage bags with junk. My mother doesn't ask to see what's in the garbage bags—as if once something is out of her sight it no longer exists—but she immediately starts rummaging through the piles that are out in the open.

"Jessie, I need these!" she says, holding up a mismatched pair of elbow pads.

"Why?"

"For when I start rollerblading. And these!" she says, grabbing a second pair.

"So you need all seven pairs I've found so far, then?"

"Yes."

"No, you don't," I say, and eventually I'm able to convince her to get rid of three pairs. Which seems pretty good, considering.

When Joe shows up, I put him in charge of emptying out my mother's car, which is the second front for the hoarding. It looks the same as yesterday: the backseat piled high with books, bags of trash, the ubiquitous Savers bags, loose papers, stuffed animals, shoes, jackets, and hats. Within her hearing, I ask Joe to put everything on the grassy boulevard next to the curb and to try to group things into piles of similar items that my mother and I will sort later—then secretly I tell him to throw out anything perishable or trashed. He can use his own judgment. I don't have time to ask my mom before tossing everything. Besides, I fear she'd find some reason for needing each precious object.

In one corner of the living room, near the sewing machines, I come upon a nest of paper bags, each filled with yarn of various thicknesses and colors. The bags sit on top of empty plastic bins.

"What's going on over here?" I ask. It looks a little more organized than the rest of the room. I pull a spool of midnight blue yarn from one of the bags.

"This is my art corner," she says. "Ooh! Pick out your three favorite colors of yarn!"

"Why?" I'm already suspicious. One of the reasons she has so many possessions is that she fancies herself an artist or inventor of sorts. Many hoarders do. As the authors of *Buried in Treasures,* the doctors Tolin, Frost, and Steketee, write: ". . . people who hoard often come up with idea after idea, saving things for all kinds of creative reasons but never following through with those plans. They have become victims of their own creativity." My mother spent close to a year trying to crochet a bikini for me even though I told her a hundred times that I would never wear a bikini at all, and especially not a crocheted one. But she ignored me and continued working on it, pulling it apart and starting over each time she discovered a flaw. That's what she does: obsess over a project, trying to get it absolutely perfect, and when she can't get it just right, she falls into a depression and finally stops. Even after she's abandoned the project, though, she can't get rid of the supplies for it, "just in case."

"Wait until you see these, Jessie—they're going to be incredible!"

"What are they? What's going to be incredible?"

"GATORS!"

"What's a gator?"

"You don't know what a gator is?" she says, stroking a spool of yarn as if it's a kitten. "That's hysterical!"

"So what is it, then?"

"It's a neck scarf . . . it's like a tube that goes around your neck—like a turtleneck, but without the shirt."

"Okay . . ." I say and start piling the yarn into the plastic bins. At least that way I can stack them, which will clear a little floor space.

Later, after I've returned to New York, she'll call me with

a new plan: "Oh, Jessie, I've come up with a great idea for my gators! African women!"

"Why would African women need gators?"

"They don't *need* gators. They're going to help me make the gators. You know how there are so many starving African tribes? I'm going to recruit them to work on my gators."

"Mom. You cannot be serious."

"I'm completely serious. They need work and I need workers."

"So basically you want to start a sweatshop of African women to make gators for you."

"Well . . ." she pauses for a long time. "Yes."

"Good luck with that," I say, and though it's months before she stops talking about them, she eventually downgrades her plan to making the gators herself and selling them from her front porch.

Hoarders' creativity can be a curse in another way as well: It makes categorization—a key part of organizing—a serious challenge. They'll spot something unique about each item and end up with many different categories containing just one object. For example, instead of forty toothbrushes, the hoarder will see one category for the blue toothbrush, one category for the red toothbrush, one category for the sparkly silver toothbrush, and so on. Since each item is one of a kind, it automatically has more value, and it can't be grouped with anything, which makes it arduous to say the least, when I find a stack of newspapers that my mom claims she "must have kept for a reason," because each one has to be scrutinized individually.

Not that creativity is the only reason she hoards. When I come upon an entire dresser drawer filled with eyeglasses, I ask my mother why she has so many pairs. Some are mangled, missing parts, or have cracked lenses.

I half expect her to tell me she's going to become an optometrist or that she's going to start a mail-order business specifically for used glasses. But, instead, her answer is simple.

"I might need them someday."

"This many pairs?"

"You never know."

"You couldn't possibly have gotten these from an eye doctor—are they even your prescription?"

"Give me those," she says, snatching the pair I'm holding in my hand. She swaps them with the ones she was already wearing. "They're fine. It's a waste of money to go to the eye doctor. If they work, they work."

"Yeah, okay, but why would you need *all* of these?"

"I told you. I might need them someday."

"How about if I get rid of half of them?"

"No," she says, her voice firm.

Okay. She's not going to budge on those, and at least they're put away. I move on to the next thing.

Much of my mother's clutter is comprised of gifts for people, gifts that she never got around to sending or simply lost track of in the mess. Still, she manages to keep track of enough of them to waste a ton of time and money sending me things: special egg-cooking devices, digital watches, and every kind of book light known to man. And since she doesn't trust the regular mail, she spends excessive amounts on UPS or, if she's slumming it, priority mail. I've begged her to stop, but she won't. No matter how many times I've told her how small my apartment is and that I don't need or want anything, she continues to send things—things that I almost always end up donating to the Housing Works store down the street.

Some hoarders have a hypersentimental attachment to their possessions; for example not wanting to get rid of a box a gift came in because that would be erasing, or at least tarnishing, the memory of the day the person received the gift. Some hoarders anthropomorphize items and take the item's feelings into account—*This empty plastic bag would be hurt if it knew it was so worthless that it was in the trash.* While my mother doesn't do either of these, she does have most of the other traits that contribute to the disorder: compulsive shopping (in her case thrift-store shopping), organization problems, indecisiveness, and perfectionism. My mother is so afraid of throwing something away now that she might need later—in other words, making the wrong decision—that she'd rather make no decision at all. Also, like many hoarders, my mother reports feeling safer when she's surrounded by her possessions, as if she can insulate herself from the dangers of the world with *things.*

Even though she's more amenable than the last time I cleaned, over the next few hours my mother edges toward a breakdown as she watches me piling her belongings into garbage bags, with the salvageable items going out to the porch for donation back to Savers. She practically cries when I find another stash of inflatable furniture and put it in the donate pile.

"I need those!" she says. "I'm going to use them, once I get everything set up."

"These are for kids," I say. "They aren't even big enough for you."

"I don't care. I'll make it work. *Please* don't make me throw them away."

"You can keep one piece. Not a whole set."

"But I need at least two pieces! A chair and one of the little couches."

"Fine," I say. "Two pieces. But that's it."

As the afternoon gets later and later, I realize that I can't put off the basement any longer. The last time we cleaned, my husband took a look around and said it wasn't that bad. This time I have no choice but to see for myself.

I take a tentative step down the stairs; they're so weak that I'm sure if I stomped hard enough I could break right through the wood. I hear my mother's voice all those times saying, "Don't go down to the basement," as she formed her fingers in a circle the size of a basketball, "There are snakes down there this wide that will eat you."

Thinking about it brings a perfect picture to my mind: a snake's giant, triangular head aimed directly at me. It was what I saw the day my mother brought me inside one of the buildings at Como Park Zoo, covered my eyes, and walked me over to a "surprise." She pulled her hand away right as a giant snake flicked its tongue at me, just on the other side of the glass.

She laughed and I screamed. The following year she left a rubber snake in my Christmas stocking. After she stopped doing Christmas stockings, she'd just randomly present toy snakes to me or leave them lying around for me to find. Begging her to stop the snake-teasing seems to simply encourage the behavior. The only explanation I can come up with is that it's another form of hoarding—letting go of the "joke" is as difficult for her as letting go of her unnecessary belongings.

But regardless of why my mother does it, I'm now absolutely terrified of snakes. I don't mean just a little afraid. My fear is phobic level, without question. The one time in recent years that I encountered an actual snake was when David and I were hiking in the Czech Republic and came across a fat one sunning itself in the middle of our trail. I burst into tears, refused to take another step, and seriously considered canceling the rest of the trip. Eventually poor David had to pull me past the revolting muscular coil—which I just knew was about to strike at any second—with my eyes closed.

That's why I haven't been down to the basement in so long. I try to clear my mind of the slithering images as I take another step, descending lower and lower, until I'm at the bottom.

Dozens of pale blue nursing uniforms my mother found at Savers hang from nails in the ceiling. I half-expect the ghostly uniforms to begin swaying, but there's no air down here. The musty, moldy scent is strong enough to remind me that the rest of the house doesn't smell bad at all. I suppose that's one good thing. In the center of the cement floor sits a four-foot-high pyramid of mildewy sweaters, looking like a bonfire ready to be lit, and that's exactly what I'd like to do, because life would be so much easier if I could just burn this whole house down.

That's when I hear it.

A low, sibilant "Ssss . . ." and then again, louder, "Ssss . . ."

My mother is standing at the top of the stairs, hissing down at me.

"Funny, Mom!" I yell and she doubles over in laughter, then immediately straightens up, looks me in the eyes, and does it again: "Sssss . . ."

I'm up the stairs and out of the house in seconds. I vow to never speak to her again. Let her clean her own disgusting house. But even as I'm pacing back and forth on the sidewalk, wishing I still smoked because I could really use a cigarette right now, I know I won't keep my vow—and not just because she has cancer. I can't keep my vow because I never can. She depends on me. She always has.

2

W HEN I WAS TEN YEARS OLD, I'D SOMETIMES TUCK myself into one of the windowsills in the hallway of my elementary school. From there I could view my mother's house in one direction, and in the other, the yellow house, where I lived with my dad and Sandy. I was bifurcated, living two very distinct lives. I'd gaze back and forth: longingly at the yellow house, and with dread at my mother's. The weight of her house was so palpable that just looking at it made my shoulders tighten.

It hadn't always been that way. The first time I saw my mother's house, when I was seven years old, was the day my dad, mom, brother, and I moved in. The house had freshly painted walls and shiny mahogany woodwork throughout, even some stained glass windows in the living room that cast shards of burgundy, blue, and green across the newly carpeted floors and over the walls in the late afternoons. A sweet balcony off one of the four bedrooms overlooked a fenced backyard filled with lilac and oak trees. I was about to enter second grade, and my brother was just starting kindergarten, at the elementary school across the street. We'd already moved more than half a dozen times in my short life, including one trip across the country.

My parents met in Berkeley, when my dad pulled his van over for the pretty girl with waist-length hair standing on the side of the road with her thumb sticking out. It was 1967 and my mother, Helen, was with two friends from UMass Amherst, from which she'd just graduated; the three girls were visiting Berkeley before their real lives started. My dad, Rick, was with two friends as well. He'd been living in Berkeley for about six months, painting houses, taking classes at the community college in Oakland, and driving a van on which he and his friends had used blue house paint to scrawl SAY IT WITH FLOWERS across the side.

One of Rick's friends slid the door open and the girls got in, smiling. Even Helen was feeling brave that day. After they settled into the back, she leaned forward and made a joke about the originality of "Say It with Flowers"—it was the slogan of a popular flower shop and Helen liked that Rick and his friends had appropriated it for their hippie purposes.

Rick laughed and decided he liked that one, the littlest one of the group, with her almond-shaped hazel eyes, wide smile, and perfect teeth.

"So where's everyone going?" he asked.

"Jimi Hendrix at the Fillmore," one of the girls said, and Rick's friend Tom laughed. That's where they'd been headed, too.

By the time they arrived, Rick and Helen had decided they'd rather stay in the van and continue talking, so everyone else went in to the concert without them.

It's hard for me to imagine this, because my mother and father are both so shy. But over the next few weeks, they walked along Haight Street and through Golden Gate Park, they went to concerts and a few antiwar demonstrations, they talked and laughed.

Helen was signed up to take a teacher training course in New Haven, Connecticut, so she could begin teaching elementary school in the fall. They kept in touch with occasional letters. One evening, about nine months after Rick and Helen had met, Rick and his friend Tom decided, while drunk, that they wanted to go to Europe. So they packed their bags and left that very night for the East Coast—figuring that would be a better departure point than California. They stopped in Providence, Rhode Island, Tom's hometown. There, they decided they needed to save some money for their trip and found jobs casting jewelry in a workshop. And given Providence's proximity to New Haven, Rick called Helen.

Helen was happy to hear from him, though a bit wary. She liked Rick but didn't want to get too attached: Her biggest fear was (and still is) being abandoned and she couldn't imagine things ending any other way. Still, he was just a few towns away. She invited Rick over to the house she shared with Yale students and workers; when he arrived they went into her tiny room and closed the door. They smoked cigarettes and a little pot. Helen was funny and witty, in the ways she still can be, and she was shy and awkward, too, which eased Rick's own nerves.

Not that first night, but soon after, Helen tells Rick about her earliest memory: She's a baby, definitely under a year old, and she and her parents are living in Connecticut temporarily, while her father is in the merchant marines. They live in a house that's built partly on a small hill. The back of the house is raised, as if on stilts, though the front is level with the ground. Helen is crying. Her mother, Esther, has no idea what to do with her. She wraps Helen in a blanket, carries her out to the back deck, and sets her down close to the edge, where the railing should have been. The deck is ten feet above the ground. Esther goes inside the house, closing the door behind her. Helen is out there alone. She cries, pumping her tiny fists in anger, rocking from side to side; when she turns far enough in one direction she sees, through the spaces between the wooden slats of the deck, the dirt and patchy grass below. Beetles live down there. She doesn't want to fall down where they are. Helen needs to keep herself from falling. Though she has no words, she cries out for her mother again and again, trying to hold still so she won't fall. She waits. Finally her mother comes back, lifts Helen up, and brings her inside.

But it was too late. Helen had been abandoned. She couldn't forget the feeling, still can't.

Rick understood being left behind. His father jumped off a bridge into the Mississippi River when Rick was nine years old, and he instantly became responsible for his younger sister and schizophrenic mother. That's part of the reason he was already so responsible, able to go anywhere and find work, even though he was just twenty-two and a heavy drinker.

Over the next few weeks Rick made the decision to stay in New Haven; he found an apartment and a job painting houses. Within a month, he and Helen were engaged.

But soon Rick began to wonder if he was too young to get married. He was so inexperienced—Helen was his first real girlfriend. Then one night, in New York City, while visiting some college friends of Helen's, the couple has an argument.

They're in the kitchen of an apartment they don't know. It's after a party and there are bottles everywhere, full ashtrays, dirty glasses, and wooden bowls with remnants of crackers. The hosts of the party are asleep; the other guests are gone. Rick mentions the future and says, "If we get married—"

Helen's on her feet in seconds. *"If?"*

"I mean *when.*"

But it's too late. Helen's grabbed a knife from the counter. She runs at Rick. He tries to block her—at five feet ten he's almost a foot taller than she is, and he thinks he can hold her back, but she's strong, stronger than usual because she's furious. Rick has just done the one thing Helen can't tolerate: He's tried to abandon her. She pushes forward at him, her teeth bared, yelling, "You asshole, you fucking asshole—"

He runs from her, around and around the kitchen table. Helen's right behind him. He makes a break for it, sprinting through the apartment. Just as he reaches the front door and turns the knob, she stops. She's gasping for air, her hand on her stomach. She's just a few yards away and with each breath her face becomes less red, less pinched. Could it all have been a joke? Is there an explanation? Rick searches her face for clues, hoping. Helen's still holding the knife. She looks at it in her hand, slowly straightens up, and walks into the kitchen where she sets it down on the table. She collapses onto one of the chairs, puts her head in her hands, and starts to cry.

But Rick is too freaked out. And he'd already been—at least on a subconscious level, which is why he said *if* in the first place—thinking about calling things off.

So he does.

They return to New Haven the next morning, both defeated. They remain friendly yet cautious as they see each other a few times over the next week. And as the days pass, Rick convinces himself that her behavior was an overreaction but not worth breaking up about. They're edging toward getting back together, at least he thinks they are, when Helen makes an announcement: She's pregnant.

They're getting married after all.

MY MOTHER'S PARENTS didn't attend the wedding, though they were invited and lived just a few hours from New Haven. They'd met my dad once before. Myron, my mother's father, said to my dad, "You're Norwegian? Norwegians are all drunks." As if he were one to talk. And they didn't like that my dad wasn't Jewish, even though they weren't observant themselves.

For the wedding, my mother wore a paisley minidress; my dad wore jeans and a jacket with a Nehru collar. Right around this time my mother was informed that her teaching contract wasn't being renewed. Helen didn't care. She'd hated teaching kindergartners anyway. So Rick and Helen, both up for an adventure, decided to go back to Berkeley, with a quick detour to Minneapolis so my dad could check on his mother.

Between Minneapolis and Berkeley, just outside Livingston, Montana, there was a car accident. My dad was driving. A bee flew into the car, ping-ponging itself against the windshield, trapped by the glass. My dad swatted at it. Right as his hand came down on the glass one of the car's tires blew out.

The car swerved, out of control—they flipped down an embankment, then tumbled over and over and over again. When the car finally stopped moving, Rick and Helen said each other's names, asking, *Are you okay?* They both answered yes. My dad's hand had been on the outside of the car, cradling the window shell; the tip of his middle finger was crushed, permanently forming the nail into the shape of a bird's beak. But when he looked down at my mother, lying still across the car's front seat, he knew something was seriously wrong. The base of her spine was bent backward—what should have been concave was convex.

"Helen," my dad said, "are you sure you're okay?"

"I think so. I don't feel any pain."

And then they heard the sirens.

Other drivers had seen the accident and called for help. Rick and Helen were pulled from the car and the bystanders were shocked that the people inside had lived.

At the hospital in Livingston, my parents were informed that my mother's back was broken. The doctor wanted to perform surgery to fuse her spine, but there was a problem: me. They couldn't do the surgery while she was pregnant, nor could they put on the body cast that would be necessary for six months after the surgery. So they put her in a brace and said she'd have to be as still as possible until I was born. Then she could have surgery.

Helen was in the hospital for a month in Livingston, then my parents carefully drove the rest of the way to Berkeley.

Within a week of my birth, my mother had the surgery to fuse her spine and then the full body cast applied. My parents went on welfare so my dad could take care of my mother and me.

Because of the body cast, my mother didn't hold me until I was six months old. Even though I know that's true—both my mother and father have confirmed it—I still have a hard time believing it. It's too easy, too heavy-handed, too forced a metaphor for my mother's inability to provide maternal warmth or comfort: not when I was a baby, not as I grew up, and not now. My mother has told me that when I was a baby—this must have been after she was out of the body cast—and I was in my crib crying, she'd stand there, unable to decide what to do, and simply let me cry. She makes no connection between those times and her earliest memory, when she was left on the back deck. She's said that when my brother was born, a year and a half after me, she considered him her chance to make up for the things she'd done wrong with me. Though when I ask what she did differently, she can't think of anything.

WHEN I WAS about a year old, my parents brought me to a protest at People's Park in Berkeley. The University of California was planning to turn People's Park, which had become a hippie campsite of sorts, into a parking lot. The protest turned violent. My dad dropped my mom and me off at a church basement where a makeshift nursing station had been set up; we waited there while he drove through the protest picking up people who'd been hurt and delivering them to the nursing station. While we waited for him, tear gas, thrown by the police, wafted in. I scratched at my eyes, howling and crying. A few years before, my dad's history class at the community college in Oakland had been hijacked by the Black Panthers, who taught their version of the class for the hour and then let everyone free. But now, my parents concluded, Berkeley had turned too violent and unpredictable. So they loaded up the station wagon and we headed to my dad's hometown.

In Minneapolis, my dad opened a used record store, called The Wax Museum, with his own record collection. At first we moved from apartment to apartment, rarely staying in one place for long. After my dad's store started doing well and he opened more—eventually he'd have eight—he did what he thought was expected of him: bought a Cadillac and moved us out to the suburbs.

I didn't know what "the suburbs" meant, but even at five years old I knew that we didn't belong there, surrounded by rolling lawns and aquamarine swimming pools. We were impostors, trying to hide our fraudulence behind the nice house and the nice car. My mother's hoarding zenith was more than two decades in the future, but she was already showing signs of excessive accumulation and lackadaisical cleaning standards. My brother and I wore secondhand clothes that were often stained or torn. Sometimes I'd look at myself in the mirror as I brushed my teeth at night and see a big smear of dirt across my cheek; I'd wonder how long it had been there. Maybe I'd even gone to school like that. I'd try to remember if people had looked at me weirdly and conclude that they had. And when I thought of the way my mother yelled at us out on the sidewalk with everyone watching from behind their perfect parted drapes, I sank even further into myself. I became shy, quiet.

My parents, on the other hand, were getting louder. Inside that oversized house they screamed, swore, and threw plates and glasses at each other while my brother and I huddled together at the top of the stairs. We cried because we didn't know how to get them to stop. Once we cried because it was Christmas Eve and we were afraid their fighting meant the next day there would be no presents—we weren't foolish enough to believe in Santa Claus. My mother had told us long ago that he didn't exist, happy to smash that illusion before it could take hold. Ditto the Easter Bunny. Ditto that ludicrous tooth fairy.

The best thing about that house in the suburbs, according to me anyway, was the remarkable laundry chute that led from the second floor to the basement, so you wouldn't have to carry your laundry down the stairs. My brother and I would pour liquids down the chute—water, orange juice, hot chocolate (though not the dregs of coffee we'd find in unwashed mugs on end tables; the coffee was for drinking while pretending to smoke one of the roaches from joints or cigarette butts that filled the ashtrays). The liquids would land directly on the baskets of clothes waiting to be washed. No one ever noticed.

The other notable feature of that house was the enormous picture window in the living room. Birds were constantly flying into it: We'd hear a plunk, and then go outside to see a hummingbird, a sparrow, a house finch dead on the ground. Eventually my dad put a big X in masking tape across the glass to warn them. It looked terrible, and I'm sure our uptight neighbors despised it, but it was better than the alternative.

My favorite times were when my dad brought me with him to work. I'd walk through the aisles and he'd let me pick out any album I wanted. I'd hover in the Linda Ronstadt, Beach Boys, and Elvis sections, choosing the Elvis imports because they were rare. I coveted an Elvis double album set from Germany and was elated when my dad let me take it home. I adored hanging out in the back room in my dad's office among the filled ashtrays and stained coffee cups, and being in the store the day a contest winner got to run through, piling everything she wanted into a cart; she was so excited and methodical as she plotted her course before the buzzer rang. I used to beg my dad to let me work at The Wax Museum once I turned twelve. That seemed old enough.

"Fourteen," he'd always say.

When I was seven, my father went away for a month. I only knew it involved drinking. During that month we visited him on the weekends in a smoky place that looked like a motel, with two beds in each room. The four of us would play the card game War, eat potato chips, and drink RC Cola because the vending machines sold only soda with little or no caffeine—they didn't want the residents trying to get high on it.

After my dad got out of rehab, my mom checked in. She decided that she was an alcoholic, too, though my dad tells me later that she wasn't. According to him, she'd have a glass or two of wine and then fall asleep while he finished the bottle and moved on to the next one. My mother also told me that she did acid while she was pregnant with me, which my dad claims is a lie. He did it all the time, he said, but she only did it once, between being pregnant with me and my brother.

Right after the rehab, we moved out of the suburbs and back to Minneapolis, to the house across the street from the elementary school. My mom's house now. Less than a year after we moved in, one evening my dad said he needed to talk to my brother and me. I whined and begged for him to wait until *Welcome Back, Kotter* was over.

He acquiesced and said nothing about my brattiness, which was unlike him. I'd come to think of his temper as his motor revving up; I was able to gauge it by the tightness of his jaw—later I could sense it even from another room, the way you can feel rain before it comes by the thickness in the air. But this time his motor didn't rev up in spite of my whining. That was my first clue that something important was about to happen.

As soon as my beloved sitcom was over, I joined my dad and my brother upstairs in my parents' bedroom. My brother was crying, huddled in my dad's lap.

My dad told me he was moving out.

"You're getting divorced?" I asked, thinking, Good. Now things will have to change.

"We're separating. We haven't decided about the divorce," my dad said. "We're taking it one day at a time." This phrase had entered my parents' lexicon during their rehab experiences; it now adorned a small plaque in the living room, where they'd also placed one with the serenity prayer, basically the Lord's Prayer of A.A.

My dad explained that he was getting an apartment and we'd

live with him there, on weekends. My brother was still crying in our dad's lap and I didn't understand why. Our parents were terrible together. If they separated, things would have to get better.

The next day at school, my parents' impending separation got around my second-grade class and for a little while I was thought of as semicool (it was the mid-'70s, so while divorce was on the rise, it wasn't as common as it is today). I'm sure I played the martyr and soaked up the attention. Once we'd moved out of the suburbs and back into Minneapolis proper, a brazen streak had snuck into my shyness: I talked when we were supposed to be reading, and I insisted to my entire class that the word "drawer" was spelled "draw," even scrawling it in capital letters on the chalkboard. I pronounced it that way due to my mother's accent and was convinced that's how it was spelled.

Sometimes my teacher, Mrs. Haynes, would threaten to send me to the principal's office for talking too much, saying I was "supposed to be shy," that that's what my mother had told her at the start of the school year, "yet here you are . . ." and then she'd laugh. Each time she said it a glimmer of hope fluttered through me: I was flattered that my mother had taken the time to meet my teacher. A kind of behind-the-scenes mothering I hadn't known about, that might, if I was lucky, sound to the other kids as if I had a normal mother who cared about me instead of one who stayed in bed most of the time, seemed happy only when her arms were full of purchases, and lashed out and pulled my hair with little or no warning.

My dad's apartment, where my brother and I began living on the weekends, was clean and peaceful. For forty-eight glorious hours a week I didn't have to make grilled cheese sandwiches and bring them to my mother in bed, try to find a place for the two cases of cucumber-scented hand lotion she'd purchased because it was on sale, or worry about her shaking me awake at

3:00 a.m. to tell me she was still furious about something I'd done earlier that day—usually "getting fresh," which I did often.

And there was another punishment, one my mother's new shrink suggested shortly after my dad moved out: My brother and I, whenever we fought, were supposed to walk around the block at whatever time it was, in whatever we happened to be wearing, regardless of the weather—which meant many midnight wintertime walks in just our pajamas.

I know she was just trying to get us to behave and to respect her, but my mother's inconsistency, strange punishments, and mercurial temper did the opposite. During the week while we were at our mother's house, my brother and I were wild: We'd play ding-dong ditch and make shaving cream drawings on our neighbors' windows and car windshields; we pointed a garden hose into an open window of the house next door, soaking a bedroom; we taunted a neighbor girl and tried unsuccessfully to get her to pull down her pants in the alley; we ran from the house at any time of the night, screaming through the streets. We even hopped the fence around the kiddie pool in the park to take late night swims.

On the weekends everything was different. We ate whatever our dad said we were eating and went to bed when he determined. Running outside in the middle of the night was out of the question—I never even tried. I didn't try because the truth was, I liked having rules. I liked knowing that someone was aware of my whereabouts, that an adult was paying attention. I felt safe at my dad's apartment. Yes, he had his motor-revving temper, but I knew how to handle it. Overall, at my dad's, things were calm. My dad not only remembered our birthdays, he even made homemade signs and hung them in his living room, one letter on each piece of construction paper, strung together with yarn and bordered by clusters of balloons. The first time

I woke up there on my birthday, I walked out into the living room and there was the sign: 9 HAPPY BIRTHDAY JESSIE 9 and I was touched that my dad had taken the time to make it. But I couldn't let him know that, so instead I said something stupid about how the "9" starting off the sentence like that didn't make sense. I'd already learned to hide my emotions.

After a weekend at my dad's—going for pizza at The Leaning Tower, to movies, bowling, bike rides around the lakes, hanging out at The Wax Museum, staying up late to watch *Saturday Night Live,* even just sitting by my dad's stereo listening through huge bug-eared headphones to Linda Ronstadt or Beatles records—I dreaded going back to my mom's house on Sunday nights. Often we'd return to an empty house. An empty and *messy* house. My mother was constantly late getting back from wherever she was—a class she was taking to get her nursing license, the library, thrift-store shopping, or "The Club," which sounded sinister but was really just a smoky house that held A.A. meetings and functioned as a sort of country club for the sober set. My dad, knowing better than to just drop us off and drive away, would always come inside with us. He'd survey the mess and start shaking his head. "This place is a goddamn shithole!" he'd yell and reach for a sponge, a broom, a mop. By the time my mother returned from wherever she was, my dad would have cleaned the whole first floor.

During the rest of the week I tried my best to keep the house neat and the clutter from piling up too badly. I did the cooking. I got my brother and myself ready for school. I even braved the snakes in the basement to do the laundry. Sometimes my mother was depressed and sleeping twenty hours straight; other times she'd be gone all day or late into the night.

The next Sunday I'd hope the house wouldn't be a disaster when we got there. Because whenever my dad deemed the house a shithole, I felt as if the words were directed right at me—either because I was responsible for the house during the week or because I'd already become the adult in the relationship with my mother. Regardless of why, every time he said the words I'd feel myself starting to hunch my shoulders a little closer together, shrinking. There was something about those words that made me want to disappear.

Two doors down from my mother's house lived a woman named Sandy and her daughter Beth. Sandy and my mother somehow ended up becoming friends, and some afternoons Sandy would come over for coffee; they'd sit at the kitchen table talking and laughing. If Sandy stopped by and my mother was out, she'd invite my brother and me over to her house. If it happened at night, she'd get out the sleeping bags, make us hot chocolate with carob rather than chocolate, and play games with us or read us stories—things my mom never did. We'd spend the night without my mother ever even noticing that we were gone.

I stepped on a cactus one day and I hopped straight over to Sandy's house, where she pulled the needles out one by one. Afterward, her father, who was visiting from California, coated my foot with cayenne pepper, claiming it had miraculous health benefits. I began to wish that Sandy was my mother. I wondered what life would be like.

My brother and I never told my dad about our mother's hair-pulling or the midnight walks around the block. But we must have let little clues slip, because after about a year and a half, my dad began to have a feeling that things weren't right at my mother's. A few months earlier, my mom had had a roommate move in to help with the bills; she was an old friend of my dad's sister. When his sister was in town for a visit, the roommate stopped by my dad's to say hello, and my dad used the opportunity to ask how things were at my mom's house.

The roommate told him that Helen was neglectful at the least, and though she hadn't witnessed any physical abuse, she suspected it. She told my dad about one incident she found particularly disturbing: late one night, I was crying, sobbing so hard I could barely breathe, having a meltdown that increased in intensity in direct proportion to the amount my mother ignored me—which was completely. The roommate, concerned about my purple face and otherwordly shrieks, asked my mother what was going on. My mother said, "Isn't it wonderful? Jessie's getting her feelings out."

My dad made a decision. He doubted he could get a court to grant him full custody, but he'd move back into the neighborhood and become more involved in my and my brother's lives. He figured my mother would agree to a one week on, one week off arrangement.

My dad had already met Sandy twice, once when he came to pick up my brother and me for the weekend and we were at her place, and once when he took us to a birthday party she threw for Beth. He knew Sandy was a big part of our lives while we were at our mom's and he wanted her opinion of our mother's parenting. He drove to Sandy's house and knocked on her door. Surprised to find him on her doorstep, and in the middle of packing for her own upcoming move across the street to a duplex she'd just purchased, Sandy asked my dad inside. She, too, confirmed the neglectful conditions. That's why she was trying to be there for us as much as possible. Sandy had no idea that my dad even cared about my brother and me, but during the next few hours, as they talked over cups of instant coffee at her kitchen table, she was relieved to realize that my brother and I had one parent looking out for us. And she was impressed when he told her about his plan to move back to the neighborhood. He even had a house picked out: a tiny red one seven blocks away, near the river. He just needed a Realtor. Sandy immediately offered her services.

Things happened quickly after that. My dad bought and moved into the house he'd chosen, and my brother and I started living with him there every other week.

And Sandy was there, too. A lot. She and my dad were dating.

It was Beth who let it slip that my dad and Sandy were getting married. She was six years old at the time, I was nine, and my brother was seven. The five of us were just sitting down to dinner at my dad's cramped dining room table. I hadn't really been paying attention and only heard her say the words "yellow house" and "married."

"What are you talking about?" I asked.

My dad looked at Sandy and raised his eyebrows. Sandy blushed. They both smiled.

"We were going to tell you tonight," my dad said to my brother and me. He explained that all five of us were going to live there, in my dad's tiny red house, while they renovated Sandy's duplex, the one kitty-corner from my mother's house, into a single-family home. After he told us, he seemed to be waiting for something. Not permission, but a reaction.

"I think it's a great idea," I said, embarrassed to show how happy I was about the idea of Sandy being my mom officially, embarrassed by how much I wanted it . . . and there was something else.

Guilt. I felt like a traitor to my mother.

She was furious. I talked to her shortly after she found out. She was in the bathtub, soaking away her problems—a habit I may have picked up from her because I do the same thing. Her giant breasts floated on the water's surface like puffy sea creatures.

"I'm getting a goddamn restraining order against him," she

declared, but her voice was so weak that it was clear she knew what she was saying was ridiculous. What was there to restrain? My dad wasn't trying to talk to her. He wasn't harassing her. He didn't want anything to do with her, and that was why her words were so sad. During the last year, she'd gotten her nursing degree and had begun dating Sam, a sour-faced yet well-intentioned man from The Club. Regardless, the idea of my dad and Sandy getting married upset her. I wished there was something I could say to make her feel better, wished that I wasn't so happy about it myself, but I was.

In the meantime, at the red house, winter was beginning to melt away. On one of the first springlike days, I went outside coatless, so happy about the upcoming changes in my life, about my new family, that I did a cartwheel on the cement walkway leading up to the house. I did a roundoff, my feet landing with a crunch on the melting sheath of ice. I'd been taking gymnastics lessons and competing in occasional meets for four years, since I was five—it was the one thing I considered myself good at. I did a quick back walkover, then another cartwheel, and then another. And then Sandy and my dad pulled up in front of the house. They got out of the car and when Sandy saw me, she said, "Jessie, come on, you really should be wearing a coat." I laughed, because it felt so good to be reprimanded in a normal way—no jaw-clenching tension from my dad followed by an outburst, no teeth-gritting and then hair-pulling from my mom. No fighting of any kind. Just concern, stated in a calm and kind way. Every time something "normal" like that happened, something you might see on television or at the house of a friend with regular parents, I'd feel my shoulders broaden just a little bit, and the cold, uncertain feeling that lived in the pit of my stomach would go away, at least for a little while.

When the yellow house was completed, with a brand new

spiral staircase linking the two previously unconnected floors, the five of us moved in, claiming spaces and bedrooms. My brother knew which room he wanted right away, so Beth and I let him have it. She and I flipped a coin over the remaining two kids' bedrooms (though over the next six years I'd often beg Beth to switch with me—back and forth she and I would move all our furniture every year or so. I was easily bored and still must be, because even now, at close to forty, the longest I've ever lived in one place is the six-year span in that house). The "yellow house" as everyone came to call it, was spacious, sparkling new, and clean. Every week my dad and Sandy gave us a new chore chart. One week I'd be in charge of cleaning the bathroom, the next week the kitchen, the next week the living room or the TV room. All three of us kids were responsible for doing our own laundry from the time we each turned ten. Most evenings we ate dinner together as a family. At the end of the night I'd go upstairs to my room and listen to the faint murmurings from the kitchen—my dad and Sandy always sat up talking at the table after we kids went to bed. Little did I know that the main topic of their conversation was the financial problems that beset them shortly after their marriage, that they were desperately trying to find a way to pay for the renovation of the yellow house, as well as feed and clothe five people. Within a year, my dad would lose his record stores and he and Sandy would be on the verge of bankruptcy.

I STILL HAD to go to my mom's house every other week. One night my mother took my brother and me to a drive-in movie. We were late and missed most of the first feature. When the second movie, *Saturday Night Fever*, came on, my mother decided it was too sexist. She started backing her boatlike car out of the lot.

"Let's not leave," I said. "Let's watch it."

"I'm not watching this crap and I'm not letting you kids watch it either."

I continued protesting as we drove along the highway toward home. Suddenly my mother flashed her gritted teeth at me and reached for my hair.

She yanked. I screamed at her to stop. My brother, in the backseat, begged us to calm down.

My mother was having a hard time driving and pulling my hair at the same time, so she did the logical thing: headed over to the shoulder of the highway and ordered me out of the car.

"It's pitch black out here," I said.

"Out!"

I got out, and—as was required in a situation like that— slammed the door behind me. She screeched off into the distance.

I started walking. It was a highway. It was night. Dark. I kept walking as cars sped past. No one stopped; I didn't want anyone to stop.

But after a while, someone did.

Her. She'd managed to circle around.

I got into the car and we drove home in silence. My mother dropped my brother and me off at the yellow house. But I'd made a decision as I walked along that dark highway: I was going to take charge of my own life now. The next day, after talking it over with my dad and Sandy, I called my mother and told her that I didn't want to live with her anymore. I wanted to live full-time at my dad and Sandy's.

She put up no resistance. She deemed it the best thing for everyone. Which was good, but not exactly what I wanted to hear. At least a "Why don't you think about it?" or "Let's see how things go," would have been nice. But she was relieved, I could tell. My brother continued with the one week on, one week off thing longer than I did, but not by much—maybe six months.

About once a week I'd go to my mother's house and have dinner with her, always doing a little cleaning and straightening up while I was there, or I'd go on weekends and try to fix up her yard. After Sam moved in, he tried his best to stay out of the way when I was over, climbing the creaking stairs to smoke cigarettes and watch the television set in their bedroom. He wasn't exactly what you'd call warm and cuddly, but he wasn't a bad guy either.

I'm sure he was the one doing the small amount of cleaning that was happening there, but it wasn't enough. Her house wasn't in a full-fledged hoarding state yet, but it was a mess and becoming junkier and junkier on the inside and the outside. And unfortunately the house hadn't magically lifted up and moved itself into a different neighborhood across town either. No, regardless of how often I wished it weren't the case, my mother's house was still directly across the street from my elementary school. Because my dad and Sandy's house was across the street in the other direction, I made a point to tell my fellow students as often as possible that I lived in that nicely painted yellow house. "See that one, right there," I'd say, pointing at the house with the adorable porch swing, gardens bursting with tulips and hydrangeas and roses, and the fence my dad had built—as straight as a set of perfect teeth—around the backyard.

Though he'd already traded it in for a Volkswagen, I'd brag about my dad's baby blue Cadillac. I thought of it as an insurance policy in case anyone found out that the weird lady who bundled up in knee-length sweaters year-round and wore a full-face motorcycle helmet while bicycling down the middle of the street—riding so slowly that a slight breeze could have tipped her over—was my mother, and those rusted, junky cars (Sam's contribution) parked outside the house, hers. Every time my class went out for recess I'd stay toward the back of the group so that if by chance my mother was outside she wouldn't see me, or worse, come over to say hello.

Sometimes I'd look around my dad and Sandy's house and marvel at how nice it was, how clean it was, how normal we all appeared. But I couldn't let myself trust it. I couldn't completely acclimate. I didn't belong there. During that time my brother and I lived with my mom through the week and my dad on the weekends, I'd turned feral. By the time I came to live with my dad and Sandy full-time, I'd been wild too long. I felt like one of those kids raised by wolves; I'd never fit in, never be able to mask my animal nature.

I tried, though. That was why I'd stand outside the school with my classmates, keeping my back to my mother's house and pointing toward the immaculate yellow house, saying, "That's me, that's where I live," even though I barely believed it myself.

Officially I lived in the yellow house, yes, but part of me had been left behind at my mother's. It was the part of me that felt responsible for her, the part that was constantly searching for a solution for her cluttered house and her cluttered mind. There was no one else to keep her from running completely amok, no one besides me who could stop her from packing the porch with "antiques," from allowing the closets to overflow with moth-eaten sweaters and the backyard to go wild. By the time I was ten years old, sitting in the windowsill of my elementary school gazing back and forth between the two houses, the weight of my mother's burgeoning problem was bearing down on me. And I had become the one in charge, in my mind anyway, of fixing it.

3

THE MORNING OF HER SURGERY, MY MOM INSISTS ON TAKING a cab to the hospital, because she has to be there at 5:00 a.m. That same morning, my dad and I drive to St. Paul to look at stoves and refrigerators for her—yesterday she confessed that her stove didn't work and her refrigerator was barely functioning. My dad knows of a place that may let her trade in her old appliances for new ones, so we're going to see what's in stock. The plan is that my dad will help get the old ones out and the new ones in while she's in the hospital. It's a big gesture, the first my dad's made toward helping, and I'm grateful.

As we pull into the parking lot, my cell phone rings. It's my mother, from the hospital.

"Guess what," she says. "Salman Rushdie is reading tonight—we should go see him!" She manages to get most of the words out before becoming engulfed by laughter.

"What's going on?" Jesus. Why does she always try to frame everything as a joke? It's just like the way she told me she had cancer in the first place.

"They're sending me home!"

"What are you talking about? You're not having the surgery?"

My dad has just opened his door, but pauses when he hears me, gauging my reaction.

"They did another colonoscopy and found more polyps. They want to test them, so now the surgery won't be until next week."

"More polyps? Does that mean the cancer is more widespread?"

"They don't know. But the good news is that we can spend more time together!"

"Okay," I say uneasily. This doesn't sound like good news, obviously. And now I won't even be here when she goes home after the surgery. Besides, I was counting on her being in the hospital for a few days so I could clean her house without interference.

"But," she says, "now the hospital won't let me leave on my own, because I had anesthesia for the colonoscopy. Can you ask Sandy to come pick me up? Or if she's busy, maybe your dad?"

I cover the phone and explain the situation to my dad. He puts the car in reverse and backs out of the parking lot.

"You're sure you don't mind, Pop?" I say after I get off the phone.

"It's fine, honey. Really."

After he and Sandy got together, if there were ever arrangements to make about my brother and me, Sandy dealt with my mom. (When my husband and I got married, my dad and Sandy had a party for us, and we invited my mother. As far as I knew it was the first time my parents had been in the same room or even spoken in twenty-five years. I was nervous about how my mother would behave at the party, but she was fine, totally appropriate—even charming. And in a weird coincidence, she showed up in a dress the exact shade of blue as the one I wore.)

When I see her standing outside the hospital entrance, my first thought is one I have frequently: Thank God I didn't inherit her enormous breasts. They hang down almost to her waist. When I was little, she'd take off her bra at night and have deep, three-inch wide gouges in her shoulders from the straps. Sandy once told me that when I was ten, she and my dad began setting aside money for me to get a breast reduction. Thankfully, I didn't need one. But why am I thinking about my mother's breasts right now? Maybe because I'm trying not to think about the cancer. It may be worse than we thought. Though we didn't know anything before, somehow now we know even less.

I switch from the front seat to the back, and my mother takes five minutes to get in and settled.

"Hi, Helen," my dad says.

"Hi, Rick," she says shyly. "Thank you for coming to get me."

From the backseat, I watch my parents attempting to make conversation. I try to remember a time when I was alone with just the two of them, but can't.

"So, what should we do now?" my mother asks, turning around to me.

"My dad's going to drop us off at your house and we're going to start cleaning."

Probably because it's impossible for me to think of my parents as together—as a couple or even as co-parents—I always say "my mom" and "my dad," rather than just "Dad," or "Mom." I didn't realize it was unusual until friends mentioned it.

"The house is in marvelous shape," my mother says, waving her hand dismissively. "You don't have to worry about cleaning anymore."

"Really? When did that happen?"

"I've been working on it," she says.

"So since I left last night, you've cleaned it? And now it's all just *marvelous*? The kitchen's all ready for your new stove and refrigerator? There's a way for the delivery people to get through?"

"Well . . . no. I guess not."

My dad's jaw is clenching; it must be hard for him to hear his daughter being so strict with his ex-wife. But it's the relationship I have with my mother, it's the way we're most comfortable: I'm the enforcer of rules, while she retreats into the role of the child. It's the way we've been for as long as I can remember, and I can't imagine us another way. And though I've long given up on convincing her that teasing me about snakes verges on sadistic and is not in the slightest bit funny, I haven't been able to give up the hope of someday getting her house clean. I worry about my mother in those conditions.

And I resent the looks of scorn and judgment thrown my way by her neighbors. Last year one of them cornered me outside, when my husband and I were walking my mom home after having lunch during a visit. It was winter, but we'd wanted a walk. We tucked my mother inside her gruesome castle and were about to head back to my dad and Sandy's when the neighbor came out of her house and started shoveling my mother's sidewalk. It turned out they'd struck a deal: a swap of lawn duties—at least in the front—for the use of my mother's garage. I don't know this neighbor's name because my mother always refers to her as "the mean lesbian neighbor."

Mean Lesbian Neighbor began glaring at my husband and

me as if we were grifters in the midst of a plan to scam my mother. But then she said, in a voice dripping with accusation, "Hey. You're her daughter, aren't you?"

I stopped walking. I turned around. "Yes. Thanks for shoveling."

"She lets me use half her garage, so I do it."

"She definitely can use the help. And I appreciate it, too." I turned to leave.

"There's concern about her," she said. "In the neighborhood."

"That's good—I mean it's nice to know that her neighbors are looking out for her."

"And I want *you* to know there's concern here."

What she was saying was clear: I should be taking better care of my mother.

"You know, I don't live here, I live in another state. I do the best I can."

"Sometimes we don't see her around for days at a time." She jabbed the shovel straight down into the snow and leaned on it. "We even called the police once—did she tell you about that?"

She did tell me. The police broke down her back door because no one had seen her for so long and she wouldn't answer her doorbell. Afterward, she seriously considered suing the police. When I asked her why she hadn't just answered the door, she said it was because she didn't know who it was; I suspected it was really a combination of her reclusive nature and not wanting anyone to get a glimpse inside her house.

"You have her phone number, right?" I said, fighting to hide my annoyance. "If you're worried about her, you could call."

"Yeah, but she don't answer her phone."

True. She'll call me either every day or not for months. Often I have to ask my dad or Sandy to tape a note to my mother's front door asking her to call me—she has voice mail but claims not to know how to check her messages. Sometimes I picture her body inside that house, dead and decaying, being snacked on by rodents, and that's when I ask my dad or Sandy to leave another note. Finally she'll call me and say she's either been too depressed to pick up the phone or too busy making some kind of political T-shirts she intends to sell for millions on eBay.

"Well . . . thanks," I said to Mean Lesbian Neighbor, and she shook her head, scowling, clearly repulsed by what a horrible daughter I am.

Now my dad pulls up in front of my mother's house and she unbuckles her seat belt.

"Thank you, Rick," she says.

"Sure, Helen. See you later."

I'm jealous that my dad gets to drive away. When he was twenty-one he had to have his mother committed to a mental institution, and though it's been a while since I've feared having to do the same thing, sometimes I can't help but resent that my father gave me a mother I'd have to take care of forever, just like he had to do with his.

"Call me if you want me to bring lunch, or if you feel like taking a break," my dad says as I get out of the car, and I feel guilty and selfish for thinking anything bad about him at all. Especially because he's the one who married Sandy and gave me a semblance of a normal family, even if by then it was too late.

"Let's not clean today," my mother says. She opens her front door and we walk inside. "Let's go to Como Park Zoo. The house already looks marvelous. You've done a beautiful job, honey."

The house looks horrible. I know the nice thing to do, the *kind* thing to do, would be to spend the next few days I'm in town talking with my mom, letting her tell me stories and pontificate on the meaning of life as she has been, but I don't want to. There is so much more cleaning and clearing out to do, and I can't stop.

"I want this house to be clean when you're recovering. I want it to be nice for you."

It breaks my heart to think of my mother, injured, alone in this house. She has no friends, not one. Sandy's offered to come by, but she's busy and their relationship, while cordial, isn't close.

"But it *is* nice," she insists.

"It isn't, Mom." I walk toward the stove. It's caked in grease and dirt, piled high with dirty pans. I'll have to clean it off before we try to trade it in. "And what's this?" I ask about the dishwasher squatting in the middle of the kitchen floor. "Why do you even have this?"

The dishwasher, it turns out, is from Savers. I can't believe she paid someone to bring it in here, that she let someone inside, and that she thought she needed it in the first place. It takes up 90 percent of the kitchen's floor space. And it doesn't even work. She needs some part for it, some part that I know without a doubt she'll never locate, and if she does, she'll never buy, and even if she does buy it, she'll never actually spend the money to hire someone to install it. So, this dishwasher will never work. But she won't let me get rid of it because when it does work "it will save so much time."

"So much time?" I say. "You live alone—you do the dishes for one person. How much time can that take?"

"You have no idea." She shakes her head as if it's the saddest thing in the world.

And considering how slow she is, maybe she's right. Often my mother seems to be moving in slow motion, or underwater. I've never seen someone take as long to write out a check, to walk one block, to get in and out of a car. And excessive slowness, it turns out, is not uncommon among hoarders. They're often slow in completing tasks and late for appointments. At least in my mother's case, the slowness is partly due to indecisiveness—each and every movement has to be considered and carefully weighed—and partly due to perfectionism and anxiety (worry about somehow making the wrong move).

I feel anxiety myself when I look at her refrigerator: It's coated with orange and yellow and brown food smears, especially near the handle; I wonder how many hours of scrubbing it will need. The freezer is one solid chunk of ice with microwavable dinners, tinfoil packets of leftovers, and bags of frozen corn, peas, and lima beans buried inside like insects in amber. The refrigerator shelves hold long-expired cartons of milk, half-eaten loaves of bread, and Tupperware containers of every shape and size imaginable. Splotches of mold in bruisey green and black hues bloom on every surface. But most disturbing are the tiny black fruit fly–looking bugs. My God. What kind of insect can stay alive inside a refrigerator?

My mom parks herself on one of the chairs at the kitchen table.

"So what are you reading, Jessie?" she says, her favorite question.

It's something I'm grateful to my mother for—she's a voracious reader, at times averaging a book a day, and I'm sure I inherited my love and respect for literature from her.

"A collection of short stories," I say, as I begin tossing every single thing from the refrigerator into the trash can I've lined with a garbage bag.

I don't feel like talking about books right now. I'm busy trying to picture a time I saw my mother clean something, and can't. Ever. Not sweeping, not mopping, not dusting. Not once. When she and my dad were married he did all the cleaning, then it fell to me, then her boyfriend Sam, and then Roger. Had the people my mother lived with always done the cleaning? Could it be possible that all of this is simply a result of never learning how to clean?

"Can I ask you something?" I say. "When you were growing up, who did the cleaning in your house?"

"No one. There was nothing to clean. We didn't have anything."

"No one?" I say, aiming a greenish bag of carrots for the trash. I'm surprised she bought them in the first place. They're much too nutritious for her normal tastes. "What about sweeping the floors? Doing the dishes? Vacuuming? Dusting? Those things still had to be done even if you didn't have much stuff. Someone had to clean."

"I guess my mother must have done it." She shakes her head angrily. "Those people. You know my father wouldn't even let me eat at the table with them. He'd say, 'I can't look at her. Get her outta here!' And I'd have to go eat in the living room, all alone."

"Why?" I've never understood the way her father's cruelty seemed, most of the time, directed singularly at her.

She shrugs. "When he'd try to beat my mother, I'd stand up for her. I'd get right between them and then he'd end up beating me instead." She's gritting her teeth and I feel bad for bringing up her childhood—it almost always leads to a downward spiral of anger and despair. But I had to ask. I'm still grasping for a reason for her behavior.

My mother continues. "I told you what my father said about the Boston Strangler, right? He said, 'Hey,'" my mother lowers her voice in an impression of a typical meathead-type guy, "'I used to drink in the same bar as the Boston Strangler, and he was a nice guy. Those girls must've been asking for it.'"

"Good Lord," I say as my mother and I laugh and shake our heads in disbelief.

I manage to pry a bag of frozen corn from the freezer's icicle tentacles and toss it into the trash.

My mom really has had a crap life—appalling parents, a bellicose marriage and divorce, then the death of her boyfriend. Since she doesn't speak to either of her siblings, she has no family other than me. And my brother, sort of. He hasn't spoken to our mom in six years, not since they had an argument shortly after Roger died. Three years ago my brother and our dad had a disagreement while my brother was doing some work on one of Sandy's listings. My brother stormed off and hasn't spoken to our dad, Sandy, or me since. It seems so odd that our mother has cancer and he has no idea. As kids, my brother and I were allies against our parents' dysfunction, but once we moved into the yellow house we drifted apart. As we grew older I'd see him at holiday gatherings, but we had no real contact other than that. I wouldn't even know how to reach him now, though I could probably figure it out. I've considered trying, so I could tell him about our mom, but she's still too wounded that my brother stopped talking to her—abandoned her—especially so soon after Roger's death.

She really has no one.

No wonder she's the way she is.

And then I glance down, into a basket of junk in the middle of her kitchen table—rather than a junk drawer, my mom has junk baskets, out in the open so she can see everything—and I notice something long and rubbery. Green. I look closer. It's a rubber snake.

My mom bursts out laughing, clapping her hands. "I was wondering when you'd notice!"

And the pity I'd felt seconds before drains away like water from a tub.

IT'S TAKING FOREVER to sort through everything with my mother watching over me, so I come up with a task to get her out of my way: I ask her to transfer a huge pile of books taking up the entire couch—where the hell has she been sitting before this?—to the empty bookshelves. Take at least half of them and put them into a box to give back to Savers, I tell her.

"But, Jessie, some of these are collectibles! Some of these books are worth a fortune! I'm going to sell them."

"Really? How much do you think this book on using Microsoft Word from 1996 is worth?" I ask, tossing it into the box.

She sighs, blinks her eyes at me. "Fine. I'll donate some of them. But only half."

A bit later, I glance into the living room to check on her progress. She's sitting on a newly cleared patch of the couch, with a cardboard box on her lap—it's one of the many boxes I've come across that contain maybe an inch of papers, or a couple small pillows, or one cowboy boot.

As I approach, I see that she's holding a photograph of Roger and her with their dog, a tiny sheltie. My mom is staring at the photo. Roger was the one person with whom my mother never fought; he was the one person who seemed to love her unconditionally, despite her many quirks. Already sick with diabetes when they started dating, Roger's condition deteriorated over the decade they were together, and eventually my mother quit her job and devoted herself to him full-time.

I met Roger only once. It was the summer of 1998, and it was the first time my mother and I saw each other after an almost seven-year silence. Looking back, it seems absurd that we didn't speak for so long—especially because our estrangement began so capriciously, almost by accident. My mother had asked me to go see her therapist with her, and even though this was the same therapist she'd been seeing for at least fifteen years and as far as I could tell hadn't helped my mother in the slightest, I agreed to go. This was also the same therapist who advised my mother to force my brother and me to walk around the block when we fought, regardless of time or weather. But I was curious about what my mother wanted to say to me that she didn't think she could say on her own.

We'd been getting along fairly well at that point, so when my boyfriend at the time and I decided to take an impromptu road trip to Canada and it happened to coincide with the planned meeting, I didn't think delaying our talk would be a big deal. Apparently, though, it was a very big deal.

"I am so sick of you letting me down," my mother said.

"Excuse me? I just want to postpone it. I'll go with you the next week."

"Just like everyone else," she said. "Always letting me down."

What was she talking about? "Mom, I don't know who you're confusing me with, but I do not let you down."

"Well . . ." she said, pausing. "You're just . . . you're just evil!"

I was so surprised that I laughed. "Really? I'm evil because I can't go to your shrink appointment with you?"

"I need a break from you!" she said. "Let's not talk for a while."

I felt stung. But not surprised. Actually, I felt stupid that I hadn't seen it coming. When she'd met Roger a few years earlier, the one wrinkle was that my mother was still living with Sam, her first boyfriend after my dad. But the wrinkle was easily smoothed out: Instead of Sam moving out of the house, he just moved into another bedroom. He was still living there. And my brother was temporarily living there, too. She'd always been unable to have more than one person close to her at a time. And at that moment she had three.

"Okay," I said. "How about if you just call me when you're ready?"

"Fine."

"Fine," I echoed, and that was that.

I figured that she'd call in a week or two. A month at most. But weeks passed. Then months.

Then years.

During that time I moved to New York; I'd see my brother at my dad and Sandy's when I visited Minneapolis and he'd report that our mom was doing well and was happy with Roger. I missed her but at the same time I was relieved not to have to deal with her. I wondered if she ever thought of me.

Five years passed like that. My brother asked me one day, when we were both visiting my dad and Sandy, if it would be all right for him to give our mom my address. She wanted to get back in touch. He assured me that she was different, that Roger was a good influence on her and that she was "calmer" now.

I said okay and about a week later I received a card from her. It said: *If you're ready to stop yelling at me, we can talk. Mom.*

That sounds really appealing, I thought, and threw the card in the trash. I figured we'd go another five years without speaking.

But a year later, she wrote again: *I'd like to talk to you again if you're ready. Love, Mom.*

It was June, and I happened to be headed to Minneapolis for a long weekend over the Fourth of July. So I called.

She sounded the same. Her accent was just as strong.

I told her about my upcoming trip to Minneapolis and she asked if I'd like to come over.

"I can make us coffee," she said. "And you can meet Roger."

"Sure," I said. And then I didn't know what else to say. "So . . . I'll call you when I get to town, then?"

"Sounds good, honey." My mom sounded strangely serene. Maybe my brother was right, I thought. Maybe she really had changed.

When she opened the door, my first reaction was surprise at how tiny she'd become. This was the woman I was once so afraid of?

"Well, hello," she said and opened her arms to hug me.

I was caught off guard. We'd rarely hugged. But I wanted things to be okay between us. We hugged quickly and then I followed her into the hallway. The floor was still carpeted then, a worn brown shag. It looked recently vacuumed. There were no piles of things, and the hooks for coats were being used. A maple-encased antique radio sat against one wall of the hallway, and next to it was a china cabinet holding fragile teacups and saucers, crystal dishes, and ceramic figurines of ice skaters and Scottie dogs.

In the kitchen, a sky blue shelf held a familiar collection of porcelain salt and pepper shakers shaped like robins, chickens, cows, and toque-topped chefs. The door was open between the kitchen and the living room and the television was tuned to a nature show.

"Roger," my mom said, "this is Jessie."

I peeked my head into the living room. It was crowded with furniture, probably twice as much as was necessary, but it wasn't unclean. Roger was sitting on the couch with his feet propped up on a footstool that was layered with pillows on top.

"Hi, Jessie!" he said. "I'd get up but I have to keep my feet elevated for now."

"It's okay," I said walking toward him and holding out my hand. "It's nice to meet you."

"Helen's told me so much about you," he said, "but it's nice to meet you for myself."

He had red hair and pale skin and looked sweet and elfin, like a man who'd say "doggone it." The kind of guy everyone liked.

"Do you want coffee, Jessie? Or tea?" my mom asked. "And I bought some Mint Milanos. You like those, right?"

"I do," I said. "And I'll have coffee, please."

"Do you need anything, Roger?" my mom called out to him.

"I'm good, Helen," he said. I couldn't tell if he truly was immersed in the show about armadillos or if he just wanted to give my mom and me time to talk, but he turned back to the television and stared at it, seemingly absorbed.

I sat down at the kitchen table while my mom poured us cups of coffee from an already made pot. She took the white bag of cookies from one of the cabinets. I glimpsed inside while the cabinet door was open and saw that it was crowded, but everything was neatly stacked. She pulled out a chair and sat across from me. Her fingers on her coffee cup were pale and slightly puffy. And I'd forgotten about my mother's bizarre thumbs: They're squished looking at the ends, like tiny troll thumbs; the crescent-shaped nail is only about a third of an inch long. I've never seen anyone else with thumbs like hers. Sitting across from her, I found her hands cute, like little paws. They didn't look like hands that had pulled my hair or shaken me awake in the middle of the night. They didn't look like hands that ever would.

She blew on her coffee, took a sip, and smiled at me.

I pulled a cookie from the bag and bit into it.

It seemed as if neither of us knew where to start.

"So how are you, Mom?"

"I'm good," she said, nodding. "How are you?"

I didn't want to tell her anything personal. It felt too risky.

"Oh, you know, things are fine," I said vaguely. "What about you?"

She told me that she and Roger had been spending winters in Florida for the past few years, about the trailer they owned there and the welcoming community of neighbors they'd found. I could picture my mother playing cards and walking on the beach. "We might not make it this year, though. It depends on how Roger's doing," she said, leaning forward.

That was worrisome. But my mom didn't sound particularly worried. I'd never seen her like this: self-sufficient. Adult. The tension—the sense that at any second she could start gritting her teeth and lash out—was gone.

After a while, I decided it would be okay to tell her a little bit about my life. I mentioned a trip I had coming up: A friend and I were going to travel in Mexico and Belize for two months. We were going to try to write a screenplay during that time.

"That sounds wonderful!" my mother said. "I've never been to either of those places. Will you take pictures? So I can see what they're like? Because I don't think I'll ever get there."

"Sure." It made me sad that she thought she'd never go. I felt guilty that I would get to experience something she wouldn't.

I went upstairs to use the bathroom, and while I was up there I couldn't help but sneak a look around. All of the rooms except the biggest bedroom weren't too bad—messy, yes, but like the rooms downstairs nothing beyond mild pack rat. Only the biggest bedroom, which had been my mother's at one point, was piled high with sweaters and shoes and orphaned hangers and empty boxes. It was hard to resist trying to straighten it up. If I thought I could get away with running downstairs, grabbing a garbage bag, and filling it, I probably would have.

When I came downstairs, Roger was in the kitchen, sitting with one of his feet propped up on the table. My mom was massaging it. "I need to get the circulation going," she said. "We have to do this at certain times each day."

"I hope I'm not interrupting you two," Roger said.

"Not at all," I said, feeling like I was the one interrupting. I picked up my coffee cup and took a sip. I was completely uncomfortable—and not just because Roger's foot was on the kitchen table. I'd never seen my mother act that nurturing. The weirdness at the door when she hugged me was compounded now by a thousand. "I actually have to leave soon," I said. "I told my dad and Sandy I'd have lunch with them."

It was true. I'd only given myself about an hour, because I wasn't sure how it would go.

"Oh, okay, honey," my mom said. "Hang on one second." She patted Roger's foot, wiped her hands on the edges of the towel, and stood up. "I'll be right back."

"She's got a surprise for you," Roger said and winked.

She came back holding two jewelry boxes—the kind made from thin cardboard and painted red, with gold lines swirling at the edges. "Sit down, honey," she said and I pulled out the chair next to hers. She opened one of the boxes and lifted out a necklace. It was made of chunky orange stones strung together on gold thread. She held it up to the light and then out to me.

"I want you to have this. Isn't it gorgeous? That stone is carnelian."

It was nothing I'd ever wear, and I knew it would just take up space in one of my dresser drawers until I eventually gave it away. But it seemed cruel to refuse it.

"It's really pretty," I said. "Thank you."

She pulled out another, this one with thick slices of jade, and an amethyst one, too. Strand after strand, she wanted to give them to me. And I had no choice but to accept them.

When I left, walking back to my dad and Sandy's, it felt like the start of something. I was nervous, fluttery in my stomach. She seemed good, and different from before, but I was wary. How long would this new and improved mother, this self-reliant mother, last?

It turned out, not long. In less than a year, Roger would be gone, my mother's true hoarding would begin, and she'd come to rely on me more than she ever had.

I pick up a paperback from the floor and toss it into the box for Savers. My mother is still staring at the photo.

"What was your dog's name, Mom?" The sheltie was gone by the time my mom and I began speaking again.

It's hard to imagine my mother having a dog because she's so afraid of them—I've seen her hang back on a sidewalk to put some space between herself and a Pomeranian—but apparently Roger surprised her with it one day.

"Buddy."

"What happened to him?" I ask.

"He ran away from a veterinarian's office."

"What do you mean, ran away?"

"It was a kennel, I mean. Roger and I went to Florida, and when we came back they said he ran away."

"What did you do?"

"Nothing," she shrugs.

That's not like her. This is the woman who used to regularly call television stations when I was a kid to complain about sexism in cartoons, who threatened to sue the Mayo Clinic because she believed Roger died for lack of funds; this is the woman who's been talking nonstop these last few days about suing her former employer. This is not a woman who backs down when she thinks she's been wronged. This is a woman who searches for instances of having been wronged, then wields them like hand grenades.

"You didn't try to sue them?" I ask.

"No."

"Did you try to find the dog? Did you put up signs or anything?"

"Oh, yeah, we did that. But no one called."

It occurs to me that possibly the people at the kennel could tell the dog was being neglected—I can't imagine my mother taking the time to brush its long fur or walk it or even remember to feed it—and said it was lost when it wasn't.

"Can I have the name of the kennel?" I want to find out the truth. It feels important.

"Why?"

"Because it's not right that they lost your dog."

She looks uneasy. "It was so long ago. I don't remember the name."

"Mom, really. Tell me."

"I think the place shut down," she says with finality.

It's obvious that she doesn't want to know what really happened. And I don't blame her.

THROUGHOUT THE DAY I come across other photographs of her and Roger together, as well as (unopened) Mother's Day and birthday cards from me; in each case the objects are on the floor under or among one of the junk piles. Someone who didn't know my mother might wonder how she could be so careless with these things.

But it isn't carelessness. It's the mental illness of compulsive hoarding. That's why she insists on keeping broken sewing machines and broken coffeemakers and a broken dishwasher hogging the last of the free space in her kitchen; that's what leaves her frozen in place whenever she needs to make a decision—in the bank, in the grocery store, in the middle of her cluttered staircase—while she mumbles to herself, weighing the consequences of choosing X, Y, or Z.

I'm at the other end of the room from my mom when I find a cardboard box under a pile of yarn, clothing patterns, two orange lava lamps, and a stack of newspapers. The box is square, about two feet by two feet, and sealed at the edges. I pick it up and give it a shake. Whatever's inside is too light to warrant a box this size.

My mother, going through a pile of papers, sees me holding the box and looks petrified.

"What's in here?" I ask.

She hesitates.

"Mom, what is it?"

"Roger."

That's a sick joke, even by her standards. I wait for her to laugh and tell me the truth.

"Really," she says.

I'm horrified. "Under all this junk? When you loved him so much?"

"I haven't found the right spot for him yet," she says, but her half smile reveals her shame. She knows it's wrong to leave him like this, but she doesn't know what else to do. She's paralyzed by indecision.

A bureau with shelves sits along one wall in the living room and I get up on my tiptoes and clear off a space on the highest shelf I can reach. I slide the box with Roger's ashes into the spot.

"He'll be safe from the clutter up there, Mom, until you find a better place for him."

"Thanks, honey." My mother sounds equally humiliated and heartbroken.

My poor mom. She doesn't want to live like this.

I wish there were a magic pill or surgery or something instantaneous to cure her, but there isn't. I wish I could convince her to stop, but I can't. Not that that's going to keep me from trying.

4

MYRON, MY MOTHER'S FATHER, WAS A RUSSIAN JEW, born in the United States to immigrant parents. He was under five feet tall, barrel-chested, with a bulldog's face and sausage fingers. My mother's mother, Esther, came to the United States from Poland—she refused to say exactly where she was from, but my mother thinks it's Lodz. Esther, her sister, and two brothers arrived in 1939, among the last of the Jewish Poles to get out. But not all the siblings chose to leave. There was a third sister who stayed behind in Poland with her husband and three children. They were all sent to Auschwitz, where they died.

My mother disagrees with me, but I think it was partly my grandmother Esther's grief and survivor's guilt that left her unable to stand up to Myron when he woke up the whole family as he came home stumbling drunk at 2:00 a.m.—among other charming behaviors. My mother blames Esther's timidity on depression and anxiety. I've suggested before that those, too, could be from the survivor's guilt, but for some reason, my mother doesn't want to hear it.

I wish I knew more about my mother's childhood. Every time I ask her, I end up hearing the same stories—the one about being left outside when she was a baby, and how occasionally when she was a teenager her parents would ship her off to stay with an aunt and uncle for weeks or even months (they'd eventually send her back because, according to my mother, she "cost too much"). There was the time Myron accused my mother of giving him a dirty look in the hallway, then flung open her bedroom door, stormed over to her dresser, and swept the one thing she cared about—a collection of glass animals—onto the floor. As my mother cried and tried to retrieve the broken figurines, Myron stood above her, laughing.

And there's one more story.

Helen is thirteen years old. Her family has just moved from one suburb of Boston to another. All of the other kids in the high school have known each other forever. She can't penetrate any of the cliques and has no friends. She's so shy that she can't say a word in any of her classes, can't say a word to any of the other students at lunch, can barely say thank you when she pays for her carton of milk to go with the peanut butter sandwich she's brought. Around this time, she starts breaking out in acne. Helen begs her mother to make her an appointment to see a dermatologist at one of the hospitals in Boston, and Esther complies.

The night before Helen's first appointment, there's a fight—Myron is slapping and shaking Esther in the kitchen. Helen runs in, yells at Myron, "Leave her alone!" and wedges her body between them. Myron's face reddens, his pale puffy lips tighten.

His fists come down on Helen's shoulders, her arms; he slaps her face. She screams but he doesn't stop, he keeps pelting her with his fists, with his open palms, until he's exhausted. Then he slams out of the house, off to the bar.

Esther, who has been trembling in the corner, walks out of the kitchen without a word to Helen. She goes into her bedroom and closes the door. Helen wants to knock on the door, wants to crawl into bed and under the covers with her mother, wants her mother to thank her for standing up for her, to run her hand over Helen's hair and tell her everything will be all right. But Helen knows better than to try. She doesn't knock. She will never knock.

The next day at the dermatologist appointment, Helen sits in a chair across from the doctor, who is behind a big oak desk. Helen's entire body hurts. Miraculously, there are no visible bruises, though she can barely lift her arms. The doctor, a young man with dark hair, green eyes, and almost translucent skin, begins to ask Helen the standard questions: "How long have you had this condition? Did either of your parents have acne?" And suddenly tears are streaming down Helen's face. She tries to wipe them away, tries to shift in her chair so the doctor won't see that she's crying, but now her whole body is shaking with sobs.

The guttural sounds are so animal that she doesn't recognize at first that they're coming from her. When she does, she's embarrassed; she feels her face flushing red, but she still can't stop.

"Miss Levine?" the doctor says, his face stern and concerned. "Are you okay?"

Helen shakes her head. She's not okay. Her father beats her. Her mother hates her. Her younger sister and brother pretend that everything in the house is okay and nothing ever happens to them. Things in that house happen only to Helen, whom no one will talk to.

No, she's not okay.

The doctor leans forward, hands Helen a tissue; without thinking she folds it into a blindfold and covers her eyes with it. She doesn't want to be here anymore, doesn't want to be anywhere. She wants to be a little kid who becomes invisible when she covers her eyes. She wants to be invisible so her body won't hurt anymore. So her father can't hurt her anymore.

The doctor comes around from his desk. He kneels next to Helen. She feels the weight of his hand on the chair next to her thigh, can tell he's resting his palm there. She can't stop crying. Will she ever stop? She's not sure.

"I'd like to help you, Miss Levine," he says. "Can you tell me what's wrong?"

Helen wants to tell him what's wrong, but she doesn't know. Not exactly. Is it that her father beats her or is it that her mother hates her? She only knows that she can't stop crying. She can't talk because she can't stop crying. She's gulping for air now. She lifts the Kleenex and opens her eyes, thinking that'll help her breathe. He's still right there; for a second she wants to laugh because this handsome young doctor is kneeling next to her as if proposing marriage. This handsome young doctor could take her away. She wants to get away, wonders if she'll ever get away, then knows she'll never get away. Never.

She cries harder.

The doctor's hand—still next to her leg, not in a sexual way but in a desperate gesture of closeness—is puffy and red. He's a dermatologist, though. Shouldn't his hands be soft and silky? Why isn't anyone what he's supposed to be? A father is not a father, a mother is not a mother, a doctor is not a doctor.

Helen can trust no one.

The doctor rises. He goes back behind his desk. He picks up the phone. "I need a psychiatrist," he says. "Now."

After that, Helen has two appointments: Once a month she sees the dermatologist and once a week she sees a psychiatrist. Somehow she even convinces Myron to accompany her to one of her psychiatrist appointments.

"He stays out late and walks home singing so the whole block can hear him, and then he comes inside the house like a hurricane," Helen says to Dr. McClure, her withered psychiatrist, the instant she and Myron sit down on the couch in his office. "Like a drunken hurricane." She's still in disbelief that Myron actually showed up and she's giddy with anticipation. Now she'll get the hell out of his house. She's going to tell the truth. It's nothing she hasn't already told Dr. McClure, but now she gets to say it in front of her father. Now she gets to see her father humiliated in the presence of a professional. A professional who will help her get out of her parents' house once and for all. "He's always drunk," she says. "Always."

The psychiatrist writes something in his notebook and looks at Myron, who remains silent.

"And he beats me." Helen doesn't turn her head, wants to look only at Dr. McClure. She didn't expect it to be so hard to say the words. She forces herself onward. "He hits my mother and he hits me."

"Only when she deserves it," Myron says, chewing on the tip of his unlit cigar, his fat fingers twirling it around.

Helen ignores him. He's an idiot, she knows. An idiot she'll soon be free from.

Dr. McClure asks questions: Are they a religious family (no), do they eat regular meals (yes), ever take vacations (no), have any pets (no), how are Helen's grades (good).

He writes down everything.

At the end of the appointment, Myron stands to leave and the doctor asks Helen to wait for a minute. Helen feels like jumping up and down. Her chest feels light and she wonders if this is what it's like to be happy, to be really happy.

"Miss Levine," the doctor says. They've had ten sessions already and he never uses her first name. "The foster care situations we have here in Boston are much worse than what you have at home. It's my recommendation that you stay there."

"Are you serious? Stay there?" Helen can't believe it.

"The conditions in the foster homes and group homes are very dire."

"But my parents, my house . . . it's dire there, too."

"I understand. But a foster home would be worse. I'm sorry."

And that's it. Nothing changes. Helen continues the appointments—they give her something to do, give her an excuse to go into Boston once a week.

The rest of the week she comes home after school and climbs directly into bed, burying herself under the blankets. She listens as her sister gets home and sits at the kitchen table with their mother, having coffee and talking about their days.

Whenever I ask my mother why the abuse was directed only at her, why her mother hardly spoke to her yet had coffee with her sister, the only answer she has is that her siblings "kept their blinders on and pretended everything was all right."

I met Esther and Myron just once. I was seven and my brother was five, and my mother had decided to try to make peace with her parents after years of estrangement. They hadn't seen each other since right before she and my dad got married. So we all drove to her parents' house outside Boston for a visit. When they opened their front door and stepped forward, I couldn't believe how tiny they were. Neither of them was taller than four foot ten. And they were round, like little silos, and gray—probably from all the cigar smoke Myron was constantly spewing. Esther wore a housecoat that was so faded I couldn't tell what color it had been originally. Myron wore workman pants and a button-down flannel shirt, even though it was summer.

They lived on the first floor of the three-family triplex they owned. It was dark inside. Dank. The wood floors were scratched and bare. It was a small space but there was room to move; it was certainly not a hoarded home. All of the furniture—the dressers in the bedrooms, the wooden stand in the hallway for mail and the telephone, the kitchen table—looked dumpy and half-broken. Stained and torn cloth doilies covered most surfaces. Cigar smoke had permeated every layer of the place. Even now the smell of cigars reminds me of Myron.

On one of our first days in Massachusetts, our parents took my brother and me to Revere, a seaside town with a famous beach. We walked along the boardwalk, inhaled the salty smell of the ocean—new to my brother and me—and ate hot dogs and fried clam strips and slices of pizza. We went down to the sand and dipped our toes in the water. My brother and I saw seagulls, white and honking, for the first time. The water was cold, much colder than the lakes we were used to in Minneapolis, but still we spread out our towels on the beach, kicked off our shoes, and shed the clothes we'd worn over our suits. My mom waited on one of the towels while my brother, my dad, and I went in. My dad pretended to be a shark, coming at us with his arms outstretched and we screamed and ran farther into the salty water, waiting as long as possible to take a gulp of air and dive under.

Another day my mom and dad decided to go into Boston for a few hours. They asked Esther and Myron to watch us. My brother and I did something—fought with each other? Ran around in a game of tag? Sassed back to Myron when he told us to shut up?—I honestly have no idea what we did, but during the few hours that our parents were gone, as Esther cried and trembled, Myron took off his leather belt and whipped my five-year-old brother with it.

As soon as our parents came back, my brother and I told them what Myron had done; Myron stood there with his fat arms crossed over his fat belly and denied it—even though my brother had welts on his back. My dad regrets to this day that he didn't pummel Myron right there. My mother was upset because her hopes for reconciliation with her parents were ruined, but she wasn't surprised. Years later, when I ask her why she left us there when she knew how horrible Myron was, she says, "I don't know what I was thinking, I really don't."

Five years after that visit, Myron became sick with prostate cancer. My mom didn't call or see him before he died, though she made a fragile peace with her mother just before she passed away six months after Myron.

Her parents even managed to screw over my mother from the grave: My grandfather had been a plumber, my grandmother a housewife, yet somehow they amassed more than three quarters of a million dollars—and their fully paid-off triplex was worth more than a million. According to my mom, the house was to be divided evenly between my mother's two siblings. Then, from the savings, my mother's sister got $500,000, her brother got $250,000 . . . and my mother got $20,000.

My mother has told me alternately that the injustice happened because she already had a house and her parents thought she didn't need one, that her father always hated her, and that her siblings convinced their parents to leave her out of the will. Who knows what's true?

My mother tried to get her siblings at least to give her something—the $20,000 covered the rest of her nursing school, which was helpful, but she was struggling at the time. According to my mom, they refused.

There's no demonstrable link between hoarding and early material deprivation. But there is a link between hoarding and *emotional* deprivation. Many hoarders report being physically or sexually abused as children. My mother was deprived of love, affection, often even the acknowledgment of her existence, to say nothing of the beatings she endured. Her cold and chaotic childhood home was the perfect breeding ground for the mental illness that would end up affecting us all.

5

MY MOTHER IS WHAT'S KNOWN AS A CLEAN hoarder—I wanted to laugh, then cry, the first time I read that term because her house is anything but clean—as opposed to a squalor hoarder. The house of a clean hoarder doesn't usually contain pools of putrid water from long-ago leaks, piles of feces from animals or humans (yes, sometimes hoarders simply toss dirty diapers, usually adult-sized, on the floor or into bathtubs), rotting food left out in the open, or decomposing corpses of rodents or passed-on pets buried beneath layers of garbage. The squalor hoarder is too ashamed to allow a plumber inside when something breaks, so the sink or the toilet or the shower goes unfixed. There's often no running water at all. Sometimes there's no heat. So compared to some other children of hoarders, and the messes they have to clean up, I'm lucky.

I'm also grateful that my mother isn't an animal hoarder, with dozens or even hundreds of dogs or cats or rabbits or chinchillas in tiny cages or sometimes running loose in a house, where the poor, often starving creatures create permanent stenches, destroy floors and walls, and leave enormous amounts of feces and carcasses in their wake. It's not uncommon for animal hoarders to serve jail time, sometimes more than once. They truly believe they're helping the animals, or even saving them. Many factors contribute to this blatant split from reality. Just to name one, animal hoarders have at least equal rates of childhood neglect and abuse as do object hoarders. Numerous studies have shown that early childhood trauma can cause dissociation, attachment disorder, and even impaired facial emotion recognition—thus, the hoarder may literally not see or understand the suffering happening among their animal charges.

In spite of my mother's horrid refrigerator, she's not a food hoarder. Food hoarders can't throw out any food item, regardless of how moldy or how many years past its expiration date it may be. The dangers of rotting food are multiple: the fumes, flies, maggots, cockroaches, and other infestations, for starters. Then, of course, there's also the fact that eating something spoiled can lead to serious health problems or even death. Many times food hoarders have extra refrigerators filled with items they just can't toss—expired yogurt, chicken broth, cheese, eggs. Just like my mother believing her house looks "marvelous," food hoarders are blind to the decay inside their refrigerators and on their shelves. One theory about hoarding is that it's a normal instinct run amok, and this makes sense, especially in the case of food hoarders. Even animals collect and store food; in fact, the word "hamster" comes from the German word *hamstern,* which means to hoard.

My mother may have a touch of bibliomania (book hoarding), but she does actually read most of her books—she just can't get rid of them afterward. "I think this is a first edition," she'll sometimes say about a ripped-up hardcover that I can tell in an instant isn't. But it's the nonsensical items, the possessions she hangs on to for no discernible reason—the unopened Savers bags with unknown contents, the childsized inflatable furniture, the decades-old cases of hand lotion—that concern me. Without those things, it would almost be possible to think of her problem as simply having a surplus of books; without those inexplicable items I could rationalize that she's just an enthusiastic collector.

Sometimes I even allow myself to indulge in this disingenuousness for a few seconds. But then my fantasy-vision expands outward, past the piles of books to the rest of the house—the floors covered in *things,* with just a narrow pathway to get through, every available dresser, table, desk covered by her potential treasures—and I'm forced to face the fact, yet again, that she's much more than a collector.

ON MY THIRD day of cleaning, I'm standing in the hallway shoveling—literally, with a shovel—old magazines, newspapers, dirty rags, and junk mail into garbage bags, while my mother sits on a chair in the doorway to the kitchen, watching. Almost by accident I finally ask if she believes she's a hoarder. I've wanted to ask her for a while, but using the word has seemed somehow too disrespectful. And I was afraid of offending her to the point where she'd refuse to let me keep cleaning. But it just slips out.

"A hoarder?" Her accent makes the word sound like hoa-da. "Of course I know I'm a hoarder."

"You do?" I stop midshovel, wiping the sweat from my forehead with the back of my hand.

"I'll tell you exactly when I knew," she says, her voice drifting off. She's always like this when she tells a story, saying "Let's see, where should I start" at least a couple times; starting, stopping, starting over; and including unimportant details that get her so sidetracked she ends up in a completely different narrative. It's common among hoarders. It's as if they're as unable to edit their words as they are their belongings. "Let me think," she says now. "Okay . . . it was that time . . . that time you and Dave cleaned. When I saw all of those things out on the lawn, I just couldn't believe they were all mine. I said to myself, 'I have a real problem.'"

I'm impressed. Surprised, and impressed. I decide to dig further. "Here's something I've always wondered: What does it feel like when you purchase something?"

She looks around the hallway at the various piles of things I've readied for shoveling and leans over to pluck an old dog toy—a dingy, stuffed yellow chick—from the mess. She brushes it off.

"It's . . . it's ridiculous." My mother actually sounds embarrassed. Normally, nothing embarrasses my mother.

"What is it?"

"Okay," she says, holding the yellow chick on her lap. "It's like I tell myself that whatever the object is, it's going to change my life."

"But I can tell that rationally you don't believe it, or you wouldn't be embarrassed by it."

"Oh, I know that it won't *really* change my life, but there's another part of me that thinks it will. I can't really explain it. But it's a thrill. It's exciting."

I've been to Savers with her before and she really does look at home there, happy and serene. If she were a zoo animal, that would probably be the habitat the zookeepers would create for her.

"And then there's this reinforcement thing, too," she continues, "because I think, well, I found a deal once, so I have to look for another one."

"But that deal didn't change your life."

She shakes her head, laughs. "I know! It doesn't make sense. See, Jessie, there's something psychological about hoarding, I know that for sure. But there's also something primal."

"I think you're right, Mom." I'm astounded at her levelheadedness and want to seize the moment. "Would you consider seeing someone about this? A professional?"

"You mean like a therapist? Oh, no. I tried that. You remember how awful she was."

"But what if I found one who specializes in hoarding? And a different kind of therapy than just talking."

"I don't need that. I just need time to clean. And now that I'm unemployed, I have it! I'm starting to think that getting fired was the best thing that could have happened to me."

"You really think it's just a matter of not having enough time to clean? What about what you were just saying about the feeling you get when you buy things?"

"But the real problem is that I don't have enough time. That's it. And now I will."

And just like that, the rational mother is gone. As I pick up the shovel, my arms are heavy with disappointment. Her problem isn't a lack of time to clean, and deep down she knows that.

Over the years, my mother has had a few different diagnoses: generalized anxiety disorder, depression, and depression with rumination (obsessive thoughts). Another diagnosis, this one self-identified, occurred a few years ago. She called me and said, "Guess what. I've got borderline personality disorder!"

"Why do you sound like that's good news?" I asked.

"It is good news—now there's a name for what I have."

I read up on borderline personality disorder, and the descriptions really did sound like her. Characterized by instability in moods, black-and-white thinking, and a tendency to see oneself as a victim and blame others for their problems, borderline personality disorder gets its name from the early belief that people suffering from the condition were at the brink, or "borderline" of psychosis.

When I read in Christine Ann Lawson's *Understanding the Borderline Mother*, "Fear of abandonment is the most common symptom of borderline personality disorder and is shared by all borderlines," and later, that some borderline mothers "may physically or verbally attack their children in the middle of the night," I picked up the phone and called my mom.

"I think you're right," I said. "I think you do have borderline personality disorder."

She didn't say anything. "Mom?"

"Actually, I hate to tell you this, but now I think I have Asperger syndrome."

That sent me on another research chase. And again, she did seem to fit some of the descriptions, especially those of long-winded and one-sided conversations, an apparent lack of empathy (she likes to use her nursing expertise if someone is injured, but she's utterly uninterested any time I have a cold or the flu), and a focus on parts of an object or experience rather than on the whole.

Whether my mother has borderline personality disorder or Asperger syndrome remains to be seen, though I'm inclined to believe that the depression she takes medication for and compulsive hoarding aren't her only problems. And she's not unique: Most hoarders have an additional psychiatric condition. Some of the most prevalent are depression, social phobia, generalized anxiety disorder, and obsessive-compulsive disorder. Personality disorders and eating disorders, as well as impulse control disorders such as kleptomania, compulsive gambling, and trichotillomania (the irresistible urge to pull out one's own hair) aren't unheard of either.

The high rate of additional conditions is one reason successful treatment for hoarding remains elusive. One approach that shows some promise is cognitive-behavioral therapy; as the name implies, it consists of examining and changing problematic thought patterns along with behaviors. For compulsive hoarders, the sessions take place either at the therapist's office, in the patient's home, or wherever the person excessively acquires objects—which could be a store, but it could also be a Dumpster. For my mother this would entail a therapist accompanying her to Savers and talking her through whether or not she really needed that twenty-first pair of sneaker-clogs.

Unfortunately, every time I've asked my mother if she'd be willing to try something like that she makes some excuse. She seems more interested in diagnosing her problems than actually *doing* anything about them.

"Oh, Jessie," my mom says now, clapping her hands over the dingy yellow chick. "Once my house is clean, maybe I could get a little dog! A sheltie, like the kind Roger and I had!"

"Mom, no," I say, my voice firm. I scoop up another shovelful of flyers and junk mail and dust balls. I can't let her start thinking about getting a dog. She wouldn't take care of it and it couldn't possibly have a good life in her possession-packed house. Besides, if she got one, she might end up getting another, and another. And then I'd have to call The Humane Society on my own mother. "Please promise me that you won't get a dog."

"I know." She sighs. "I can't."

Relief floods through me, then sadness for her. What's wrong with wanting a dog? It's a normal desire. I have my own little dog waiting for me back in New York; it doesn't seem fair that I can have one and she can't.

"But Jessie," she says. "Maybe someday I could have one?"

"Definitely. Someday. Let's just get your house in shape and get rid of your cancer first, okay?"

"You're right."

I would love to see my mother get a little sheltie. I'd love to see her in a clean house, lying on a comfortable couch, reading a book with the dog snuggled up next to her, a cozy quilt tossed over them for warmth. It's easy to picture. I'm just not sure it'll ever happen.

THE FIRST TIME I noticed my mother's unusual relationship to possessions, I was five years old. It was before my parents separated, during the two years we lived in the big house in the suburbs. One morning before school, my mother asked me to tell my kindergarten teacher to keep me longer that day because she wanted to go thrift-store shopping. "Just take the afternoon bus home instead," my mom said.

We were sitting in the U-shaped booth in the kitchen, my mother feeding my brother warm cereal from a bowl as I chewed on a piece of toast.

I didn't like the idea. It seemed too unorganized, too haphazard. My dad had already left for work, so I couldn't ask him to intervene.

"Can't you just be home in time?" I pleaded.

"Just tell the teacher you're staying for both the morning and afternoon sessions today. Don't worry so much. Kids do it all the time."

Did they? I had no idea. I was so shy I could barely say a word to my teacher, so I couldn't imagine approaching her about this. But my mother kept insisting. That entire morning at school, I tried to get up my nerve to tell the teacher about my mother's plan, but I couldn't do it. Such an easy thing to do, but I couldn't do it.

I shuffled out the door at the usual time and rode the school bus as always, hoping that by some miracle my mom would be home when I got there. I walked up the long snowy driveway, looking through the big picture window for signs of life inside. I tried the door. Locked. I rang the bell. Nothing. It was a typical Minnesota winter day: freezing and windy and snowy. I stuffed myself between the heavy door of the house and the screen door, trying to protect myself from the wind. I stayed like that for a long time, occasionally pulling off my mittens to blow on my fingers in an attempt to thaw them. When my mother finally came home, her arms were loaded with purchases. My brother, his face wrapped in a scarf, lagged behind her lugging the bags she couldn't carry. I knew what was in them: salt and pepper shakers, sweaters, patterns for clothes she'd never sew.

"What are you doing here?" my mother demanded when she saw me. "I told you to tell your teacher—"

"You could have given me a note," I said, running inside as soon as she unlocked the door. "You could have called!"

I had a feeling that's what other mothers would have done. Still, no matter how angry I was with her, I was angrier at myself. I shouldn't have been so shy. But as I began to warm up, I looked around at all of her new acquisitions and thought about how she'd chosen these *things* over me, and I grew angry at her once again.

Sometimes I wonder if my mother felt strange, being Jewish, tiny, with dark eyes and hair and her strong Boston accent in a land of blond, Nordic giants. She's shy and self-isolating, and was then, too. Maybe she coped with her loneliness by shopping. Maybe that's how it all started. The problem is she never stopped.

WHEN I'M FINISHED cleaning for the day, my mother insists on taking me, my dad, and Sandy to her favorite Thai restaurant for dinner. My eight-year-old cousin, Billy, who lives next door to my dad and Sandy, joins us. Billy's favorite thing to do is go out to eat. He keeps up on all the local restaurant news. Once I asked him what he thought of a new café in the neighborhood and he said, "The lunches are okay, but the entrées at dinner are fabulous." For Christmas he asked for and got a sushi maker. What I'm saying is that he's a sophisticated kid.

Still, it isn't quite appropriate, when, on the way to the Thai place, my mother starts talking about dying and how she's ready for it, and how she's STILL an atheist in the proverbial foxhole. My mother, Billy, and I are in the backseat. My dad and Sandy are in the front, trying to work out the best way to get to the restaurant. My mother seems prepared to hold forth on death for the entire ride, but then I notice that Billy's gotten quiet and is frowning. I ask her to stop.

"Okay," she says, unbothered. It turns out she's got another subject all lined up: the waitress at the Thai place we're headed toward and how extremely hard she works. "You just wouldn't believe how hard . . . it's incredible." My mother actually chokes up as she says the words.

It's a Wonderful Stranger. Family members often notice hoarders fixating on one person who is *absolutely perfect,* usually someone who doesn't know the hoarder well—a doctor, a clerk at the bank, a hairdresser—though sometimes it's a new friend. That person is lavished with praise to the point of worship. In my mother's case, that person becomes the center of her world and pretty much all she'll talk about. *So-and-so is just so wonderful, you wouldn't believe . . ."* that is, until the person does something that disappoints my mother. When that happens, the Wonderful Stranger is quickly discarded. (It turns out the Wonderful Stranger concept is identical to a feature of borderline personality disorder called "splitting," in which a person is idealized and then suddenly despised and rejected.) I've seen my mother do it again and again. One friend got a face-lift. One didn't hire my mother for a nursing job the woman didn't even know she wanted. And in many cases, I never found out the exact crime.

I remember weeding my mother's front garden once while she sat on the steps watching—I was maybe eight or nine—and her best friend Sue walked by across the street. They didn't acknowledge each other.

"Mom," I said. "There's Sue, right there—aren't you going to say hi?"

"No," she snapped. "Of course not."

"Why not?"

"Because she's a goddamn lunatic, that's why."

"Since when?" This was a woman my mother had seen at least three times a week for months. I had heard them having conversations about their childhoods, about the fact that they'd both had alcoholic, abusive fathers.

"Since always," my mother said. "It just took me a while to figure it out."

I never learned what Sue did, but the aftermath was the same as the others: *It happened again, just like always. I start to trust someone and she turns on me. She starts putting me down.* My mother crawls into bed for a few days, depressed. She emerges from her chrysalis self-righteous and enraged. *I don't know what I was thinking being friends with her.* And then it's on to the next Wonderful Stranger, who may or may not become an actual friend. And repeat.

When we arrive at the Thai place, because of my mother's nonstop talk about how hard the waitress works, I'm half-expecting to see some broken-backed, hundred-year-old woman hobbling from table to table, maybe blind, or at least deaf. I'm also expecting the place to be semi-nice, since the restaurant is far out in the suburbs and my mother apparently makes the drive regularly. Instead, we're greeted by thin, stained carpeting, frameless prints on the walls, bare lightbulbs hanging from the pockmarked ceiling, and the smell of old grease wafting through the air. Maybe, I think, they spend their budget on fine ingredients rather than décor. I can see my dad and Sandy, who are extremely healthy eaters, eyeing each other; they're skeptical.

The five of us have just walked in the door when a tall Thai woman approaches holding menus. She's maybe thirty-five and is sheathed in a red satin dress.

My mother takes a step toward her and says, "Oh, hello, Lalana," in a high voice. "It's so good to see you. How are you?"

The World's Hardest Working Waitress doesn't know who my mother is.

She looks baffled by my mother calling her by name. I'm embarrassed for my mom, but she seems not to have noticed. And the waitress quickly recovers and politely answers, "I'm fine thank you, how are you?"

"I'm doing okay," my mother says, as the waitress leads us to a table and hands us menus. No, you're not, I can't help but think, you have cancer.

When the World's Hardest Working Waitress comes back to take our order, my mother smiles up at her, and, I could swear, even bats her eyelashes.

"Oh, Jessie," she says, pointing to an item on the menu, "get the fish. The fish is incredible here!"

"I'll have the fish, please," I say.

"I'll have that, too," my mom says. "And an order of the chicken wings. Should I get two orders?" She looks over to Sandy at the end of the table.

"That's okay, Helen," Sandy says. "Rick and I aren't that hungry. One order should be enough."

"Okay," my mom says, obviously disappointed.

My dad and Sandy order something with tofu and vegetables and Billy gets a platter of various appetizers.

The food is so greasy that it's almost inedible. Billy is the only one who seems to even mildly enjoy it—and that might be for the novelty of it, since he rarely gets to indulge in such greasiness. My mother is too busy talking about the World's Hardest Working Waitress to notice what she's eating; every time the woman walks by on her way to or from the kitchen, my mother leans forward and says, her voice overflowing with reverence, "Oh, my God. How hard she works."

Billy starts teasing my mom, though I don't think she realizes it. "So, do you think the waitress here works hard, Helen?" he asks, in his cute, perpetually hoarse voice.

"Like you wouldn't believe," my mom replies, shaking her head and gnawing at a chicken wing. After a minute she switches topics, back to dying. "Maybe I should donate my body to science," she says dreamily.

"You haven't even had the surgery yet," I say. "You don't know what your prognosis will be."

"I have a feeling, though."

My dad and Sandy are talking about something else—probably how bad the food is. It takes me a little while to notice that Billy's quietly looking down at his plate, no longer touching his food. He's frowning, just like in the car.

"Mom," I say. "Let's talk about something else." I gesture toward Billy.

"It's good for him to know about death," she stage-whispers at me.

"Helen, please," Sandy says.

I feel bad that I didn't stop my mom sooner, before Billy got upset. But I guess I'm just used to her inappropriateness. It's nothing new. When I was ten years old and already living full-time with my dad and Sandy, my mother invited me over for dinner one night. When I went upstairs, I peeked inside her bedroom. She was living with Sam and their king-size bed took up most of the room. It had no sheets on it. The floor was piled high with clothes—they reached the height of the naked bed, so it was as if the entire room was one level, a few feet above the actual floor. And there was a smell. A strange chemical yet musty scent I didn't recognize. Downstairs, I said something to my mom about the state of her bedroom.

"I'm too busy to clean," she said.

"And it smells weird."

"That's from sex," she said, matter-of-factly. "That's the smell of semen."

"Gross, Mom," I said. "Thanks."

During the meal, Sandy barely touches anything on her plate. My dad, Billy, and I eat a little, and my mother eats heartily, though she admits that the fish isn't so good this time.

"I guess the waitress was working too hard and she left it in the fryer too long," Billy jokes.

My mother laughs. And while I like that she can laugh at herself—to say she doesn't get offended easily is an extreme understatement—her immunity to criticism makes it difficult to get through to her about her house, her yard, her car, even about the way she dresses. She's so spectacularly unself-aware that I can barely believe she gets by in the world. That's why I was so shocked when she admitted to being a hoarder.

She's still going on about the waitress.

In the meantime, muscles I didn't even know I had ache from the twelve-hour days I've spent hauling bags of garbage out of her house. Sandy and my dad, struggling with their real estate business, work twelve-hour days themselves.

Each time my mother mentions the waitress I can see my dad's jaw clench, his internal motor revving. Even Sandy looks agitated. Their barely touched plates are pushed to the side; only my mom and Billy are still eating.

"We all work hard, Mom," I say.

She shakes her head. "Not like her. She's just incredible."

6

AS HAPPY AS I WAS WHEN MY DAD AND SANDY GOT married, and as relieved as I was when I started living in the yellow house full-time, I was never able to shake the feeling of being too abnormal for a normal family. Not that things were completely normal in the yellow house: Merging the two families proved difficult. Often it felt as if we were two separate families living under one roof—me, my dad, and my brother in one, and Sandy and her daughter Beth in the other. My dad, my brother, and I would go to movies while Sandy and Beth stayed home and sewed together or gardened. It was almost as if the remodeling my dad and Sandy had done to turn the yellow house from a two-family duplex into a single-family home simply hadn't worked.

It wasn't anyone's fault. Sandy made an effort with my brother and me, taking each of us out separately for our own special days—a picnic at one of the lakes, shopping, or miniature golfing. She even arranged for me to visit a private zoo one of her clients had access to, where I got to pet a bobcat and a timber wolf and sit on the back of a tiger—later I found out a man with an aimed rifle had been standing behind me the whole time, just in case. My dad didn't make as much of an effort with Beth, figuring she'd always gotten plenty of love and affection, whereas my brother and I had a deficit and needed all of his attention.

But it wasn't enough.

My dad and Sandy said later that when I was thirteen, it was as if a switch flipped inside me—I went from being an agreeable kid who liked to help around the house, to a desperately unhappy drama queen.

My dad and I bickered constantly, especially when, around the age of fourteen, I started dressing in a style he didn't like—dyeing my hair bone white or fire engine red (these days not at all wild, but in 1983 it was extreme, especially in Minneapolis), wearing ripped jeans, flannel shirts over T-shirts, and combat boots, and coming home with albums made by bands with names my dad found both nonsensical and repugnant: Dead Kennedys, Hüsker Dü, JFA, GBH. ("The Dead Kennedys! That is the height of disrespect!")

My dad was embarrassed to be seen with me. When we'd go to the movies he'd require me to cover my hair with a baseball cap. And when, at fifteen, I told him that I wanted to get my nose pierced, he forbade it. By now my dad and I were almost always in some kind of argument. Because my absence meant relative peace at the yellow house, my dad and Sandy never said no when I wanted to spend the night somewhere else. So I spent the weekend at my friend Tara's house, where our friend Jennifer pierced my nose with a brooch and a couple ice cubes.

I was terrified to come home, but eventually I did, bringing

Jennifer and Tara with me. Sandy and my dad were talking at the kitchen table. My friends and I walked past them, and I covered my nose with my palm as we did. Immediately my dad demanded, "You did it anyway, didn't you?"

"Run," I said to my friends and we bolted up the spiral stairs to my room.

In seconds my dad was pounding on the door. "Goddammit, Jessie. I told you not to do that!"

"Stay here," I said to my friends, and went out into the hallway, closing the door behind me. My dad walked toward me, but I ran past him, for some reason into his and Sandy's bedroom. I turned around and there he was in the doorway.

"It's my life," I yelled. "I can do what I want."

He grabbed my arm and stared at the nose ring for a few seconds. "Jessie! Why?" He shoved me backward and I fell onto his and Sandy's bed.

"What the hell?" My dad had never been physically violent with me before. He was only a few feet away, and without thinking I kicked him in the stomach. I was wearing combat boots, so I know it hurt. But I didn't wait for his reaction—I sprang off the bed and out of the room.

I threw open my bedroom door and told my friends that they should leave.

"No way," Jennifer said. "We can't leave you."

In spite of what had just happened, I wasn't afraid. I knew my dad wouldn't really hurt me. And I didn't want my friends to see him like this. I loved my dad and I couldn't bear the thought of my friends thinking badly of him. My dad had saved me from my mother; my dad told me I was a good kid and believed I was good, even though I wasn't. My dad would do anything for me. This raging man wasn't my real dad—this was merely his temper. Besides, it was my fault that he was so angry.

"I'll be fine," I told my friends. "Really."

They reluctantly scurried past me, down the stairs, and out of the house. It was summer and the windows were wide open. I could hear Jennifer out on the sidewalk yelling, "You're an asshole! You shouldn't treat your daughter like that!" Her voice faded as she and Tara hurried toward the bus stop.

I was already feeling guilty for kicking my dad. I walked toward his room to apologize, right as he was coming out. When I saw how red and angry his face was, I got scared. My first impulse was to get out of the house, but I was already past the staircase opening. The only way down to the first floor was by scaling the metal bars surrounding the stairs. So I climbed over the top and began working my way down.

I'd gotten over the side and was hanging by my fingertips onto the edge of the floor, which was the ceiling of the living room below, when my dad stomped one of his feet near my fingers. Even though it was only about a six-foot drop, I was reluctant to jump. But the next time his foot came down inches from my hand, I did.

I ran out the front door, looking around for my friends, but they were already gone.

I walked right past my mother's house and didn't even consider going in. Instead, I ended up sitting in the park next to the elementary school, swinging on the swing set until it was dark.

When I got back to the yellow house, my dad had regained control of himself. He asked if we could talk in his office and I followed him into the small room, taking my usual spot in the chair across from his desk. My dad had finally quit his three-pack-a-day smoking habit two years earlier, and though his skin had lost its yellowish hue and he'd repainted the eggshell-colored walls of his office, I could still smell old smoke.

"I owe you a big apology," my dad began. "I never, ever should have acted like that."

"I'm sorry, too," I said. "I shouldn't have gotten my nose pierced."

"Let me see it, anyway," my dad said, and leaned forward. "It's not that bad."

"Do you want me to take it out? I'll take it out if you really want me to."

"No, honey, it's really not that bad. It's actually kind of cute."

"Well, it's a good thing we had that blow-out fight then, right?" I said, attempting humor. But I was confused. Why had we fought, anyway?

"Listen, honey. I can't tell you how sorry I am for how I acted. I'm absolutely ashamed of myself. I can't believe I tried to smash your fingers."

Suddenly my perfectly unhurt fingers ached. I cradled my hands together in my lap.

"But you weren't really trying to smash them. My fingers were right there. If you'd really wanted to, you could have."

My dad shook his head. "I have to be honest, in spite of how painful it is to admit."

"I don't believe you," I said. "And besides, I kicked you in the stomach, so we're even."

"We're not even. I'm the adult here. I shouldn't have let things escalate like that." He plucked a pencil from the cup on his desk and twirled it around. I stared at the fingernail that looked like a bird's beak, as I always did. I'd seen him cry only once, at his mother's funeral just a few weeks before he and Sandy got married, but when I looked at my dad's face that night in his office, his eyes were watery.

"Dad, it's okay, really."

"It's not." He sighed. "I guess I've just let things build up. And you seem so unhappy. I want you to be happy, honey."

That's how my dad and I did things: a big blowout, then calm talking, with no hard feelings afterward. Anger was a cancer to be excised, and the way that happened was through verbal venting; you couldn't fault someone for trying to be honest and open, after all.

Unfortunately, this explosion-then-bonding didn't prove to be such a winning strategy with friends and boyfriends later. Shockingly, it turned out that my habit of yelling at the slightest provocation and thinking that what I said in anger didn't carry over into calmer times didn't go over so well with normal people. It took me a long time to realize that regardless of how angry I may feel, some things shouldn't be said. Or done.

But I didn't know that then. After each fight, I felt closer to my dad than I had before. And the nose-piercing fight was no exception. By the end of our talk that night, we were laughing, friends again.

I didn't believe my dad when he said he'd been trying to smash my fingers. If he'd really wanted to, he could have. But that didn't matter. Nor did it matter that after that horrible fight we were friends again. That fight, our worst yet, was the beginning of the end of my days in the yellow house.

LATER THAT YEAR, I was arrested for underage drinking and my dad forced me to start seeing a shrink. I'd already begun asking my dad and Sandy if I could move out, into an apartment. I made decent money at my job selling magazine subscriptions over the phone. My dad and Sandy said of course I couldn't move out, I was fifteen years old. So I started threatening to run away to New York. I wasn't really going to run away, and I didn't seriously expect to move out before I graduated from high school. Nobody else I knew had. But I kept bringing it up because I needed things to be different—and at that point I could envision only external change.

I was anxious, I was depressed, I was shy, I was obnoxious. I was intensely unhappy. And a bizarre shift had taken place: Back when I was seven, eight, and nine, during the time I lived with my mom through the week and my dad on the weekends, I was wild at my mother's and calm and respectful at my dad's. Now it was the opposite. I was rude and out of control at my dad and Sandy's and when I went to my mom's house I'd fall immediately into my role of cleaning, organizing, and offering advice on everything from hairstyles to jobs to nutrition.

The change I was craving came a few months after I turned sixteen, on Mother's Day. My dad was furious because I hadn't gotten Sandy a card. "After all Sandy's done for you!" he yelled as I lay sprawled across the brown sectional sofa in the TV room, twirling my nose ring around and around.

"It's just a Hallmark holiday," I said. "It's total bullshit."

"Maybe so, but Sandy deserves to know she's appreciated. And do the dishes!"

It was my turn and this was the third time my dad had asked me. I could feel his temper revving up, but I didn't care.

"I'll do them when I'm good and ready," I said.

My dad grabbed my arm and pulled me up from the couch; I struggled and ended up squished against the wall.

"That's it," I said and ran past him, up to my room, where I threw a change of clothing into a backpack. I walked out of the house and to the bus stop. It was a Sunday, which meant the buses ran infrequently, and it was late, too. I called my friend Mary from a pay phone in the bus shelter. I'd met Mary recently, at an all-ages Otto's Chemical Lounge show at the 7th Street

Entry. She was eighteen, an art student at the university, and she had her own apartment.

When she answered the phone I asked if I could spend the night. She said yes.

Even before I got on the bus, a familiar guilt began settling over me. I was such a fuckup. A terrible daughter.

I called my dad when I got to Mary's apartment. I didn't want him to worry. He had an idea: I had a shrink appointment coming up, and he suggested that he meet me there. I covered the phone and asked Mary if she'd mind if I stayed with her for three days, and she said not at all.

"Okay," I told my dad. "I'll see you then."

During those three days, Mary asked me if I wanted to officially move in—an extremely generous offer, because it was a two-room apartment. When I met my dad at the shrink's office, the first thing he said was, "I know you're not happy. What can I do to make you happy?"

"You can let me move in with Mary."

He agreed. Apparently he'd taken my threats about running away to New York more seriously than I'd meant them; if I moved in with Mary, he'd at least know where I was. We left the appointment and drove back to the yellow house, where I packed up my few belongings and strapped my mattress to the top of his car.

Because I owned almost nothing, moving into Mary's apartment took twenty minutes. When my dad left, he hugged me and shook Mary's hand. I had to restrain myself from following him down the stairs and getting into his car with him. I was too young; I hadn't really meant my juvenile threats. But it seemed too late to back out. And now Mary was counting on me to help with the rent.

The first few nights felt like an extended sleepover with a

fun girlfriend: We ate macaroni and cheese out of the pan, we made prank calls to boys we liked, and in a not-so-wise move we gave each other homemade tattoos with sewing needles and India ink. But despite the fun, I missed my dad and life at the yellow house. I felt awful for the way I'd acted toward my dad and Sandy. Sandy, who I'd wished was my mom, who'd tried so hard to blend our two families and make the new family in the yellow house work. I'd taken her for granted, and worse. And my dad, who'd stepped in and taken me from my mom's house once he realized what was happening there.

A few days after I moved in with Mary, a letter came for me. A letter from my dad. In it, he said that he knew, no matter how dark things got or seemed for me, that I was going to be okay. That I was strong and that I could do anything I wanted. He said I was always welcome at the yellow house. After all I'd put him through, my dad still loved me and still believed in me. I'd been planning to pay my rent with earnings from my magazine subscription job, but in the letter my dad offered to pay it. I only had to pay my food, clothing, and bills.

I started going back to the yellow house every Sunday. I'd bring my laundry and we'd eat lunch—Sandy, Beth, and my brother, too, if they were around—and then we'd go to a movie. Sometimes my dad, who is a relentless audiophile, would take me with him to stereo stores to scout out gear. He'd buy a few pieces of equipment and then back at home he'd test out the sound quality of one turntable cartridge versus another, one set of speakers versus another, one subwoofer versus another. We'd take turns sitting in the prime listening spot in the living room, and judging by the high notes in Mozart's *The Marriage of Figaro,* the mid notes in a Beatles song, and the voice quality on an Emmylou Harris record (later Aimee Mann), we'd decide which pieces could stay and which ones had to be returned.

Afterward, my dad would drive me back to Mary's and in the car I'd tell him about school, or whatever job I happened to be working, or whatever boy I happened to be dating. I could tell my dad anything and I wanted to, because he always gave me the best advice.

I'd wanted to move out, and I should have been thrilled. And in many ways I was. But moving out of the closest thing I'd ever known to a normal house confirmed the suspicion I'd always held: There was something wrong with me. Something had turned in me, gone rotten during those years I lived mostly with my mom, and now I just couldn't fit into a family.

Almost all of my friends were older than I was. One of them helped me get a fake ID with my picture on it, so I could go to bars to see bands with my friends. Though I continued to go to high school, half the time I forgot how old (or really how young) I actually was. I felt both too old and too young at the same time.

I moved constantly: After a few months Mary and I decided two rooms weren't enough, so we found a bigger place. Six months after that, we amicably parted ways, each moving into bigger places with groups of people. I moved seven times in two years.

I hardly owned anything and I liked it that way. I was writing poetry and snippets of stories in spiral notebooks, and when I got to the end of one, I'd toss it out. I wish I still had the letter my dad sent me the first week I lived at Mary's, but like most things, it wound up in the trash. I even threw away the Polaroids from the day Sandy took me to the private zoo, including one in which I, wearing an emerald green halter top that she had made for me, sat on the back of a tiger and smiled nervously. Throwing things out wasn't a conscious attempt to avoid being like my mother—I just didn't like the thought of being weighed down or tied to one place. I liked to be able to look around wherever

I was living and know that I could be out of there in a matter of hours if I needed to. I'm still like that.

MY MOTHER AND I saw each other every few weeks or so after I moved out of the yellow house. I'd stop by while I was visiting my dad and Sandy on a Sunday, and my mom would sit at her kitchen table, drinking coffee while I did the dishes or organized the pantry. Sometimes we went shopping together, to Target or one of the thrift shops: Ragstock or Savers or the Salvation Army. Ragstock's main location was downtown, in an enormous warehouse filled with barrels of musty second-hand clothes. You had to practically climb inside the barrels to find the best things and you had to dedicate hours to the hunt. My mother was friends with the manager, Sharon, who was the buyer for all the Ragstock stores. Sharon saw everything as it came in and if something struck her as "very Helen," she'd put it aside for my mom. She also gave my mother discounts on the already bargain prices. I liked going there with my mom—I hadn't yet begun to see excessive shopping as a link in my mother's mental problems. I liked watching her laughing with Sharon, seeing my mother's natural sense of humor and charm come out. I even liked the look of concentration on her face as she dug through the barrels, the satisfaction when she found a particularly pretty cashmere sweater, maybe one with beads or sequins—"Oh look, Jessie, it's from the 1940s," she'd exclaim.

My mother had never seen one of my apartments before. None of my friends had ever met her. But one day when I was seventeen and had just started my senior year, I met my mother after school for a late lunch at Peter's Grill downtown. The lunch went well—she was in a good mood, and funny. Her sense of humor has to be just right: not too repetitive and not too esoteric. After lunch we headed to Target, and her driving didn't even bother me.

At Target she let me buy anything I wanted. I picked up a packet of condoms from the shelf and put them into the cart. I was testing her. Other than the weird semen comment she made when I was ten she'd never talked to me about sex— though Sandy had embarrassed the hell out of me by forcing me to look at *Our Bodies, Ourselves* with her when I was eleven. As we strolled through the wide Target aisles, side by side, my mother glanced down at the condoms in the cart and said, "Oh, Jessie, that's great. Why don't you get another pack, too?" So I walked back to where they were and plucked a second box from the shelf. I felt weirdly close to her—as if we could make up for the fact that we'd never had anything like an intimate conversation by purchasing an item associated with another form of intimacy. During lunch I'd felt a connection to her as well. In fact, that day I felt closer to her than I had in years.

I was living then in a crummy apartment above a crummy liquor store. When my mom and I left Target, I didn't want our good day together to end. So instead of having her drop me off as I usually did (always ducking as we got close to my place so I wouldn't be spotted in her junky car), I invited her to park in the liquor store's lot—momentarily not caring who saw me getting out of her rusty boat—and see my apartment.

"And I have a surprise to show you," I said. I was in the midst of a short-lived attempt to get over my fear of snakes and had recently purchased a baby one. During my years at the yellow house I'd had a succession of frogs, chameleons, hermit crabs, and fish. I spent hours on aquatic homes for my creatures and became a regular at a pet store in one of the malls. The first time I'd seen the snake in the store, I knew it would be the perfect way to cure my phobia. It was a rare red rat snake. Only eight or so inches long, its ruby-colored body was barely wider than a pen. Eventually it was supposed to grow to five feet, but I figured that knowing the serpent since it was a baby would neutralize any potential fear before it could even begin. So I spent all the money I had on the snake, using my fake ID to prove I was over eighteen. The first time I held it in my hand, felt its surprisingly not-slimy-at-all skin crawling over mine, watched it uncoil and writhe smoothly across and around my pale wrist, I was proud of myself. I felt brave. Every time I held the snake, stroked its fragile body and tiny triangular head, I'd think, I did this. I could barely believe it.

And now here I was taking another risk. One even more frightening than a snake.

"What's the surprise?" my mom asked as we walked up the stairs to my apartment. She was usually the one—always the one—who said she had a surprise for me. It had never been the other way before.

"You'll see," I said and unlocked the door. As we walked in, I called my roommate Christine's name, but she didn't appear to be home. We'd lived together only a few months and weren't close, though we got along fine. I recognized a steamy, burning smell: The radiators had come on that day.

"This is the living room," I said, holding my arm out toward the bare white walls and the curved couch that fit into one corner with a scratched-up coffee table in front of it.

"And that's the kitchen," I said, pointing toward an almost empty room with a warped linoleum floor. It was big enough for a table and chairs but we didn't have them.

"I'd say you and your roommate are minimalists," my mom said.

"More like broke," I said, though she was right. We took a

few steps down the hallway and I pointed to a closed door. "This is my room."

I reached for the doorknob and that's when I remembered where the snake's aquarium had been that morning when I'd left for school: on top of the radiator. I flung the door open and ran to the glass rectangle, my mother following closely behind asking, "What is it? What is it, Jessie?"

The snake was dead. Lying on its back, its mouth was wide open, as if it had died screaming. And then I saw the mealworms. I'd left the mealworms in the cage for the snake to eat and now they were crawling into the snake's mouth, possibly trying to save themselves from the literal cooking going on inside those four glass walls. Horrified, I moved the aquarium from the heat source and set it on the floor. My hands were shaking. Because of my stupidity, I had killed an animal. How could I have been such an idiot? At first my mom didn't say a word, choosing instead to scrutinize my bookshelf, but finally she turned to me.

She was laughing. "Why would anyone have a pet snake, anyway?"

"I bought it to get over my fear."

She stopped laughing, but was still smiling. "What fear?"

"Are you serious?"

She didn't answer. I wanted her to comfort me, to acknowledge that I'd been brave or even that my snake fear was a direct result of her teasing—but all she did was stand there with a smile on her face as if she could start laughing again at any second.

I'd been a fool to think things could be different.

Things would never be different.

I thought of the last time she'd ever pulled my hair: I was twelve and had reached her same height. We were in her kitchen. Her hand lashed out, but I was faster: I caught her forearm. Our eyes locked. My hand gripped her arm, holding it up in the air.

"Those days are over," I said. "You will never do that again."

She tried to laugh, but couldn't. She knew I was right.

And there we were, in my apartment after what I'd thought had been one of our best days. Our eyes were locked once again. Between us, on the floor, was the aquarium with the dead snake inside.

And like my erstwhile pet, the hope I'd allowed myself that day was gone. My mother didn't know how to comfort me. She only knew how to laugh at me. I should have known better, and a part of me must have, because I wasn't entirely surprised. I had come to expect disappointment from her. For the day I'd temporarily tamped down that expectation, pressed down on it as if it were snow I could harden and climb over, but it hadn't melted away. It never would.

My mother made some excuse about needing to leave. I walked her to the door and then I listened as her car rumbled to life below my window, waiting to take a breath until she was gone.

7

AT MY MOM'S, I'VE GOTTEN TO THE DIFFICULT PART OF cleaning. Shoveling garbage into bags, sweeping up the remains, and emptying and scouring a refrigerator is easy, but trying to decide what to keep and what to toss among three-foot-high stacks of old bills and baskets of papers with scribbled phone numbers and addresses is much harder. And since this is my penultimate day of cleaning, I'm going fast. At one point I'm about to toss what looks like a piece of junk mail when my mother snatches it from my hands.

"Jessie! That's about a class I have to take to keep my nursing license."

I set it on a shelf, with the edge sticking out so she can find it. I'm hoping she'll go back to work, just to give herself something to do, though she says she's enjoying being unemployed and is still obsessed with suing her former employer. I've never worried about her money situation—no matter how loony and quirky she can be, my mother has always been able to take care of herself financially. Except now she won't give me a straight answer about how much money she has, and I've realized, by the state of her kitchen, that she eats every single meal out. And then there are those Savers bags with the receipts stapled to the top. If I added them up I'm sure they'd equal thousands of dollars. All wasted.

Finally, in a stack of papers on top of a dresser, I find a bank statement.

It's for $35,000. I was expecting it to be for ten times that amount, at least.

"Mom, please tell me you've got another account. This can't be all the money you've got."

She grabs it from my hand and examines it. "It's not. I've got way more than that."

"Good. How much and where is it?"

"It's around here somewhere . . ."

"But do you have any idea how much you actually have saved? We need to make you a budget. I need to know that you have enough money to live on."

"I've got plenty! And besides, I'll have a lot more once I sue those motherfuckers."

The nest egg I assumed she had was one way I tried to make myself feel better about her hoarding; I always figured that someday I'd be able to convince her to sell her house and buy a condo. And this seems like the perfect time to do it. The problem is, I'm beginning to wonder if she could afford to buy one, even if I could convince her.

And it's partly my fault.

We were speaking again, but still not in regular contact, when I found out from my dad, who'd heard from my brother, that my mom's boyfriend Roger had died. Since Roger had been sick the whole time they were together, I knew this day would come and I'd always dreaded it.

When I found out Roger had died, I tried calling, but she didn't answer. I called again and again. She'd turned her answering machine off. The next day I sent flowers and kept trying to call; a few days after that I received a rambling, unsigned letter from her with words that ran to the edge of the paper and trailed right off the page. Finally, after a week, I reached her. She cried and cried—who wouldn't?—as I sat on the other end of the phone line and listened. I wished I could do more.

We began talking on the phone almost every evening. (Or, rather, she talked, and I listened.) It was the spring of 1999, and I was living in Brooklyn with a roommate and working as an editor at an online magazine in Manhattan. I didn't have much of a social life. I'd broken up with a boyfriend a few months before, and because many of my friends had been his pals first, I found myself invitation-less in the evenings and on weekends. I didn't really mind though; I was good friends with the people at work, and often that "work" consisted of playing laser tag or staying up all night watching bad wrestling movies in the name of research.

I used the weekends to work on a novel. The evenings were for my mother. Over the weeks, then months, she began to cry less during our phone calls. She began talking about things further in the past than Roger. And she began apologizing. "I know I was terrible to you. I feel so bad about it. I just had no preparation," she'd say. "My parents were both so sick. I didn't know how to take care of you kids. I'm so sorry."

I'd always say it was fine, that I forgave her. My feelings were more complex and I was more confused than I let on, but I had no idea what else to say. I didn't know what I wanted from her.

Was I supposed to forget the hair-pulling and all the other chaos because she said she was sorry? I wished I could. I wanted it to be that easy. "I turned out fine," I'd say, and she'd usually respond, "It must be because of your dad and Sandy."

Whenever my mother asked about my life, I was wary of giving her any personal information. I feared that she'd use it against me. She'd done it before: diagnosing me with the "trait that ran in the family" of failing to maintain friendships because when she asked about a friend from elementary school, I hadn't a clue what had become of her. And then there were the snakes: She latched onto that fear of mine—which she'd created, no less—and wouldn't let go.

So I was hesitant. I tried to keep things at a superficial level: what I was reading at the time, the stories I was editing at the online magazine, that I loved sushi and Ethiopian food. Small things. One night I happened to mention the student loans I was paying off and she said, "That's excellent news!" sounding more excited than I'd heard since Roger's death.

"It's excellent news that I'm in so much debt?" I owed more than $30,000.

"Jessie, this will give me something to live for!"

"You're kidding, right?" I asked, but I already knew she wasn't.

"I'm going to help you pay off your loans . . . I'll send you money each month. It'll give me a goal. That's what I need."

At the online magazine, I was making the most money I'd ever made—$40,000 a year. My loan payments were high, though, around $500 a month; each month I paid as much as I could afford over the amount because I hated the idea of being in debt. Since I thought she had more-than-ample riches squirreled away, letting my mother help with my payments didn't seem like a bad idea, especially if it gave her a goal, but there was something about it that made me uncomfortable. It smacked of exploiting her grief. Also, I suspected that giving money was the only way my mother knew how to express love, and worse, that she saw it as her only value. Plus, declaring my student loan payments "something to live for" was just beyond sad.

"I'm not sure," I said.

"I'll send some every month. And little by little, we'll chip away at it."

Other than showing up for work on time when she had a job (an amazing feat for her, when I think about it), my mother had never kept to a schedule in her life. She was always forgetting appointments, and when I was a kid, she often forgot to pick me up from places when she was supposed to. So I knew she wouldn't keep to her self-imposed schedule of sending me money, and frankly, I didn't want her to.

"How about this," I said. "You can send it when you want, *if* you want to. But no pressure."

I told myself that if she sent money, I'd accept it, but I'd never ask.

Around this time I decided to fly to Europe with an airline voucher I'd received for getting bumped from a flight. One of my friends was touring with a band called the Residents, and I made plans to meet her in Prague and then continue on to Paris, where I'd attend a week-long writing workshop. I told my mom about the trip, and she sent me money even though I hadn't asked. I cashed her check, convinced that her bank account was bursting.

My friend's band played three shows in Prague, and on the last night, I happened to sit next to a very cute guy who scribbled things in a tiny notebook throughout the first part of the set. I knew he was American because when I'd asked if the seat next to him was free (praying that he spoke English because I could only say "please" and "cheers" in Czech) he'd replied, "It is. It's all yours."

Between songs, we started chatting. He was probably gay, I decided, because of his perfect posture, stylish haircut, and fashionable hipster clothes. Plus, he wasn't flirtatious or sleazy in any way. His name was David and he was in Prague for the summer, but lived in San Francisco where he was getting a master's degree in history. When he asked what I was doing at a Residents show in Prague, I told him I was there with someone in the band.

"Oh, really? Who?" he asked.

The Residents are secretive about their identities, disguising themselves in oversized tuxedoes with giant papier-mâché eyeballs covering their faces. Over their thirty-year career, there's been speculation that members include everyone from David Bowie to Lou Reed to Iggy Pop. The nonpermanent members like my friend aren't as clandestine, but she'd sworn me to secrecy about the others.

"I can't really say who I'm with."

"You can't remember?" David asked, the hint of a smile on his lips.

"No," I said, "it's just that, you know, they're incognito."

He looked surprised. "I just had lunch with the drummer today. His name is Mark."

Oh. "Were you interviewing him?"

He looked confused. I pointed to his notebook.

"Oh, no, I'm not writing about them. I was just jotting down random things—poetry type stuff, but don't tell anyone." He smiled.

It turned out that he couldn't have cared less about the band but had met the drummer earlier that day at a mutual friend's apartment; in fact, he'd sat at the end of the row of seats in case he wanted to leave early.

"Okay." I said. "I'm here with the female singer. The one in the chicken mask."

When the show ended, I asked David if he knew of any good dance clubs—my friend and I had already decided that was how we wanted to spend our last night in Prague. David not only knew of some (more proof that he was gay), but while I waited for my friend to come out from backstage, he spent five minutes drawing me a map of all the best places on a napkin. On a whim I asked if he wanted to join us—he was sweet, and besides, I knew my worse-than-nonexistent sense of direction would render the map useless.

None of the dance clubs was open, so we ended up at a smoky, loud, expat bar. While my friend was talking to some Italians, David asked how long she and I had been together. I practically choked on my beer.

"We're just friends," I said.

"It's just that earlier, when you said you were with her, I thought you meant *with* her."

"Right," I said, laughing, and then added, "Not that there's anything wrong with it. I mean, you're gay, aren't you?"

He shook his head. "You're not the first person to think that, but no, I'm not."

Interesting, I thought, and scooted my barstool a little closer to his. David told me some of Prague's fascinating history, and he made me laugh, which I've always been a sucker for. We stayed perched on our stools, talking and laughing long after my friend, exhausted from performing, said good-bye and went back to the hotel. My train for Paris was leaving at 6:30 the next morning, and when it got to be 2:00 a.m., David and I decided to just stay up. He offered to go with me to retrieve my bag from the hotel, and then take me to the train station when it was time.

And that time came way too fast.

As David carried my bag through the echoing halls of the station, I tried to convince him to get on the train with me. And he would have, except that he didn't have his passport with him; besides, in two days he had friends flying in from London. It wouldn't be right, he said, to leave them on their own.

Though I'd known David less than twelve hours, the good-bye was difficult.

The writing workshop was horrible. And I couldn't stop thinking about David. So after my third day in Paris I called him and asked if he wanted me to come back to Prague.

"Of course," he said and I got right back on another train.

For three days we binged on hearty dumplings, goulash, and rich thick beer, rode the trams among Prague's perpetually making out teenagers, drank pumpkin/ginger/forest-flavored Becherovka, gawked at the withered, centuries-old hand in the church of St. Jacub, relaxed at a secret teahouse where you had to pull on a silk rope to be allowed in, walked and walked over narrow cobblestone streets and through the sprawling chess-piece castle, and talked, talked, talked.

Our second good-bye was even more difficult.

I had to take a bus back to Paris to catch my flight home, and during the long ride I made a surprisingly easy decision: David couldn't leave San Francisco because of his graduate program, but I could leave New York. I'd lived in San Francisco for three years prior to moving to New York and still had warm feelings for the city and plenty of friends there. I called him from the Paris airport and asked what he thought of my idea. I listened closely for any hesitation from him, but there was none. He was just excited. He even suggested that once he graduated we could travel around Europe for a while, move back to New York if I wanted, or both. So within a few days of my return to New York, I began making arrangements to leave again.

I'm not normally impulsive. I usually agonize over big decisions, or any decision, really. That might have been why my dad and many of the people I knew in New York thought I was crazy to make such a hasty move. But not my mother. My mother was thrilled about it.

And she took credit for it, too. "It's because I gave you that money that you could go to Europe, and that's how you met him! You wouldn't have met him if it wasn't for me!"

It wasn't exactly true—I certainly would have gone anyway, though the money she gave me enabled me to not worry so much about things while I was traveling. And I definitely appreciated the help with my student loans, especially as I watched some of my former classmates struggling. Still, she was in the midst of grieving Roger's death, so I let her think what she wanted to; it did me no harm. If it made her feel better to take credit for me meeting the man who would become my husband, so be it.

Of course, now that I'm looking through her cluttered house for bank statements, hoping to find evidence of another account somewhere, I regret taking those checks from her. I didn't keep track at the time, but over the course of five years she had to have given me at least $15,000. I never should have taken a penny.

"Mom, please," I say now. "What are we going to do about your finances? I need to know how you're going to pay your bills."

"I'm going to put some coffee on. Do you want some?" she asks, before she turns away and walks toward the kitchen. Yesterday we went to Target and bought her new sheets, towels, and a coffeemaker.

I begin sorting through a pile of sweaters on top of one of her dressers—picking up each one, folding it, and shoving it into one of the empty drawers. I just need to clear some surfaces. The next time I come here, if I find the sweaters untouched in the drawer I'll sneak them out and donate them to Savers.

Eventually she comes back, sipping a cup of coffee. "Jessie," she says, "don't worry about me. There really is more money."

"Are you being serious?"

"Yes."

I knew she had another stash somewhere. My dad and I couldn't have been off by that much, there's just no way.

"Where is it? Another bank?"

"It's not in a bank," she says, and I don't like her mischievous tone.

I know where it's going to lead. "Don't say it—"

"Cat beds!" She practically falls on the floor laughing. "Just wait until you see them!"

I hoped at first that she was joking about the cat beds, but while cleaning I've come upon notes for other "inventions," including a "money clip," a "shopping list holder," a "paintbrush holder," and "knee pads." Could she really be that clueless?

It's possible.

And I'm afraid her cluelessness will end in homelessness. It's always been a worry of mine. Since Roger's death she's said numerous times that she wanted to move: to live in a trailer (or that step van) in Florida, to become a traveling nurse, and for a while she was talking about just selling her house and renting an apartment with roommates—refusing to believe me when I told her how much rents were. As much of a problem as her house is, I've always felt she was safe tucked away there.

But I can't keep coming back here and cleaning like this, and the things that need repairing aren't going to fix themselves. This house is just too much for her.

And then, toward the end of the day, I finally find a letter from another bank.

I tear open the envelope. It's a savings account. With $10,000 in it.

"Ah, there it is," my mother says, standing next to me.

"That's all your savings? This, plus the other account . . . that's forty-five thousand dollars. This is everything you have for when you retire?"

"Yeah," she says, smiling as if it's an enormous sum.

"You must have more money—what about all those years of working overtime? Where did all that money go?"

"I don't know," she says meekly.

All those Savers bags. Every meal eaten out. All the doubles, triples, quadruples of identical objects.

"Oh, Mom. What if you can't work again after the surgery, or if you have some kind of emergency? You could be completely wiped out."

"I'll be fine," she says, waving away my preposterous concern. As always.

That evening, when I'm done cleaning, I call my dad and he comes to pick me up. I get into the car and sink into the seat. Leaving her house is always like being inside the funhouse at the state fair—mirrored and dark and vaguely menacing—and getting to the end, when you walk out into the sunlight.

"Rough day?" my dad asks as he pulls away from the curb.

"You could say that."

"At least there's just one more after this."

"Right," I say, too tired to explain that that's the problem: Tomorrow's my last day to clean and I haven't gotten nearly enough done.

As soon as we walk in the door, Sandy hands me a glass of red wine. "I had a feeling you'd need this," she says. "This and a nice warm bubble bath."

"Thanks," I say, "and you're right." I head up the stairs, where

I fill their claw-foot tub and climb in. When I emerge my muscles still ache, so I take some Advil. I put on one of Sandy's fuzzy bathrobes and go downstairs. Sandy's making curried chicken and the house smells like peppery curry and sweet coconut milk. My dad comes into the kitchen and grabs a nonalcoholic beer from the refrigerator, then sits down at the table.

"Guys," I say, "I really need some advice." I pour myself more wine from the bottle on the counter, then walk over and sit down next to my dad.

"Of course, honey, what is it?" he says. My dad's good at advice. He's still one of the first people I go to with a problem.

"I need to figure out how to get my mom's house in decent shape so she can sell it. You guys know contractors, right? I thought maybe I could tell you what's wrong with the house and you could call your contractors."

"Honey," my dad says, "your mother's house is not *your* problem."

My dad and Sandy have been telling me for years to detach from my mother and her hoarding. But I can't.

"Yes, it is my problem," I say. "Who else is going to look out for her? Who else does she have?"

"Well . . ." my dad starts, but then his voice trails off.

I put my head in my hands. "Jesus Christ, what am I going to do?"

Sandy comes over and puts her hand on my shoulder. I lift my head in time to see her shoot my dad a look. "Don't worry, sweetie. Of course we'll help you. What have you seen inside the house that needs fixing?"

"For starters, I'm pretty sure her basement's partially flooded, but I can't stand to be down there long enough to thoroughly check"—here I can see my dad's jaw clenching; he knows all about my mom's snake-teasing and it drives him crazy—"the rain gutters need to be replaced, and I'm pretty sure there's a family of squirrels living above the front porch. And that's just what I can see. I know there's more."

"Just from driving past it I can tell you that the exterior needs repainting," Sandy says. "And the window frames need replacing."

My dad takes a sip of his nonalcoholic beer and shakes his head. I understand his frustration: He remembers how nice the house used to be when we all first moved in thirty years ago— he remembers because he did a lot of the work himself. He's an excellent carpenter. My dad and Sandy left the yellow house five years after I did, and they're now in what they consider their dream house, and not just because my dad designed it and did much of the carpentry. It's a 1920s bungalow with shiny red oak floors and trim and perfect Arts and Crafts details: from the crown molding with dentils to the wainscoting to the built-in bookcases and intricate American Craftsman fireplace, mantel, and overmantel. Their house was even featured in a coffee-table book about bungalows. My dad and Sandy spend vacations swooning over homes, going to Pasadena to look at bungalows, touring Frank Lloyd Wright buildings throughout the Midwest. In many ways their lives revolve around nice houses. I have no idea how I could have one parent who's a connoisseur of beautiful homes while the other wrecks her house through hoarding.

"She's destroying that house," I say. "I have to get her into a condo before it's too late and she has nothing."

"The problem is that those repairs cost a lot of money. But if she doesn't do those things, she won't be able to sell it," Sandy says.

"Won't be able to sell it at all, or just won't be able to sell it for much?" I ask.

"At all," Sandy says.

"But honey, don't worry. She'll be fine," my dad says. "She's probably got a million bucks in a mattress somewhere."

"She doesn't," I say and tell them what I've discovered about her bank accounts. "And that's all, I'm sure of it."

"That can't be," my dad says. "Where did it all go? All that overtime?"

"If you think about it, she only worked a little overtime when she was with Roger, then she didn't work at all during the last year he was alive—all those really intense long hours were after he died. So the major overtime was only for about six years."

"Still," my dad says. "That's a lot of overtime."

I'm stabbed with guilt. "I shouldn't have cashed all those checks she sent me—I should have known better." Though I realize $15,000 wouldn't make *that* much of a difference to her now, it would have made a slight difference. I just didn't know that her irresponsibility extended into financial matters. I thought that was one area of her life I didn't have to worry about.

"And she won't qualify for social security for two more years," I say.

"Do you know how much she'll get?" my dad asks.

"I have no idea, and neither does she. She claims to have thrown out those letters you get every year telling you about social security benefits." I laugh, but it sounds more like a bitter snort. "Those would be the one thing she gets rid of."

My dad pushes back his chair. "We can figure it out."

We go into his office and he sits down at his computer. We get her social security number from the power of attorney papers Sandy signed. It takes five minutes online to learn how much her monthly payments will be once she qualifies. And it's not much.

* * *

THE NEXT MORNING, when I arrive at my mother's to clean for the last time, I bring some harsh news: From now on she can spend only $900 dollars a month, because that's how much she'll get from social security. I want to get her into the habit now. I've decided to not harass her anymore about selling her house, at least until after the surgery. I've given her enough stress. And there's more to come: I tell her that she's got to curtail her favorite activity, shopping. No more Savers.

"But Jessie, look what I found," she says, and is suddenly fanning dollar bills in my face. Hundred-dollar bills.

"Where did that come from?"

"From the bank! I went this morning. I wanted to have some cash on hand in case I can't get there while I'm recovering after the surgery."

"How much is it?"

"Three thousand dollars!"

"From your savings account?"

"Yes."

"Give it to me," I say, and go over to the bureau where I've put envelopes, pens, and pads of paper. I grab three envelopes and on each I write one of the upcoming months: May, June, and July. I put $900 in each one, and seal them. I give her the extra $300 and tell her to put it in her wallet. "And that should last you until the end of the month."

"Where's my wallet . . ." she says, walking away, looking down at the floor as if it'll magically appear there.

"It's in your purse, which is hanging on one of the hooks near the front door."

I find her in the hallway a few minutes later, still looking through her purse.

"Will you remember where those envelopes are?" I ask.

"Yes."

"Where are they?" I want to make sure she pictures the location, to help her remember.

She squints her eyes in concentration and speaks in a dreamy tone: "In that cabinet where the record player is . . . in the top drawer."

"And you'll be able to make each envelope last for a whole month?"

"Oh, yeah. That's not a problem."

"Good. Now come on," I say. "It's our last day to clean, so we need to get started."

"Let's not clean today! Let's go out for Mexican. I know a place on Lake Street that has the best guacamole." She always says the "mole" part of guacamole as mole, like the rodent. My husband and I pronounce it that way now, too; it started as a joke but now we just do it all the time without thinking about it.

I miss my husband. I miss my life—my real life. This is my secret life. I haven't told any of my friends about my mother. They might know vaguely that she has some "mental issues" but that's it. It's easy to explain that I'm visiting my mom because she has cancer and needs surgery, but how do I explain that what I'm really doing is gutting her house of trash, digging through years of muck, and speaking to her as if she's a five-year-old?

She's looking at me expectantly.

"Mom, I want your house to be clean for when you're recovering."

"It is," she says, opening her arms. "Jessie, it's marvelous."

Since I've been in Minneapolis, I've hardly let myself worry about her cancer. But it is *cancer*. And now, looking at her hopeful face, barely wrinkled even at sixty-three, I think, What if this is the last time I see her? What if something happens during the surgery or her prognosis is terrible?

"Okay, I'll tell you what, Mom. Let's clean until one o'clock and then we'll go to the Mexican place for lunch."

At the end of the day, after the guacamole and then a few more hours of cleaning, I survey the results. It's better. Much better, though there's more to be done. The living room is still packed with too much furniture, four cardboard boxes need to be gone through, and something needs to be done with the overflow of books that wouldn't fit on the shelves. But at least the house is back to the mild pack rat but not unsanitary state it was in when Roger was alive. That's something. And for now, it'll have to do.

8

THE NEXT MORNING, ON THE WAY TO THE AIRPORT, I ASK my dad to stop off at my mother's house so I can say good-bye. My dad waits in the car. Early tomorrow my mom's going into the hospital; we're supposed to find out at some point between now and then if the new polyps are benign or malignant. Those results will determine how much of her colon will need to be removed during the surgery and give the doctors some idea of her prognosis.

My mom opens the front door and steps aside so I can pass. She follows me in, holding her arm out toward the living room and the kitchen as if I've just won a prize on a game show. "You've done such a marvelous job. Just look at it! Ooh, Jessie, here," she says and goes over to the china cabinet we unearthed from a mountain of clutter in the hallway. It was actually in great shape, even neatly organized on the inside. It holds ceramic figurines, china cups and saucers, and a collection of clutches and other small purses. "Here," my mom says, opening the hutch's glass door. "I want you to choose something to take home."

I select a boxy red purse that looks like it's from the '40s. I don't really want it—it's just another thing I'll have to give away or find space for in my tiny apartment—but I can tell my taking it would mean a lot to her.

"Oh, Jessie, you can take that to Italy with you! It will be perfect there."

"Sure," I say, knowing I won't.

"Thank you for all you've done, honey," my mom says.

"I wish I could've done more."

"No, it's gorgeous."

"You'll go through those today, right?" I point to the cardboard boxes we didn't get to.

"Sure," my mom says.

"And you'll call me from the hospital tomorrow, right?"

She nods.

"Or sooner if you find out about those other polyps."

"Okay."

"Are you going to be all right here on your own?" I feel so bad leaving her. But I have to get back to New York—one of the classes I teach meets tomorrow and I can't cancel another one.

"Oh, yeah, I'll be fine."

I hug her good-bye. It's awkward in the way it's always awkward.

And then my dad honks his horn and I head for the door.

ON THE PLANE back to New York, the aching sets in. My back, shoulders, and arms, from all the hours of hauling, scrubbing, sweeping, cobweb clearing, and stacking. I'm so sleepy, but something's keeping me from drifting off: the papers at the lawyer's office, putting my mother's house in my name—they're a thick chain around my neck, an anchor ready to drag me down. I fear, however irrationally, that the lawyer will forget our deal and accidentally file them. I cannot be legally responsible for that house. I do *not* want that house.

There's one other thing that keeps me awake: my ankle. It itches like crazy. A cluster of five or six welts that look like mosquito bites, only smaller. I scratch them, but the itching only intensifies. It must be some kind of poison ivy I got when I went for a walk with Sandy a few days earlier along the Mississippi River.

When my dad dropped me off at the airport, he gave me sixty dollars and told me to treat myself to a cab home rather than take the subway. So after the flight lands, that's what I do. David and I live in a walk-up building, on the fifth floor. "Free exercise!" we said when we moved in. Usually the stairs are no problem, but today I'm moving a little slow. When I finally open the door to our apartment, David comes toward me and lifts my backpack from my shoulders. He sets it on the floor and puts his arms around me.

"The Magpie," he says, using his nickname for me.

Our dog, Abraham Lincoln, is hopping around, trying to put his paws on my calves, his mini hot dog–size tail wagging.

"I'm so happy to be home," I say, my face against David's chest.

"Look," David says and pulls away from me. He points to the tall two-person table against the wall in our living room.

"You didn't," I say, walking toward the table.

"I went this morning."

It's a feast from Sahadi's, the Middle Eastern deli in Brooklyn that we love: hummus, baba ganoush, olive-flecked pita bread, a wedge of creamy Saint André cheese, a circle of goat cheese brie, the garlic-tinged flatbread crackers I like, two sa-mosas, this sun-dried-tomato and feta-filled pastry that David and I constantly crave, juicy black olives, and fanned-out slices of pear. Behind the spread is a bouquet of orange gerbera dai-sies.

"You are too good to me," I say and slice off a piece of the Saint André. "Thank you." I take a bite of the cheese and bend down to let Abraham Lincoln lick the rest off my finger.

"I wasn't sure how hungry you'd be," David says, "but I fig-ured we can save it for tomorrow if we need to."

"Famished," I say, and put my hand down on the floor for le-verage as I stand up. A sharp pain shoots from my wrist to my shoulder. "Ow," I say, as I stumble to my feet. "My mom's house really beat the crap out of me."

"I'll give you a massage, if you want," David says in the fake-reluctant tone we use with each other sometimes as a joke.

"Maybe if I take a long bath first you won't need to," I say, reaching for a slice of pear.

"It's o-kay," he says in an exaggerated singsong, and I know he means it, that it really is okay, but I still hate asking David to do those kinds of things. It's leftover humiliation from when I became so helpless that he had to do almost everything for me.

IN 2001, JUST a few months after David and I had gotten married, we were living in San Francisco and I was working as a producer in the online division of a business magazine. They'd hired me because of my experience at the online magazine in New York; I'd neglected to mention during the interview that I understood nothing about business, nor was I even remotely interested in it.

I was greedy for all the dot-com money that seemed to be flowing endlessly: David had just graduated from his master's program and begun working as a writer at a weekly newspaper in San Jose, and our plan was to save as much money as possible, then go traveling around Europe for six months to a year. After that, we'd move back to New York.

Not long after I was hired at the business magazine, my department launched a huge website redesign, which meant long hours and weekends. My boss, Eric, assured me that there would be a big bonus when the project was done.

I didn't mind the long hours at first. When I got sick of being there or was annoyed that I couldn't go with David to review a restaurant or a band because I had to stay late at work, I'd picture lingering in a Roman trattoria over a plate of luscious pasta, enjoying a velvety beer in a rustic Prague pub, or strolling the wide boulevards of Paris. The bonus from the redesign was going to help make those things possible. And regardless of my long hours, I was waking up early each morning to work on short stories at home. The writing I did on my own was what mattered to me. The magazine producer position was just what I did for money.

When my fingers became heavy and fatigued and my wrists began aching, I figured it was probably from my long hours on the computer, but I knew I'd have time to rest after the redesign. I was too busy to pay that much attention to the pain anyway. My company had begun laying people off, and with each round of layoffs, I acquired new responsibilities. I'd look over from my monitor to see Eric standing in the doorway of my office. "So, they let Jonathan go. I'm going to need you to be in charge of updating the stock tracker."

The following week, he'd say something like, "It looks like Carla's been laid off. Can you handle updating the white-paper page? Thanks." He'd walk away before I could say no or ask what a "white paper" was. Not that I would have said no. I wanted that bonus.

It was a job I'd disliked from the beginning, and with each passing week and each new round of layoffs, there was more and more of it. My fatigued fingers became stiff, tingly, and numb. My aching wrists began to throb and burn. The pain traveled up from my hands to my forearms, all the way to my shoulders and into my neck, which became perpetually sore. One day I mentioned the pain to Anna, one of my few remaining colleagues. She promptly diagnosed me with something called "repetitive strain injury."

"What's that?" I asked.

"You've heard of carpal tunnel, right?"

"Yes, of course." Carpal tunnel was rampant in San Francisco. Walk into any office on any day and there would be half a dozen people sitting at their keyboards typing away while wearing bulky black wrist braces; or peek into the freezer of any break room and you'd be certain to find ice packs with people's initials on them. I'd always thought of those people wrapping ice around their wrists and wearing braces as slackers or whiners.

"So," Anna continued, "carpal tunnel only relates to a certain nerve in your wrist that can get hurt from overuse. Repetitive strain injury encompasses all the nerves."

"Okay. Repetitive strain injury." I didn't care what it was called. Once this redesign was over I'd be able to rest my sore hands, and then I'd be fine.

"Or you can just call it RSI, like most people. I've had it for years," Anna said, shaking her bony hands as if to warm them. She was small, about my size, and pale. "That's why I keep my hair short. So I don't have to hold up a blow dryer."

That seemed extreme, but I didn't tell her that. Anna advised me to file a workers' compensation claim because that way my medical bills would be paid even if I was laid off. I didn't want to file a claim. I didn't think I'd *have* medical bills, and I didn't want to be a whiner.

Instead, I stopped my routine of writing before work. Surely, I thought, cutting a few hours a day from the keyboard would help my hands heal. I wasn't happy about it—the writing I was doing at home was the only thing (besides the promised bonus) that made going to an office every day bearable. But I figured it was temporary, just until my hands got better.

Only, they didn't get better. Finally, a few weeks after Anna suggested it, I filed a workers' compensation claim.

At my first doctor's appointment, I was prescribed 600-milligram ibuprofen pills and given exercises to build up my "horribly underdeveloped" trapezius muscles. Dr. Olsen also restricted my keyboard time to six hours a day. She said I should be better in a few weeks.

Back at the office I showed Eric the form limiting my keyboard use, but he continued to pile on the duties anyway. And my pain continued to worsen. Every click of the mouse sent a sharp shooting pain from my fingers to my elbow; every keystroke seared the nerves and muscles in my wrists.

When I was back in Dr. Olsen's office three weeks after my first appointment, she was surprised to see me, especially when I told her the pain had gotten worse. At home, I could no longer carry my laundry to the laundry room, chop vegetables, or even hold the phone up to my ear for more than five minutes when my mom or my dad and Sandy called. My hands were almost always aching or burning, or worst of all: numb. Each day I found something else that aggravated the pain, which meant each day I had to ask David to do yet another task for me—and I hated asking anyone, even David, for help.

I learned of a hand injury doctor who was supposedly the best in the Bay Area, and I went to see him, hoping he could help me. Dr. Chatterjee said my case of repetitive strain injury was severe and most likely permanent. I promptly pushed the word "permanent" from my thoughts. He changed my work restriction from six hours on the keyboard a day to four and prescribed hand therapy three times a week.

My hand therapist, Gloria, asked me to rate my pain levels on a scale of one to ten as she took an inventory of my symptoms. We were sitting across from each other over a small white table. She had me lift hand weights and pull on yellow rubber resistance tubes to determine my muscle strength and muscle loss. The room was bright, with lots of windows and seven other tables like the one at which I sat, each occupied by a hand therapist and a patient. Most of the patients were small-boned women like me, but there were a few men with broad shoulders and muscular chests who looked wildly out of place.

Gloria had blue eyes and gray-streaked black hair that she pushed behind her ear with the back of her hand. I got the feeling she was keeping a secret, and months later she would tell me she was dating a man who was not quite divorced. "So," she said, setting down her clipboard, "can you think of anything you might be doing to contribute to your nerve pain? Are there any other activities you could cut out?"

I caught myself gritting my teeth and yawned wide to stretch my jaw, though it did nothing to release my frustration. I had just told her that I wasn't doing laundry, carrying groceries, cooking at all, or using a keyboard at home, and that I'd stopped writing with a pen entirely (the pinching necessary to hold it cramped my fingers); I'd also begun getting my eyebrows waxed so I wouldn't have to pluck them (again the pinching and the cramping); and I'd purchased a headset for talking on the phone. When David and I went to our regular sushi place across the street from our apartment, I ate with my fingers rather than chopsticks. Like my colleague, I'd stopped using a blow dryer and was trying to accept my hair's natural waves (and frizz). I'd even swapped our ceramic coffee mugs for lighter plastic ones. "What else could I possibly stop doing?" I asked.

Gloria studied my face. "You're wearing earrings. I bet you put them in this morning. Why not get some small hoops and leave them in? That way you won't have to do the squeezing motion every day." She made a lobster-claw gesture with her fingers to demonstrate, and at the sight of it my wrists began to tingle and burn.

I stopped wearing earrings altogether.

The layoffs continued at my company, but still not me. The only thing that kept me from walking out was that holy grail of a bonus I was supposed to get after the redesign.

The third time I saw him, with my symptoms continuing to worsen, Dr. Chatterjee added another physical therapy to my growing repertoire: trigger point release. I began seeing Kathy, a gentle giant of a woman who worked on the knots strewn throughout my upper back, swapped chicken mole recipes with me, and ended our sessions with a soothing stroke down my spine and a reminder to broaden my shoulders and carry myself in a way that left me "open to life's experiences."

Because I was so afraid of doing something that would exacerbate my symptoms, I relentlessly monitored myself for pain. At any slight twinge—and I had many twinges—I'd scan my hands, wrists, and arms for nerve, tendon, or muscle pain. At least fifty times a day I asked myself what my pain level was from one to ten. It became a constant refrain, my mantra.

My husband and I had been married only three months when I became injured, and as the weeks, then months, passed, my hand injury began to affect our sex life—how could it not, when any new way I moved made my hands hurt? Besides, when you're in chronic pain, sex isn't exactly appealing. Not that I felt sexy in any way. I felt weak and helpless and infantilized. I couldn't even clip my own fingernails and toenails—David had to do it for me.

But the worst humiliation happened one night when David and I went out to dinner. It was an old-school, red-velvet-draped place in North Beach and David was including it in an article. We ordered creamed spinach, iceberg wedges with chunky blue cheese dressing, big steaks for each of us, and a nice bottle of red wine. My hands had been particularly achy that day; even holding the heavy steel fork to eat the salad was difficult. But I tried to ignore it. The steaks arrived perfectly done—red in the middle and yet slightly crisp on the outside. I reached for my knife with my left hand, but froze as a sharp pain shot through my wrist and up the inside of my arm.

"What is it?" David asked.

"Nothing," I said and sliced into the meat. I was determined not to give in to the pain. But I felt like someone was poking a hot knife straight into my armpit from below. Each time I sawed off another piece the pain got worse. I'd eaten less than a quarter of the steak when I set my utensils down.

"Are you okay?" David asked, and I started crying. I hid my face behind a red cloth napkin. David reached over and put his hand on my shoulder. The weight of it hurt.

"Sorry," I said, and glanced down at his hand. He knew what I meant because it had happened before. He moved his hand from my shoulder to his wineglass and took a sip, frowning almost imperceptibly as he set it down. In some ways this was harder for him than for me.

"I hate my evil arms," I said.

"I don't. I love your arms."

"You're joking. Why would you love my arms?"

"They're part of you," he said. "And I love you."

"I talk to them sometimes," I said without thinking, and regretted it when I saw the mildly horrified expression on David's face.

"Maybe you shouldn't tell me things like that," he said, but he was smiling. "Here," David said, pulling my plate closer to him. He began to cut my steak into bite-size pieces and for a second I hated him for being able to do it; then in the next second I hated myself for putting him in the position of *having* to do it.

I was thirty-two years old. Much too young to be this feeble. I didn't eat another bite.

The next day I went to my boss's office and asked him to lay me off. I was willing to forgo the bonus. For the Europe trip and the move back to New York, we'd just have to be on a very, very tight budget.

Eric agreed to let me go instead of the person who was next on the list. I was among the last round of employees to receive a severance package before the whole company collapsed, soon after.

We wanted to leave for Europe, but everything had to be put on hold until my hands were better—if I left San Francisco before my doctor deemed that I'd reached my "maximum recovery level," I'd lose all future medical coverage related to my injury.

In addition to my thrice-weekly hand therapy appointments with Gloria and twice-weekly trigger point release sessions with Kathy, I began getting full body massages once a week from a woman named Marilyn, who welcomed me to her apartment with a big hug every time and smoothed the knots in my neck with warm stones. Our chatty appointments sometimes lasted for two hours though she was being paid for only one.

I saw a chiropractor. I tried acupuncture. I floated in a rehabilitative pool and was the youngest person in it by forty years; I ignored the women, in their flowery bathing caps as they stood off in a corner and whispered speculations about why someone so young might be there. I was tempted to tell them I'd been bitten by a shark, but then they might ask to see my scar and I didn't have one. I saw an "intuitive healer" who claimed that she could see my organs and discern which vitamins and minerals I was lacking—conveniently, her office was located inside a vitamin store and I left with close to two hundred dollars' worth of products. I tried a sensory deprivation tank. I went to a repetitive strain injury support group where I was told that I needed to switch from being a "do-er" to a "be-er." At the end of the meeting, instead of clapping we all snapped our fingers.

I tried qigong, meditation, gemstone therapy, Reiki, Feldenkrais, biofeedback, a wheat-and-sugar-free diet.

My whole life became appointments with Gloria, Kathy, and Marilyn and then my standard every-three-week session with Dr. Chatterjee. I walked to all of my appointments, no matter how far away they were, just to kill time. Killing time became one of my daily goals. There was no such thing as pleasure anymore; there was only constant pain. I couldn't even hold up a book without my hands and arms going numb, so I started getting books on CD from the library. I'd lie on our living room floor—on my back, with my feet on a chair to force the blood to my upper body and arms—and listen to the books until I fell asleep.

I asked Gloria one day: "If I fell into a coma for a year, would that be enough time for my muscles and nerves and tendons to heal?" I'd been daydreaming about being comatose.

"You have a crush injury," Gloria answered. She explained that this meant the muscles covering the nerves had become so tightly knotted that they created pressure on the nerves. "Would a year in a coma help?" she said, repeating my question, "I'm not sure. The damage is most likely permanent."

"But you said 'most likely' permanent. So it's not *definitely* permanent."

"I'll tell you what you need to do," she said and wrapped the arm we'd just dipped in warm wax in a plastic bag. After the other arm was waxed and wrapped, too, I'd lie down on a table and she'd massage my shoulders as we let the paraffin wax do its supposed wonders on my circulation. "What you need to do is start listening to your body."

"I already do," I said, and was glad she didn't ask me to elaborate.

We hate you, my arms told me often. *Anything you love, we will take away.*

By the time I passed the one-year anniversary of being injured, my arms had nicknames: "bastards," "traitorous wretches," and when I felt generous, they were "poor things." I rubbed them, hoping to wake them up, I wrapped them in heating pads and lay on the floor, trying to breathe the new, correct way Kathy the trigger point release therapist had shown me: into my abdomen and not shallowly into the top of my chest. It turned out I'd been doing everything wrong, including breathing.

Sometimes, as I lay on the floor, I'd imagine chopping the bastards off; I'd picture them separated from my body, right at the top where the shoulder meets the rib cage, sliced precisely with the cool steel of a machete. Some days I thought that might hurt less. Some days I felt a tingle of life at the tips of my fingers and I'd imagine blood circulating through them, filling them with oxygen, and I'd feel hopeful.

Because of my years in gymnastics, I'd always had strong, well-defined arm muscles. I'd always hated my legs, scrawny and so pale that you could see the blue veins running under my skin like rivers on a map, but I liked my biceps and triceps. One day while getting dressed, I glanced down at my arms and I thought I was being tricked: These were not my arms. Somehow I was looking at someone else's arms. These were the arms of someone who was fat and lazy. They had no muscle tone whatsoever. None. These arms were flabby and shapeless. Weak. Useless. These arms could never take care of me. These arms could never keep me safe.

"Chronic pain can create patterns in your brain that keep the pain cycle going even without stimuli," Dr. Chatterjee told me one day. "And one thing that can stop that cycle is a low dose of an antidepressant. I'd like to prescribe one to you."

His examination room was all-white, except for a colorful poster of the different kinds of infection you can get from not washing your hands.

"No thanks. I'm not depressed," I lied. Depression was for weak people. Depression was for people like my mother.

"This is about stopping the pain patterns in your brain," he said and explained it again.

"I'd rather not." I considered myself opposed to antidepressants. My mother had been on them for decades and they'd done her no good. For all I knew, the pills had made her worse.

"That's your choice. But I want to be clear about the severity of your injury," he said, his dark eyes serious. "This is permanent. You'll never be able to return to your previous job." He tapped the end of his ballpoint pen on the white counter.

So I couldn't be a producer at a business magazine, I thought. Big deal. But then panic struck. What about writing? Did he mean I could never use a keyboard again?

"Let me think about the antidepressants," I said and left the appointment in a daze. I hadn't ever told Dr. Chatterjee about being a writer, mostly because I feared he'd attribute my injury to writing and not my job, which would jeopardize my medical coverage. But there was also a part of me that didn't want to think about what was beginning to seem inevitable—physically, I could no longer write. I had a feeling that if I told my doctor the true impact of this injury, I'd start crying and never be able to stop. Just like my mother, all those years ago in the dermatologist's office.

By this point, Roger had been gone a few years, and my mother was working eighty to one hundred hours a week. I hadn't yet seen her house in its post-Roger hoarded state. Over the phone, my mom still talked about how much she missed Roger, but she also mentioned how much she loved her job and her coworkers. She always asked about my repetitive strain injury, and when she offered advice: "Use heat, then ice," I wouldn't mention that I already knew that from Gloria. My mother sent me heating pads and gloves with special, heatable beads inside and I didn't tell her that we didn't have the microwave necessary for the gloves. We'd talk a few times a week, then she'd disappear for months until I asked Sandy or my dad to tape a note to her door—just like before and after.

Also as before and after, I didn't let myself count on her in any way. I knew better.

Instead, I counted on Gloria, Kathy, and Marilyn, the women I saw for my appointments. I could unfurl myself in their offices, allow them to nurture me in ways my mother never had. As awful as it was, I grew used to living in this world of appointments and pain and even looked forward to seeing my "ladies," as David and I had begun to call them.

But one night after David and I returned home from a party, I was horrified to realize that I'd just blathered on to an acquaintance for an hour about whether or not I should take Dr. Chatterjee's advice and try an antiseizure medicine that had been found to decrease numbness in extremities. I couldn't believe this is what my life had become. I had nothing to say that wasn't related to RSI. If someone asked me what I did, I'd say, "Well, I've got this injury . . ." as if that was my job, or worse, who I was.

The next time I saw Dr. Chatterjee, I asked him to write the Permanent and Stationary report, which would allow me to leave San Francisco and still be eligible for medical care elsewhere. I didn't tell him, but I had begun to believe I wouldn't get better until I left the city. (How similar this was to my thinking, at sixteen, that moving out of the yellow house would solve my problems.)

I'd never had to change out of my clothes for an exam with Dr. Chatterjee, but this time I was in a gown. He tested my reflexes. He had me close my eyes and tell him when I felt sensation in my fingers (as he pricked them with something resembling an ice pick); using a small metal and wire contraption that looked straight out of the nineteenth century, he tested the strength in my fingers, wrists, forearms, biceps, and triceps. He squeezed and poked and prodded, asking page after page of questions, filling out the report as he went.

Though I'd heard many times that my injury was permanent, I wasn't prepared for Dr. Chatterjee's verdict about my work restrictions.

"Fifteen minutes a day on a keyboard, maximum," he said, jotting it down on the report.

"Excuse me?" I thought—I hoped—I'd misheard. "A day? Fifteen minutes?"

"That's right. You'll have to find a job where you won't need to use a keyboard. You could be a teacher," he suggested, his hand on his dimpled chin. "Although writing on a chalkboard might be difficult . . ."

"You don't understand," I blurted out. "I'm a writer."

"You are?" He set down the report and picked up my chart, opening it to the first page. "It says here that you were a . . . an online producer."

"That's what I did for a job. What I *care* about is writing."

"I see." He was really looking at me, maybe for the first time in the year-plus that I'd been his patient. "Well, Ms. Sholl, you should probably rethink that."

I felt like taking the stethoscope from around his neck and choking him with it. I felt like snatching the pen from his fingers and stabbing him in the eyes.

I said, "Someday I plan to write about this whole experience."

"I hope you do." But I could tell his words were perfunctory. He didn't believe I ever would. And that conviction was as painful as anything I'd felt during the entire time I'd been injured.

David and I finally left San Francisco. We made the cross-country trek in a rented van to my dad and Sandy's, where we stashed our belongings in the attic of their garage, and then we flew from Minneapolis to London. We lived for a few months in Paris, spent time in Amsterdam, and traveled through the Czech Republic; we stayed in Rome for three months, where as part of my professional retraining package, workers' compensation paid for me to take a course in teaching English as a second language.

By the time we returned from Europe and moved to Brooklyn, I'd had RSI for almost two years and it had been that long since I'd gone an entire day without pain. One of my friends in New York had developed RSI a few months earlier so I asked her for doctor recommendations. Hers was all the way out in Queens and he had a tendency to keep patients waiting, she said, but he was also the best.

When I arrived, the waiting room was so packed that patients spilled out onto the red brick stoop in front of his building. I waited more than an hour and a half past the time of my appointment until finally, Dr. Walker, a lanky man in his early forties, emerged from the back of the office and ushered me into what looked like a 1970s basement rec room, complete with wood paneling. A vinyl examination table sat in the middle of the room. The earth-toned carpeting had flecks of popcorn in it and on his desk were a few more—all escapees from the opened bag of Smartfood in front of his monitor.

Dr. Walker gestured toward the exam table and I climbed up. He sat down at his desk.

"So," he said, scooping a handful of popcorn from the bag, "tell me your story."

I did. He took notes as I spoke and then he washed his hands at the little sink in the corner. He squeezed the muscles in my forearms and had me flex my wrists and bend my fingers. He took more notes. I realized I'd been holding my breath for most of the time since I'd finished telling him my story, so I exhaled, then took a deep breath into my diaphragm, the way Kathy had shown me. Dr. Walker set down the clipboard he'd been using and clapped his hands together. "Well, this one should be easy."

"What should be easy?"

"Fixing you up," he said, sounding completely confident.

I couldn't believe my friend had sent me to a crazy man. "This is permanent," I said.

"It's not always permanent." He smiled. "Lots of my patients have recovered."

"No offense, but that's not what my doctor in San Francisco said."

He raised his eyebrows. Then he laughed. "Look at you: You're young. You're healthy. There's no reason you can't get better."

"But I've tried everything! If there was a way to heal from this, I would have."

Why was I getting so frustrated? Why was my voice shaking as if I was holding back tears?

"Ms. Sholl, just because you've had a hard time getting better doesn't mean you *can't*."

"Okay, then how?"

"Here's what we're gonna do . . ." Maybe it was his optimism that made me more open to the idea, but when he suggested I take a low dose of antidepressants to break the pain cycle, as Dr. Chatterjee had, I said yes. Dr. Walker also told me I should start taking lessons in something called the Alexander Technique from a woman he'd been sending patients to with excellent results. He asked me if I'd ever done yoga.

"I used to love yoga," I said. "But I can't do it anymore because it's bad for my wrists."

"Bah," he said, with the motion of throwing something worthless over his shoulder. "Do yoga. Don't be so fearful." He tossed a few kernels of popcorn into his mouth. "So. Sound like a plan?"

I wanted to ask him more questions—maybe even for the phone numbers of the patients he'd supposedly cured. But there were so many people out in that crowded waiting room, all wanting a turn with this man, all wanting to be told they could get better.

"Okay." I hopped off the table and held out my hand to him. I'd stopped shaking hands after too many ruffians (both men and women) crunched mine, and now I was testing Dr. Walker: If he squeezed my hand too hard, he was a quack who didn't know what he was talking about. If he was gentle, then maybe I'd trust him.

He took my hand in both of his, barely touching it but forming a protective shell around it. He tilted his head downward and looked me in the eyes. "You will get better. It's important for you to believe that."

I turned my face away, embarrassed because I was tearing up.

When I left his office, the day had turned overcast. During my long walk to the subway, I thought about how I'd felt when Dr. Walker said I could recover. Behind the shock, then nervousness (that he was wrong or crazy, that I'd injure myself even more) and behind the excitement (was it really possible? using a keyboard? writing with a pen?), there was something else, tucked way far back. As I continued walking, the feeling crystallized. Sadness. If I were to get better, there was something I'd have to give up.

The Ladies. During my appointments with them I'd felt babied, cared for, mothered. It was my first time, really, and I had to admit that I enjoyed it. Even though I was in New York now, I knew I could find an East Coast equivalent to the Ladies. When I thought about it, that was exactly what I'd been planning to do. I easily could.

Or, I could choose not to. I'd grown accustomed, even possibly dependent, on that ersatz mothering. But it was time for me to stop looking for nurturing in physical therapy offices—I had a feeling that I wouldn't get better until I did.

There were ups and downs, but it wasn't too long before I had my first pain-free hour, then morning, then day. I took my first, then second, third, fourth tentative strokes on the keyboard. I did yoga and I began lifting weights at the gym. I did pushups and even tried boxing classes. And one day I realized—out of the blue, as I carried a bag of groceries home from the store— that I was no longer helpless and weak. I was strong again.

AFTER DAVID AND I are done feasting on the Sahadi's delicacies, I turn on the hot water for the bathtub and dump two cups of Epsom salts under the running faucet. When I climb in and close my eyes one thought cycles through my mind, a little louder than all the others: My mother has cancer. My chest aches with worry, with sadness, with grief. But the ache is dulled, as if rising from the bottom of a deep well. Over the years, I've tried to put layers between myself and my mother—I don't tell her details about my life, I don't expect anything from her, I try not to be surprised or disappointed when she forgets my birthday or teases me. If the layers were foolproof, she wouldn't affect me at all, but they have protected me. Now that she's sick, my worry and sadness and grief are buried beneath those same layers. The feelings are there, just blunted. At the bottom of them is the inescapable fact that she's my mother, and I love her.

When I get out of the bath I wrap myself in a giant towel, open the sliding wooden door to our closet, and flip through the clothes on my side.

"Is there anything of yours I can get rid of?" I ask David, who's sitting on the couch reading a travel magazine.

"I just did that a few weeks ago," he says. "I'm good."

I reach for a pair of black pants I haven't worn since last summer. They can go. Ditto for the blue and gray button-down plaid shirt I've hung onto only because it's vintage and in good shape. Both of them go into a paper bag to bring to Housing Works. I do this often.

Because I'm the opposite of my mother: I save nothing. I've given away stereos, televisions, vintage love seats, bookcases. I can't find my diploma from graduate school and I have a feeling it ended up in the garbage during one of my purges. I even love getting to the end of a bottle of shampoo or conditioner, or a tube of toothpaste. It's exciting to throw things into the recycling bin or the garbage. Whenever I buy a new article of clothing I toss something else to make room. I get a thrill each time I discard something. Getting rid of things is liberating.

It's invigorating.

It's easy.

And I'd do anything to get my mother to agree.

9

I TELL MYSELF: COLON CANCER IS SUPPOSEDLY ONE OF THE most treatable cancers, my mother doesn't seem sick at all, and she needs to stay alive so she can continue to drive me insane. I tell myself these things to keep from worrying about her. Not that they work. My first full day back in New York I'm only half-present as I clean our apartment, take the dog for walks, teach my class, and make dinner. The other half of my mind is on my mother.

Except for the sliver absorbed in what's happening on my ankle. In the last twenty-four hours, the bumps have spread. What started as five or six individual welts is now a solid patch of rash about three inches square. And the rash really itches. I'm afraid I'm going to permanently scar myself from all the scratching, so eventually I coat it with Neosporin and cover it with a Band-Aid to keep from clawing at it.

My mother calls me that night. She's all checked into the hospital and she's got good news: The new polyps were all benign. That means that when she has the resectioning surgery the doctors will have to remove only the area of the colon around the one cancerous polyp.

"That's great news, Mom! So the surgery's tomorrow, then?"

"It's scheduled for the day after tomorrow."

"Why do you have to wait so long?"

"I really don't know. But I don't mind. I like it here."

"Really? Why?" But then I think about it: Of course she'd like it—she's getting waited on, she's got people around her. Nurses. "Are you bonding with the other nurses? Is that why you like it?"

She laughs. "Actually I don't think they like me very much."

"Why not?"

"Oh, they're just uptight."

"Mom. What did you do?"

"I just put up this sign . . ."

Dear God. "What kind of sign?"

"Just asking them to please wash their hands before they touch me. You don't know what kind of infections you can get in hospitals."

"Yeah, but now the nurses are going to think you're annoying. It's rude, Mom. I'm sure they wash their hands constantly."

"It's just a little sign. I leave it on the table next to the bed."

I want to point out the ludicrousness of worrying so much about germs, given the state of her house, but I bite my tongue. Besides, who knows? Maybe she's right.

We talk for a while more, and then as we're about to get off the phone, I remember the mysterious rash. "Hey, Mom, you don't have any weird bumps or bug bites, do you? I've got this patch of *something* on my ankle and I can't figure out what it is."

After a few long seconds she says, "Oh, no. You're not going to like this."

"What?"

"I think I know what it might be." She pauses. "And you're *really* not going to like it."

"What is it? Tell me."

"I think it's . . . body lice."

I wait for her to laugh, but she doesn't. "You are kidding, right?"

"I wish I was."

Immediately the itching spreads from my ankles up through my legs and into my torso, my arms, all the way to my fingertips—invisible lice are crawling over my entire body.

"What makes you think that's what this is?"

"I bought a pillow at Savers and I think it had lice on it. Or, wait a minute, maybe it wasn't at Savers. No. That's right, this was from a consignment shop in St. Paul."

"But why would you use it if you thought it was infested with lice?"

"Well, I didn't know it had lice at the time," she says as if I've just asked the most absurd question she's ever heard.

"Why would you buy a used pillow? That's like buying a used bra or used underwear."

"It's one of those pillows that I like—you know, with the arms attached? And it was such soft corduroy. I couldn't resist."

I know which one she's talking about. The so-called "husband pillow" was on her bed.

"After I slept with it a few times, I noticed my feet itching in the morning—"

"Your feet? Wouldn't it be your head that was itching?"

"No, it wouldn't. I was sleeping with it down by my feet. But I used the RID cream and I thought it was cleared up."

"You knew about the lice and you still didn't throw it out?"

"Well, it's one of those ones I like . . . and I washed it after I figured out the lice. I thought it was gone."

Her voice is high-pitched and whiny. I feel like yelling at her, but I don't. It's not her fault that she acts like an idiot sometimes. It's the hoarding that compels her. Once again I wish I still smoked. Instead, I walk to the refrigerator, grab a bottle of white wine, pour myself a glass, and take a sip.

"Jessie? Are you still there?" my mom asks.

"How am I supposed to get rid of this?"

"I thought you hung up on me." She laughs. "Is there a drugstore open near you?"

"This is New York City. Of course there's a drugstore open," I snap and take another sip of wine. "Sorry for being a bitch, Mom, but I can't believe I have . . . body lice." I can barely say the words.

And what really upsets me is that her hoarding is now affecting my life all the way across the country. Mentally, yes, she affects me wherever I am, but I always thought I was safe from the physical aspects of her disorder once I stepped on a plane. I was wrong. Not even the 1,200 miles I've put between us can protect me.

"You just have to go to the drugstore and get some RID. It's for both head and body lice. Get the spray and the shampoo. You'll need to put the shampoo over your entire body and sleep with it on. And use the spray on your bed and your couch."

"I'm not sure about spraying that stuff in my bed or on the couch—what about Abraham Lincoln? He weighs ten pounds. His system can't take those chemicals."

"Please, I'm telling you, you have to spray! And get Dave to use the shampoo, too. If you don't both do it, you'll just keep reinfecting each other. Oh, and you have to wash everything you've touched since you've been back, and in the hottest water possible."

"Okay, okay," I say. "The problem is that we don't have a washer or dryer in the building and the nearest Laundromat is two blocks away." I look around the apartment, quickly assessing everything I've used since I've been back: the clothes I've worn, the sheets on the bed, the blankets, the pillows, the couch cover, the bath mat, the bathroom towels, the kitchen towels, my jacket. "God, this sucks," I say. "It's going to take a whole day to wash everything."

"I'm so sorry . . . and please tell Dave I'm sorry, too!"

"It's not your fault, Mom," I say, though in reality I think it is her fault. No one held a gun to her head and forced her to buy a used pillow. My poor husband is teaching tonight and won't be home until after 10:30. He'll come home tired and hungry, and instead of relaxing and eating he'll get to smear lice shampoo over his entire body.

"Jesus Christ," my mom mumbles. "Maybe I still have it. Now I'm going to have to tell those nurses to treat me for lice."

"Hey, at least you can take down that sign you made—they'll definitely want to wash their hands now, at least *after* they touch you."

But my lame attempt at a joke isn't met with my mother's usual free-flowing laughter.

"I really am sorry about this," she says.

"I know you are, Mom. Look, it's okay. It'll be okay. Just take care of yourself in the hospital. You're the one with cancer."

And I do forgive her, but it's so humiliating and frustrating that I'm running to Rite Aid at ten o'clock at night to buy RID. I want to have everything ready for when David gets home. He's going to have to slather the stuff on as soon as he walks in the door. And Abraham Lincoln: I have no idea how to treat him.

It turns out there are three shelves dedicated to lice-killing measures and insect repellants. I stand there under the fluorescent lights comparing the prices of RID versus the generic brand, looking at the lengthy list of chemicals I've never heard of, and whenever I sense anyone approaching I turn around and pretend to be looking at the aspirin across the aisle.

I can picture the exact moment I was infested. Her bedroom was packed like all the other rooms, filled nearly wall-to-wall with folding card tables and TV trays, every surface layered with stuff: crumpled McDonald's bags, empty Pringles cans, raggedy books of crossword puzzles and acrostics, half-full two-liter bottles of Pepsi and Orange Crush. A tall white bookcase sat empty against one wall (a smaller bedroom, next to hers, was packed floor to ceiling with paperbacks). While taking it all in and trying to decide where to start, I spotted a pyramid of empty liquor bottles on a table in one corner of the room. But supposedly my mother hadn't touched alcohol in thirty years.

"What are these doing here?" I asked my mother, who was standing in the doorway.

"I don't know," she said, coming closer to inspect them. "Wait a minute, I bet they were left over from when I had that asshole guy living here! That guy . . . you know, the guy who was going to work on the house in exchange for a place to stay. I can't even remember his name now."

"The superstar handyman?"

"Yes. That guy."

He was an acquaintance of one of her neighbors and my mom had met him only once before she hatched the plan. All she knew about him was that he was seventy-five and supposedly fantastic at fixing things. I didn't love the idea of him moving in—at least not until she got to know him—and advised my mother against it, but she struck a deal with him anyway. The arrangement lasted only a few months, just until she figured out that he wasn't planning on doing any actual work. He'd been gone for at least a year, though.

"This was that guy's room?" I picked up one of the liquor bottles and put it into a bag for recycling. "Did you *share* this room with him?"

"No, no," she started laughing. "This room was his and then I moved into it after he left."

"And you didn't bother to throw out these bottles?"

She shrugged. "I guess I forgot they were here."

Okay.

What else did she forget? Did she even change the sheets? I looked over at the bed, a tiny twin bed from when I was a kid and lived here. The question of whether or not she changed the sheets was irrelevant. There were no sheets on the bed at all.

"Oh, Mom." Suddenly I was completely depressed. "How can you live like this? It's so . . . sad. How can you stand it?"

"Frank! Oh, Jessie! That was his name. Frank."

I want my mother to have a normal life. I want her to have a clean house, clean sheets on a comfortable bed. I want her to *want* that. But as I swept under her bed, I found a garbage bag's worth of Häagen Dazs bar wrappers, clumps of dust and hair, combs and Q-tips and soda cans and bottle tops and paper coffee cups and more crossword puzzles. I felt like crying and almost did as I put sheets and blankets on the bed and organized the pillows.

Including *that* pillow.

I dusted the windowsills and swept the floor. I tried to get my mom to give up some of the back massagers and foot soaking tubs and those contraptions you put into a bathtub to make an instant Jacuzzi, all unopened in their boxes, but she wouldn't part with them. And I understood why: They're all devices meant to give comfort. Without Roger, she has no one to give her comfort. Who ever hugs my mother, besides me when I visit twice a year? Who ever touches her?

And now that I have body lice, who will touch me?

Finally I toss three bottles of RID shampoo and one can of RID spray into my red basket and go stand in line to pay for them—though the store is almost empty, there's still a line; there's always a line—and as I scratch at a new welt that's forming on my arm, the first one outside my ankle area, a hazy memory of another infestation in my mother's house begins to take shape. Rodents. It happened right after my parents separated, when my brother and I lived with my mom during the week. The rodents weren't mice and they weren't rats—they looked like three- or four-inch long fetal kangaroos. None of us had any idea what they were. It was as if some alien spacecraft deposited them in the house at night, and in the mornings we'd find them. Once I found one in a shoe—discovering it as I slipped my foot inside. No one will confirm the existence of these otherworldly creatures, but I remember them, and they're what I'm thinking of as I purchase my poisons from the night clerk at Rite Aid and make my way home.

MY MOM DOESN'T call me the next day, and when I try to call her the afternoon of her surgery, I can't get through. The phone in her room is busy. I'm pretty sure she's taken it off the hook. She always makes herself unavailable when I most need to reach her. Every Mother's Day, Christmas, birthday, her phone is off the hook. She clearly doesn't want to be disappointed if no one calls, but by making herself unavailable for disappointment, she also negates any chance of being pleasantly surprised. I've told her this a million times but it makes no difference. I always end up waiting for her to call me.

And she finally does, the day after her surgery.

"I feel fine," she says when I ask. "Totally fine. Now I just have to wait for the doctors to tell me the results from the tissue samples. That's when I'll find out about the chemo."

"So you're not in any pain at all?"

"No, none."

It's one of my mother's many paradoxes: She can talk for hours about the emotional traumas she's suffered at the hands of her father, her siblings, bosses, ex-friends, even bank tellers, but her threshold for physical pain is off-the-charts high. My dad told me that after she broke her back in the car accident she never once complained about the pain. And she had to have an emergency appendectomy not long ago—*emergency* because she waited so long to go to the hospital, thinking the odd feeling in her lower back would pass.

I'm the opposite. I'm constantly gauging how I feel, touching the glands on my neck to see if they're swollen, looking at my tongue as I've seen acupuncturists do (though I have no idea what I'm looking for), asking my husband if he'll feel my forehead and tell me if I seem feverish. My dad is the same way and I think I got it from him.

My mom starts talking about how one of the nurses there has a dog the same size as Abraham Lincoln and my mother plans to knit it a sweater.

"Mom?" I say, interrupting her. "I need to ask you about these . . . lice."

"Oh, no. I didn't mention it because I was hoping they were gone."

"They're not."

"The nurse is here," she says abruptly, and then I hear her speaking in the high voice she usually reserves for children and pets, "I'll take more of that pudding, please. The butterscotch— it was just delicious!" Then she's back to me, her voice low and muffled, as if she's covering her mouth and the phone's receiver. "Jessie, what's going on with the lice?"

"It seems to be getting worse. The rash that started on my ankle has moved to my arms."

"I told you to get that RID!"

"I did. In fact I did it two nights in a row just to be safe. And I've washed everything."

"You didn't get Dave to do the RID, and now he's reinfecting you."

"No, he's done it twice, too. And he doesn't have any of the bites that I have anyway. The thing is, from what I've read, this doesn't seem like body lice. You're supposed to be able to see them crawling around in the seams of your clothes and I can't see anything. And I've washed every item of clothing I've worn since I was in Minneapolis, not to mention all the sheets and blankets and towels, plus I've scrubbed the entire apartment from top to bottom."

"We-ll," she says, drawing out the word, "then I've got some bad news."

"What?"

"I think it's something else."

"What could it be?"

"Scabies."

I've heard of scabies: It's the thing that homeless people and junkies get—it's disgusting. Suddenly body lice seems quaint.

"Mom, please tell me you're kidding."

"Unfortunately, I'm not."

"Jesus Christ. Well, why do you think that?" While researching body lice online, I'd come across mentions of scabies but didn't pay attention because it seemed too absurd.

"It just sounds like it," my mom says. "And if the RID isn't working . . . and, well, I had it once before—I got it in the nursing home. It's really common in nursing homes."

"How long ago was that?"

"About ten years ago."

I can tell she's lying. I can almost always tell.

"How long ago was it really, Mom?"

"Maybe five years."

"You knew before that that's what this is. Why did you even bother telling me to get that RID crap? You must have known it wouldn't work."

"I—I'm not sure," she says. "I really didn't know for sure. I was hoping."

I sit down on the couch and start up my laptop, with the phone pressed against my ear.

"This is really frustrating," I say, thinking, She's got cancer. She's in the hospital. You can't lose it on her when she's in the hospital.

"Listen, this isn't a big deal—but you are going to have to go to the doctor and get this cream. It's called permethrin. You put it on at night and then wash it off twelve hours later."

I type "scabies" into Google and get a series of horrific images and some articles. They seem to be a parasitic mite that lives underneath your skin and feeds on human blood. The pictures make my skin crawl. I grab a notebook and start jotting down some things that are supposed to be natural cures: tea tree oil, eating raw garlic, something called "neem," which is an Indian plant or leaf or herb, I can't quite tell.

"Mom, what about you? What are you going to do about

the . . . you know . . ." I can't even say the word "scabies" out loud,
I'm so repulsed. "You know, the . . . bugs."

She starts laughing. "Oh, don't worry—I've had to do this
millions of times for patients at the nursing home. I'll just tell
the nurses that I've been exposed to it and they'll treat me."

"But what about getting them out of your house? You have to
disinfect it. I mean, you're not going to be able to do all the loads
of laundry and mop your floors and—"

"Oh, Jessie, do you have the internet at home?"

"Yes," I say and don't mention that I was already online. I
don't want her to think I wasn't paying attention.

"See how long they can live on surfaces. Maybe by the time
I get out of here I won't have to do anything to disinfect my
house."

"Hold on," I say and click through a few more pages. "Okay,
it seems like most websites say they can live seventy-two hours
in clothing and on furniture and floors."

"I've already been in here for three days," she says, "so it's
fine. By the time I get back there, everything should be safe.
Now when you go to the doctor, don't forget to get some medicine for Dave, too. And then you'll have to wash everything, of
course."

Again. I've already done two loads of laundry each of the
three days I've been back. "This is getting expensive, Mom."

"I'll pay for it; don't worry."

"How? You have no money. Unless you get another job,
you've got to keep to your allowance until social security kicks
in."

"Correction!" my mom says, suddenly excited. "I only have
to keep to that allowance until I win my lawsuit against those
motherfuckers! Did I tell you I've already got an appointment
set up with an employment counselor? Her name is Marcy and

she's going to help me do all the paperwork to sue those mo—
Oh, hello," my mom says to someone. "It's the nurse with the
pudding. Oh, wait a minute, the doctor's here, too. Honey, I've
got to go."

"Is this about the chemo?"

"I'll call you later," she says, and is gone.

10

"I'M SO EMBARRASSED," I SAY TO DAVID AS I DOWN COFFEE and put on my shoes at the same time. "I can't believe what I'm about to go to the doctor for."

"Don't get so stressed out," he says. "It'll be okay."

My husband's on the couch with his laptop, clearly waiting for me to leave and the commotion to stop so he can resume working. He's got a ton of research to do before we leave for Italy, where he's going to be working on a book project. For this first stint, we'll be there about six months—he's leaving at the beginning of July and I'm meeting him there three weeks later, after my summer classes are done. We'll be living in a tiny village north of Rome and are still trying to find an apartment there, as well as sublet ours here in New York. Before my mother was diagnosed with cancer we were already stressed out about all the arrangements we had to make, not to mention the fact that we've both been taking any freelance writing or editing work we could find and scrimping and saving every penny. Plus we're both studying Italian, which comes pretty easily for my husband, not so much for me.

Now I've got the additional joy of these rash-inducing parasites to contend with. I'm just grateful that David doesn't have them. He didn't seem fazed when I told him last night that what I thought was body lice might actually be scabies. Nothing surprises him about my mother anymore.

"And then she doesn't even call me back last night," I say, fuming. I have no idea if she found out about the chemo or if the doctor was there for another reason. I finish tying my Pumas and bring my coffee cup into the kitchen, where I set it in the sink.

"Go," David says. "Just get it over with and you'll feel better."

"You're right," I say. Then I lean down to kiss him and run out the door.

The doctor's office I go to takes walk-ins and it can get crowded. I have a regular doctor there and usually make appointments with her, but this time I'd rather see someone I don't know.

When I arrive, there are only three people in the waiting room, all of whom are staring at the TV in the corner. Dr. Sanjay Gupta is discussing strategies for combating heart disease. I sign in and the woman behind the desk hands me a clipboard and a short form.

I fill in the lines asking for my name and the date. Next to "reason for visit," I write "insect bites." I hand it back to the woman and take a seat across the room from the television, pulling down the sleeves of my shirt so none of my skin touches the upholstery of the chair—if I got this from a pillow, then it's contagious through objects and I don't want to infest anything.

After about twenty minutes, a nurse calls my name and leads

me into one of the examination rooms. She takes my temperature and her hand brushes against my arm as she pulls the thermometer from my mouth.

"Um," I say, "I think I have something contagious—you probably shouldn't touch me."

"Sure, hon," she says as if she's heard it before. She writes down my temperature in my chart and I don't bother asking what it is before she leaves the room.

The doctor who comes in a few minutes later is a guy in his midthirties, about my age.

"So, what can I do for you today?" He's looking at the sheet of paper I filled out in the waiting room. "You're here for insect bites?"

I pull down my sock to show him the rash. "Actually, I think it's . . . scabies."

He leans down to get a better look, but doesn't touch me.

"Yes," he says, straightening up. "That looks like it could be scabies, though the bites are usually smaller than that. You're sure they're not mosquito bites?"

I nod. My face is beet red, I can feel it. "I got it from my mom. She did a really boneheaded thing and bought a pillow secondhand and didn't wash it."

Even though I'd practiced what I was going to say the whole way here, it's hard to get the words out. I'm honestly not sure what's worse: that I have this in the first place, or that I got it from my mother.

"That is boneheaded," he says. "I'll prescribe you permethrin. Does she need a prescription, too, or does she have a doctor?"

"She's in Minneapolis and she's taken care of medicine-wise. But if you could prescribe enough for my husband, too, I'd appreciate it. Although he doesn't have any bites."

"This is highly contagious—if you're sleeping in the same bed, sharing towels, etcetera, he needs to do the medicine, too." He jots down something in my chart and then starts filling out a prescription.

"Also, I have a dog. Can he get it?" I've read conflicting things online about whether scabies can live on animals.

"No. That's not a problem," he says, shaking his head. "Animals can't get scabies."

Well, that's one good thing. And he says it in a kind and completely noncondescending way. Usually the doctors here are in and out of the room in three minutes or less, but he's not rushing me at all. I have a sudden urge to explain the connection between my mother's mental state and this parasite. Maybe this doctor could even help. As a health professional, he might know something about hoarding that I don't. "My mom's got a problem with . . ."

I can't bring myself to say it.

The doctor stops writing and looks at me with an earnest expression. "Yes?"

". . . she's . . ."

He's still looking at me.

"She's got cancer," I say, and my eyes fill with tears.

The doctor nods with concern. "What type?"

"Colon. But she had surgery and she's going to be okay," I say quickly, even though I don't know that for sure.

No. She *is* going to be okay.

She has to be.

The doctor nods again and smiles sympathetically. After a few seconds, he flips my chart closed and tears the prescription from the pad. He stands and hands me the slip of paper. "Don't worry—" he glances at my chart—"Jessica. Do this cream head-to-toe tonight, sleep with it on, and then wash it off. If you really want to be sure it's gone, do the treatment again one week later. I've given you refills in case. Your husband needs to do the treatment at the same time. And wash everything."

"Thank you," I say and jump off the examination table. I feel a little better already, just having the prescription.

The doctor holds out his hand to shake mine.

"Are you sure I should shake your hand?" I ask. "I've read that even shaking hands . . ."

He pulls his hand back. "I don't think it's a problem, but I suppose just to be safe." He looks embarrassed. "Good luck with your mom. I hope she recovers quickly."

It's a long walk home, thirty or so blocks, but it's a nice day and I need the exercise. I call my husband from my cell phone to see if by chance my mom's called. She hasn't.

"But I do have something to tell you," he says. "Right after you left, I noticed something on my chest."

"No."

"Yes. I have a bite on my chest. It really fucking itches."

"Just one? Maybe it's a mosquito bite?"

"It's not. I can tell. The weird thing is that at first it was just this itchy spot—but when I scratched it, this welt started forming. I know it's what you have. It is. I have it, too."

Goddammit. "I'm so sorry. You shouldn't have to deal with this."

I shouldn't have to deal with it either, but she's *my* mother. David's always been so patient with her—letting her go on and on when we go out to lunch, letting her take forever in the used bookstore she insists we go to afterward, not to mention the time he helped clean out her house.

"I'm sorry," I say again, mentally searching for a way to make this better. "You should go to the gym and go in the sauna. I read online that the sauna can help kill these things. Then we'll do this cream tonight and be done." We both love the sauna, so this isn't an outlandish suggestion.

"I've got so much reading to do," he says. "But then again, I can't exactly concentrate."

"I'll make dinner tonight so you don't have to worry about it, okay? You can read before and after, even *during* dinner if you want."

"Okay, thanks. That sounds good."

"One more thing," I say. "When you go to the sauna, make sure that you sit on a towel. Don't let any of your skin touch the wood or anything in the locker room at all."

It kills me to have to say that to my husband. We're lepers; there's no question.

"Fine," he says and hangs up.

I'm walking through Madison Square Park. Shake Shack is just opening up and the smell of grilling hamburgers is already filling the air; about twenty people wait in line for their meaty meals, BlackBerries and iPhones in hand. They're all well-dressed, in stylish white blouses and black skirts and suits and neatly coiffed hair. I bet none of them has had scabies. Most of them probably haven't even heard of it. I bet they'd be utterly revolted if they knew that at this very moment, walking right past them is a girl with a parasite living under her skin. Walking past them as if she has every right. She has no right to be among normal people anymore. She knows.

It's something she's known for most of her life.

I was eight years old, spending the night at Vanessa Erickson's house. Her father worked at the Minnesota Orchestra and they lived in the ritzy part of our neighborhood, in one of the big houses along the river. Her mother was sleek and gorgeous, with wide blue eyes and porcelain skin; Vanessa was an exact miniature of her. I didn't like being around Vanessa's parents.

They were too perfect. Too pretty and wealthy and clean. Vanessa and I were friends because we were in the same third-grade class, as well as the after-school gymnastics program. I still lived then mostly with my mom, and neither Vanessa nor any of my other friends had ever been there.

Vanessa's parents were out somewhere, and a babysitter watched us, letting us take a bubble bath together as we sometimes did, running a wide-toothed comb through each other's sudsy hair. Then we watched part of *The Carol Burnett Show* while drinking hot chocolate made with real milk and loaded with marshmallows. Afterward, the babysitter got us into our respective twin beds, leaving Vanessa's bedroom door open a crack. We giggled and talked late into the night, looking up at the high arched ceiling, at the sliver of moon coming in through the window.

We woke to the sound of her parents saying our names. They said them quietly, as if they didn't want to alarm us. They stepped forward and scooped each of us out of bed. "We want to show you girls something. We need you to dress up a little bit."

I borrowed a pink dress from Vanessa. I had no idea where we were going. It was late, but as we drove over the dark streets, I wasn't afraid.

We pulled up to a house with a wide, circular driveway and got out of the car. An orchestra played on the lawn, under a giant oak tree. Tear-shaped lights hung from the tree's fat branches. Waiters in tuxedoes walked through the crowd carrying trays of filled champagne glasses. The women's hair was up; some had strands of pearls threaded through. They wore sleeveless satin dresses and several of their skirts trailed on the lawn, but they didn't seem to care. It was a scene from Cinderella's ball. I'd never seen anything like it.

"Isn't it beautiful?" Vanessa's mother said. "We wanted you girls to see it."

Hot anger flared inside my rib cage: They brought me there to show off, to brag that this was the life they led, a life I could never have. Because it was beautiful, yes. And I didn't belong there, among such beauty. I didn't even belong with a friend whose parents went to events like that. Not when I had a mother at home who wore the same ratty knee-length sweater coat year-round; who chased me out of the house gripping a hairbrush, not so she could tame my tangled locks but so she could hit me with it; a mother who was already showing signs of a mental illness that would render her unable to differentiate between trash and treasure.

It would be years and years before I understood that Vanessa's parents hadn't been trying to show off at all. They'd merely wanted their daughter and their daughter's friend to see something they found beautiful, to see what was possible. All I knew then was that I had no right to be there. And all I wanted to do then, as now, was disappear.

WHEN I GET home, my husband's gone—to the gym, I assume. Abraham Lincoln greets me at the door, running in happy circles, his little tail wagging. I pick him up and walk toward the front room, where the phone is.

This time when I call, my mother answers.

"Oh, honey, I'm so glad you called!"

"I've been calling, Mom, ever since last night. What did the doctor tell you?" I sit down on the edge of the couch, wishing David were here in case the news is bad.

"You're not going to believe it! There was no cancer anywhere in the tissue samples—no cancer anywhere besides that one polyp."

"So what does that mean?"

"It means I don't have to have chemotherapy. I just go home and this is over."

"Over, over?" I can't quite believe it.

"I think so, yes." She sounds as surprised as I feel. "I have to be on a special diet for a while and I'm not supposed to lift anything over twenty pounds."

"That's amazing. So when can you leave the hospital?"

"They want to keep me until tomorrow. Do you think you could call Sandy or your dad and ask them to drive me home? Your dad called me a few minutes ago but I didn't think to ask."

"Really? No offense, but why would my dad call you?"

"He wanted to tell me that he went into the house and took care of the stove and refrigerator since I've been in here," she says.

I knew he was planning to do it, but I didn't know exactly when.

"Now what happened at the doctor?" my mom asks, lowering her voice. "Did you get the permethrin?"

"Yes, I did," I say. "And now David has these things, too."

"Really?" She laughs, but I can tell it's because she's nervous.

"Yes, really."

"Listen, they're easy to get rid of. The nurses treated me and now I'm fine."

"I hope you're right," I say. "I feel so repulsive. And I teach a writing class here in our apartment, but I can't have anyone over until I know these things are gone. I mean if they lived on that pillow, maybe they're in our couch, or in the rug, or—"

"Jessie, I'm so sorry about all this," my mom says. She pauses for a few seconds. "If it makes you feel any better, you'll never have to clean my house again. It looks so fantastic with everything you did to it, and I bet your dad made the kitchen just gorgeous. I promise you, I'm going to keep it that way."

I know why she thinks keeping her house clean would wipe this parasite-infestation slate clean: She realizes the depth of my obsession with her house. Over the years I've sworn off asking about it so many times—but because my compulsion to try to fix the situation is probably equal in strength to her compulsion to hoard, I always eventually cave. "So, how's your house?" I'll ask, while telling myself, *Shut up shut up shut up,* and when I hear that she has "the most beautiful bureau" from a yard sale waiting on her porch, she just needs to find someone to bring it inside for her, or that she's just spent the last four hours at Walmart buying three different kinds of pizza stones so she can do a taste test—now she just needs a bigger kitchen table to fit all the pizzas—I'll begin the begging/bribing/bullying: *Please just try to bring one box of stuff a week to the Goodwill; if you get it clean enough you can rent out one of the bedrooms to a university student and not have to work; don't you realize your house could be condemned?*

But she just laughs off my various attempts and nothing changes. Nothing will ever change. I should know that by now. So why don't I?

WE DO THE permethrin cream, but three days later not only are David and I still itching, we're still getting new bites. I can't touch anyone—when I meet a friend for dinner at my favorite Ethiopian place I make sure not to have any skin-to-skin contact at all. I don't even let any of my clothes brush against hers. I'm terrified of passing this on and I'd rather die than admit to anyone besides my dad and Sandy that I have it. I tell my writing class that David and I suspect we were exposed to bedbugs and that I want to have our place fumigated before anyone comes over—we begin meeting at a nearby bar instead. My husband

and I eat cloves of raw garlic three or four times a day and take drops of grapefruit seed extract (which supposedly kills parasites) as well as capsules of neem leaves, apparently a cure-all in India. I take baths laced with tea tree oil and scrub every surface of the apartment, sweep, mop, and vacuum constantly.

A week after the first permethrin treatment, we do the second one. It doesn't help. David and I are both so itchy and continuing to get more and more bites. But perhaps the worst part is the amount of time we're losing. Hours that could be spent writing, looking for freelance work, studying Italian, not to mention all the research David needs to do: All those hours are lost to what we are now calling "the bugs." Because we can wear things only once—and that includes the sheets, blankets, and towels we use—we have to do laundry every day. Thankfully our neighborhood Laundromat is large, with lots of employees, so no one seems to notice our daily pilgrimage with two stuffed laundry bags. That, or anyone who *does* notice isn't saying anything. I start going to the sauna at the gym almost every day, picturing these parasites cooking to death under my skin. I stay in the sauna for thirty, forty minutes, once almost an hour. Afterward I slather myself with tea tree oil and pray that no one in the locker room notices its pungent aroma or the red welts around my ankles and up my calves or the chicken pox–like rash across my waist and hips.

My mother is back home, claiming to feel great, and enjoying the kitchen my dad fixed up for her—he didn't just replace the stove and refrigerator, but also swapped out a gigantic shelving unit for a new one that fits perfectly between the wall and refrigerator, holding more things but taking up less space. She tells me over and over again how *marvelous* it is, and about all the things she's going to cook once she can eat regular food again.

She sounds toned down, though, her voice and inflection weak and muted, and I know it's not just because she feels awful about the bugs—which she does. It's because she had to go off her antidepressants before the surgery. Hers can cause constipation, which is not what she needs with a colon that's still healing. At first I didn't detect a difference in her personality, but now that she's been off them for a few weeks, I can. And I don't like it. She sounds sad, even when she's telling me how much she loves the new kitchen and how grateful she is to my dad and Sandy for helping her. Her words are slow and thick.

I ask when she can go back on her medication.

"Not for a few more weeks," she says. "But I'm okay."

"You don't sound okay. Can you call your doctor and see about starting again? At least at a lower dose for the meantime? You really sound terrible."

"I'm okay."

"Maybe you could take a drink of water? Your mouth sounds really dry."

Is she so un-self-aware that she doesn't even know when she's thirsty? Or is it the depression? I have no idea, but I do know that I feel very sorry for her right now—and that's the only reason I don't tell her how truly upset I am about the bugs, about how much they're disrupting my life.

"Hold on," she says and sets down the phone. She comes back, gulping something. "I'm doing this experiment where I mix juice with water, to make the water tolerable. It's not bad."

She perks up a little and I let her go on and on, talking about something she saw on the news, about something her career counselor Marcy said, about their latest ploy for the lawsuit. I let her talk even though it makes me feel vaguely abused—no, "used" is the right word. But I don't ask her to stop. She has no one else.

My normally extremely patient husband's patience is beginning to wear thin, though: He snaps at me one day as he comes home from the Laundromat. He fears these bugs won't be gone before we leave for Italy.

"They will be. I promise," I say, though I'm not so sure myself.

AFTER I'VE BEEN back in New York for about three weeks, my dad tells me that he's noticed this strange itching around his ankle, and some bumps there that look like mosquito bites but he can tell aren't. He's afraid that he's got the dreaded S-word, too.

"Are you sure it's not something else?" I ask. "Is there anything else it could be?"

"They're just like the ones you described and they itch like hell," he says. "Dammit! I must've gotten infected when I was dealing with your mother's stove and refrigerator. I scrubbed the floor right before we put the new ones in. I was even on my hands and knees."

"Can you go to a doctor and get some permethrin? Do you have a regular doctor?"

"I don't have a regular one, but I can go to that clinic on Franklin Avenue I suppose," he says, sighing. "But I thought you guys haven't had any luck with that medicine?"

"That's true." I've already told him about how at first it'll seem like it's worked, but after a few days one of us will get new bites. "According to some things I've read, though, the itching can last for up to a year after they're gone, so maybe the bugs are gone and we just can't tell the difference. But I don't think so. I have an appointment with a dermatologist next week."

"Oh, great. If the medicine doesn't work, why should I even bother getting it?"

"Because maybe it will work for you, or maybe the doctor

you see will know of something else to use. Please go to the doctor tomorrow. And get some medicine for Sandy, too."

"She won't take it," he says. "You know she won't."

I do know. Sandy's approach to health is strictly alternative. Coming from her, the term "Western medicine" has almost as much contempt as the phrase "pinko commie" had during the McCarthy era. That's why neither my dad nor Sandy has a regular doctor. That's why they have only catastrophic health insurance.

"There are some natural cures I'm sure Sandy would agree to take," I say, "like tea tree oil and garlic . . . though I haven't had any luck with them so far. Obviously. But it's worth a try."

I lift my pants cuff to look at my chewed-up ankle. My forearms and wrists have red bites all over them, too. It's early May and getting warmer out, and I can't wear skirts or even short-sleeved shirts.

"What's really sad about this," my dad says, "is that for once, we were all coming together. Sandy and I wanted to help your mother get through this cancer . . . and she ruined it by infesting us with some goddamn parasite—"

"I know Dad, I know. Believe me. But it's not worth raising your blood pressure over. Yes, having this sucks—really, really, sucks—but they're not permanent. There's a cure, we just haven't found it yet. Just, whatever you do, make sure Sandy doesn't get them."

THAT NIGHT WHEN my mom calls, I tell her about my dad having the bugs now, too. I say he must've gotten them from being inside her house.

"That's not possible," she says. "Besides, when he was in my house I'd already been in the hospital for three days . . ." she drifts off and I hear her mumbling. "*No, four* days, so that can't be how he got them. He must have gotten them from you."

I walk to the refrigerator, grab a bottle of white wine, and open it. I can't talk to my mother anymore without something to distract me, either the internet or wine.

"I highly doubt that, Mom." By now I'm an expert on scabies transmission. Prolonged touch—the kind that occurs when you're handholding or sleeping with someone—is the main culprit. Supposedly skin-to-skin contact is necessary. But I got them from that pillow, I know, because my mom and I never touch. We rarely hug, and when we do there are layers of clothes between us. I got them after being in her house and now my dad has them after being in her house. The house being the common denominator, it's pretty clear that somehow this parasite is living there.

Through the phone, I hear a sort of screechy gulping noise. She's crying.

Here's a crazy fact about my mom that doesn't seem crazy to me: Normally, there are two things—and only two things—that make her cry. John Lennon's murder and the Bird Man of Alcatraz.

When my brother and I were kids and feeling evil, we'd say, "Mom, what about the Bird Man of Alcatraz?" and she'd immediately start crying. "All those years he spent locked up, taking care of those birds," she'd say through her tears. "Yeah, the Bird Man, so sad," we'd taunt, trying to get her to cry harder. (Evil, like I said.)

Later, after we got older and stopped teasing her like that, she'd do it to herself by saying, "I just can't believe what happened to John Lennon," sometimes saying it twice before the tears began to fall.

The reason it doesn't seem that crazy to me is that I went through a similar phase a few years ago, while reading a stack of books about the Holocaust for a novel I was researching. The more I read, the more gutted I felt. I'd only have to think about the Holocaust and I'd begin weeping; I couldn't even say the words without my voice cracking. Commercials for 90 percent of the shows on the History Channel would leave me in a puddle, and when I went to the Anne Frank house in Amsterdam I barely made it through the museum without collapsing.

So although the two subjects that make her cry seem a little random, I understand how a certain topic can trigger tears. She's told me many times how disconnected she feels—from people and from her own emotions. Maybe crying over seemingly random events is a shortcut to emotion, not unlike the way some cutters claim to cut themselves in order to feel something. Or it could be an avoidance tactic. Maybe there's something out there she doesn't want to feel. By feeling strongly about *this* you don't have to feel strongly about *that*. So the tears over John Lennon or the Bird Man of Alcatraz don't seem crazy to me. What's crazy is to hear my mother cry about something else.

And she's still crying.

"Mom?"

"I feel so bad for what I've done. I gave you these things . . . and now your dad, too!"

"It's okay. Nobody blames you," I lie. "It's not your fault."

"It *is* my fault."

"Well, technically it is, but we don't hold it against you. It's not like these things are fatal. Annoying, yes, embarrassing, yes, but no one's going to die. And we *will* get rid of them. Okay?"

"Okay."

Things could be worse, I tell myself, much worse.

And soon, they will be.

11

I DIDN'T REALIZE IT AT THE TIME—I DIDN'T REALIZE IT for years—but David and I may have gotten Abraham Lincoln from an animal hoarder. It was 2003, right around the time I began to use a keyboard again after recovering from repetitive strain injury. David and I had just moved from Brooklyn into Manhattan, to an apartment building that allowed dogs. We'd been waiting years, literally, to get one. We knew we wanted a rescue dog and we knew he or she had to be small and portable, so we could bring him traveling with us. On a website that allows users to search for animals by age, size, and gender, we entered our criteria and up popped a photo of a one-year-old black Chihuahua mix with huge eyes and enormous batlike ears.

The dog's name was Milton and he was in Hartsdale, about an hour's train ride from Manhattan. I called and spoke to

Penny, who ran the shelter, and a few days later David and I took the subway to Grand Central and then a train. It was dark when we walked out of the station. In the parking lot, a rusty brown car sat idling; a woman opened the passenger side door and called out, "Are you David and Jessie?" I detected an English accent.

"Yes," we said.

"I'm Maureen," she said, "I volunteer with Penny sometimes."

"Come on in," the driver, who I assumed was Penny, said. Her voice was muffled because she was leaning over the backseat, shoving blankets, dog toys, empty boxes, and down comforters or coats—I couldn't tell which—onto the floor to make room for us. Her hair was gray and messy, and when she finally looked up, she seemed dazed and hyper at the same time. Her owlish glasses were smudged, her clothes baggy and disheveled.

She was my mother.

I hesitated to get into the car, but after David did, I followed.

"I can't show you Milton at my house right now because there's too much going on there," Penny said as she pulled her car out of the lot.

Too much going on there. Right. That sounded familiar.

"So we're going to my husband's office," she said.

"Is that where Milton is?" David asked.

"Milton's right here," Maureen said, and opened up her coat. He was snuggled on her chest like a baby. Even in the dark car I could see that his black eyes were watery as he clung to Maureen, shaking. His long, deerlike snout was set in a grim frown, his big ears flattened against his head as if he wanted to be more streamlined for flight. I reached my hand toward him so he could sniff it and he growled at me.

What I knew about him from Penny was this: When he was

a few months old he was brought to a veterinarian because one of his front legs was broken. The veterinarian set his leg, but the couple who'd dropped him off never returned to claim him. So, Penny had told me over the phone, he'd been living at the veterinarian's office for the last year. I figured he frolicked all day with the other animals being treated or boarded there and that he must've been fed well and gotten lots of attention from the staff and customers. It didn't sound like a bad life.

When we got to Penny's husband's office—a nondescript, gray-carpeted room in a nondescript building—Maureen tried to peel Milton off her chest, but he was digging in to her brown sweater. She tried again. Suddenly there was a loud screeching noise, and then another, and another—at first I thought it was a smoke detector. But it was Milton.

I'd never heard a dog sound like that. I didn't even know it was possible.

"How long have you been taking care of him?" I asked Maureen. He was obviously really attached to her.

"I just met him today," she said, her brow wrinkled as she stroked his back. "It was just a few hours ago, actually."

David and I looked at each other, alarmed. Milton was clearly neurotic.

Penny came running over then, leading a dog on a leash— I had no idea where it came from, but it looked like a shih tzu.

"Here's Oliver," she said. "I thought you might be interested in him. He's a purebred."

David and I both shook our heads no. He was way too big. We had a ten-pound limit because that's the maximum weight most airlines allow for pets in the cabin. Penny had said that Milton was seven and a half pounds.

Finally Maureen managed to peel Milton off her chest. David and I were sitting cross-legged on the floor and she set the trembling pooch on my thigh. He hung on as if he'd finally found a safe raft on a violent ocean.

"Look how scared he is," I whispered to David. I didn't want Penny to hear me because I didn't want her to decide we couldn't have him. Over the phone she'd grilled me about whether we'd grown up with dogs—even wanting to know the breeds, what our attitudes were about hitting pets (I thought she was joking, but she wasn't), and how many hours David and I worked each week. Apparently one guy had been interested in Milton before us but when Penny found out he had a full-time job, she turned him down—even though his office was dog friendly and he was planning to bring Milton to work with him. She was pleased when I told her that David and I worked mainly from home and thrilled when I assured her that one of us was almost always there.

She'd also told me Milton's tail was docked, and as he clutched my thigh his two-inch nub was tucked tightly against his Cornish hen–size hindquarters. I could feel his sharp claws through my jeans. The noxious smell coming from him made me wonder if he'd ever had a bath in his life. And he was so skinny that his ribs were visible. What kind of vet's office had he been living in?

"Milton," David said softly as he pulled a Liv-A-Snap from the bag we'd brought and reached it out to him. The little dog only growled in response.

Penny was hovering at the edge of the room, watching us, still holding the shih tzu's leash.

"So," David said and I could tell he was trying to sound casual, "what exactly was Milton's life like before this, again?"

"I told Jessie already. He was at a veterinarian's office," Penny insisted. "It's where I take my other rescues. I kept seeing him there in his little cage—"

"In a *cage*?" David and I said at the same time.

Penny hung her head and her straggly gray hair covered her eyes. "Yes. I kept seeing him there so eventually I asked the veterinarian what happened to him. She told me about the couple leaving him and I offered to find him a home."

I reached down and covered the poor dog with my palms. I had a feeling he'd been in the cage the entire year he was there, probably twenty-four hours a day.

"What kind of veterinarian would treat an animal like that?" I was livid, too upset to worry about Penny deciding we couldn't have him.

"Well, if you don't want him that's fine." Penny seemed to be shrinking and puffing out her chest at the same time.

"That's not what I'm saying," I said.

"So you *do* want him?"

David and I looked at each other—did we want a dog this damaged? One of our friends had the cuddliest dog, who'd sit in anyone's lap, and that's what we'd had in mind, too. And we needed a dog who would be adaptable to new places, because we intended to travel.

"Can we think about him over the weekend and let you know on Monday?" I asked.

"I've got no room for him this weekend," Penny said. "If you don't take him now he'll have to go back into the cage, starting tonight."

Maureen had been sitting at one of the desks, scrolling through her BlackBerry. She looked up and said, "I would take him, but I've got two large dogs and I fear they'd trample him."

"You'd really put him back in a cage?" David asked Penny.

Penny shook her head. "I'd have no choice."

I looked down at Milton, so helpless, wrapped along my thigh. I was covering his body with my hands and he was starting to shake a little less. There was no way I was letting this dog go back into a cage.

"Let's take him," David and I both said.

"Great," Penny said. "I know you'll give him a good home. I can tell."

I shifted Milton to my shoulder and David and I got to our feet. "Do you think it's a problem for us to change his name?" David asked Penny as he wrote her a check for $350—a little high for a shelter dog, but we didn't care.

Penny shook her head. "He didn't really have a name—we just started calling him Milton when we put the ad up."

"He didn't even have a name?" I asked, feeling my teeth begin to grit.

"Un-be-liev-able," David said as he handed Penny the check. She shoved it into her pocket.

We didn't have any kind of carrier so I just zipped my parka over him and kept it that way during the ride in Penny's car back to the train station, the train to Grand Central, and the subway. His almost-lethal smell wafted up to my face every so often, but I didn't mind. While David and I settled on the name Abraham Lincoln, the pooch stole glances up at me; through the course of the journey home, the glances got longer and longer, and by the time we got to our apartment he couldn't take his eyes off of me.

The first day we had him, rather than walking, he slunk along the floor like Gollum from *Lord of the Rings*. The second day he began walking instead of slinking, and that's when we noticed his limp. He wouldn't put any weight at all on his back, right leg. I called Penny to ask her if she'd noticed it—supposedly he'd stayed at her place for a week between the vet's office and us. No, she said, and suggested that maybe he hurt it when he was playing with the other dogs at her house. She offered to pick him up and take him to the veterinarian to have him checked out.

"I don't want him going back to that vet," I said, picturing the post-traumatic stress disorder he'd get just by entering that office.

"I've got a few vets I go to. I'll bring him to another one to have his leg x-rayed."

"Are you sure? I mean, we already adopted him; he's our responsibility."

"Well, I guaranteed you a healthy dog, so I want to do this."

"Okay," I said, though I was a little nervous about letting him near her. I didn't trust her.

Maureen came to pick him up. She told me she was probably going to stop volunteering with Penny and find another animal group instead—Penny's chronic disorganization was driving her crazy, she said. Chronic disorganization, I thought, that sounded familiar. Maureen said she couldn't bring Abraham Lincoln back to us that night, but would bring him the next day. He looked terrified, shaking as I handed him over to Maureen, who set him inside an open, blanket-lined cardboard box. I teared up as they drove away but I told myself we needed to get that leg checked out.

That evening, Penny called.

"His leg is permanently disfigured," she said the moment I answered the phone. "The vet says he was probably born like that. He'll always limp."

My first reaction was annoyance, then disappointment. David and I loved going for long walks and we'd wanted a dog who could come with us along the river or across the city.

"Is he in pain?" I asked.

"She didn't say. But if you want your money back, you can have a refund."

"What? You mean return him?"

"Yes."

I paused. "Let me talk about it with my husband and call you back."

Of course, neither of us seriously entertained the idea of returning him. We already loved him.

Maureen brought Abraham Lincoln back to us the next day and David and I were elated to see him. He looked happy to see us, too, even wagging his tiny tail for the first time we'd witnessed. The next day we brought him to a veterinarian we'd heard good things about. She gave Abraham Lincoln a thorough exam and x-rayed his leg. On the x-ray we could see that his back right leg was twisted about ninety degrees, at the hip. His right knee actually faced the left leg, rather than straight ahead. "I can't say with one hundred percent certainty," our new veterinarian said, "but it's likely he was born this way."

"Could it have been caused by sitting in the same position for too long?" David asked and explained what we knew about Abraham Lincoln's background.

"Well, yes. Depending on how old he was when he went into the cage. If the bone was still soft it could have reshaped itself this way."

Unbelievable. How could a vet have treated an animal that way? How could anyone?

"Also," our veterinarian said, "his front left leg appears to have been broken at some point. And it wasn't set very well."

"That's not a surprise," I said. I asked her if she thought Abraham Lincoln was in pain when he limped. I couldn't bear the thought of his little leg hurting each time he took a step.

"Does he go for walks with you?" she asked.

"Yes," David said. "We walked him here—we live about twenty minutes away."

She moved Abraham Lincoln's leg around in her hand. Thankfully he'd warmed up to her within a few minutes. "He seems flexible other than that one spot and he's not yelping when I move it. On the way here, did he try to stop or did he just keep walking?"

"He didn't stop," I said.

"Then I'd say he's not in pain. His limp might look bad, but he doesn't know any different. As he gets older, though, you'll want to keep an eye on that other back leg, because it's picking up the slack."

The next day I called Penny. I asked for the veterinarian's phone number, saying I needed it because I wanted to find out what she'd fed our new dog. The real reason was because I intended to file a complaint against her. What she did to Abraham Lincoln was abuse and I wasn't going to let her get away with it. My intention must have been obvious.

"She just made a mistake. She liked to see him there."

"Liked to see him there? He's not a painting! What she did was wrong."

"He ate puppy chow," Penny said, and hung up.

I called back, but she wouldn't answer. I didn't have a phone number for Maureen, but she'd given me her email address; I wrote to her numerous times, but she never responded. I considered calling every veterinarian's office in Hartsdale, but I didn't know for sure that's where the vet was, and besides, what veterinarian would ever admit to treating a dog like that?

Years later, when I learned that sometimes animal hoarders will cloak their behavior behind the pretense of running a "shelter," and occasionally sell some of their charges for money to feed the rest, I started wondering about Penny. Her story about Abraham Lincoln living at a veterinarian's office just didn't make sense. And there was her car. Her chronic disorganization. The fact that we had to meet "Milton" at her husband's office rather than her house. And Abraham Lincoln smelled so absolutely putrid when we got him. As a small, short-haired dog he shouldn't have smelled like that. (David and I have gone two or three months without bathing him and he doesn't smell bad at all.) The first few times we took him out, he looked startled and cowered when the wind blew, as if he'd never been outside in his life. And then there's his weight: In the first few months with us, his ribs became less and less visible as he went from seven and a half pounds to nine pounds, then ten.

In the beginning, David and I babied Abraham Lincoln (and still do), showering him with toys and treats and soft fluffy places to lie down. We wanted him to know that he wouldn't be hurt or neglected again, that he was safe and loved. It sickened and enraged me that someone had hurt him. And the intensity of my feelings triggered unexpected fury toward my mother: Why hadn't she felt the same protectiveness toward me? Once, when I was eight or nine, she even allowed a friend of hers to slap me. When I went crying to my mother about it she just shrugged and said, "She must have had a good reason."

Abraham Lincoln is better now, but he hasn't gotten over the trauma of whatever happened that first year. He's distrusting of strangers and he flinches at the sight of a raised hand or the sound of a shoe scraping on concrete. And he's completely conflict-averse. If David and I are even slightly bickering, or if I happen to yell in response to something annoying on television, he'll immediately leave the room.

After I began putting the pieces together, I tried to find Penny's phone number. Maybe she wasn't an animal hoarder, maybe she'd rescued him from another hoarding situation and for some reason thought he'd sound more appealing if he came from a vet's office. I just wanted to know the truth. I had to at least try.

I searched our entire apartment, but I couldn't find Penny's phone number anywhere. Nor her email address, or even Maureen's. Why hadn't we at least kept the receipt? I didn't remember the name of Penny's organization, and David didn't either. Had I tossed out her contact information during one of my purges? Perhaps. All I know is that it was as if she'd vanished.

12

THERE'S A WOMAN IN CALIFORNIA WHO'S INTERESTED in subletting our apartment while we're in Italy, and she's willing to pay all six months upfront—a necessity because we won't be able to deposit checks while we're abroad. Another plus: She won't be arriving in New York until six weeks after we leave, which is surely long enough for any remaining bugs to die off. A friend of hers who lives in our neighborhood is coming over to look at the apartment, and the morning of the appointment, our buzzer rings twenty minutes earlier than the time we'd set. David and I, still in the middle of cleaning, shove the broom and dustpan into the closet and buzz her in.

"I'm Isabel," she says when I open the door. She doesn't apologize for being early, nor does she wait to be invited in—just steps into our apartment, her champagne-colored skirt and jacket shimmering in the sun that streams in through the skylight above the living room, her practically egg-sized diamond ring temporarily blinding me with its glare. Next to her, in my cutoff jeans, flip-flops, and tattered tank top, I feel like a hideous slob. Abraham Lincoln's growling at her from his bed in the corner, so David picks him up. Isabel reaches into her beige, buttery leather Marc Jacobs bag, pulls out a credit card–thin digital camera, and begins snapping pictures. David and I give each other a *what the hell?* look.

"The bathroom's this way, I assume," Isabel says, striding toward the front of the apartment; she stops at the entrance to our narrow galley kitchen and snaps away. I follow behind her, noticing the two coffee mugs in the sink I hadn't had a chance to wash, the ever-so-slightly chipping paint near the handle of one of the cabinets, and the wedding pictures I've affixed with a magnet to the refrigerator. I hold my breath as she steps toward the photos. I don't want her looking at those.

"The bathroom's here," I say from behind her and she takes a step back. Without a word she walks into our minuscule bathroom. I'm surprised when she shoves aside the shower curtain, but at least she doesn't photograph the tiles that are still dingy in spite of the twenty minutes I spent scrubbing them last night.

"Do you have any questions?" I ask as she moves past me, to the front room of the apartment.

She snaps more pictures—our old IKEA couch, the television set, the desk we've fashioned from a bookshelf where I usually write. Even the Persian-style rug on the floor. She looks out the window, to the sea of yellow cabs rolling down Seventh Avenue. "Does the apartment get loud with all the traffic?" she asks, "because I don't know what kind of sleeper Carolyn is."

"Sometimes this room does, yes. But that's it."

She nods once. "I think I've seen enough," she says, slipping her camera into her jacket pocket.

"Good, because we've got someone else coming to look at the apartment soon," I say as we walk through the hallway toward the front door. I'm clearly lying—she's only been here a few minutes and she arrived early—but I don't care.

"These floors are pretty scuffed, no?" Isabel says, pointing down.

I can't see why a subletter would care about gouged floors, but all I can think to say is, "It's an old building."

"Ri-ght." She hitches her thousand-dollar purse a little higher up on her shoulder as David opens the door for her.

"Bye," he says sarcastically.

"All the best," Isabel says, and David closes the door behind her.

"'All the best'? Who says 'all the best'?" I ask David.

"I was tempted to let Abraham Lincoln bite her," David says and sets down our dog, who runs over to the door and barks at it.

"I was tempted to grab her hand and hold it long enough to give her the bugs," I say.

"Magpie! That's awful."

"I'm kidding," I say. "Half."

THAT AFTERNOON I have an appointment with a dermatologist about the bugs. I've seen him before because I have so many strange moles on my back that I need to get them examined every year. Twice before today I've stood in front of this man naked while he went over every inch of my skin.

"No," he barks when I tell him that I think I have scabies and that I've done the permethrin cream three times but it hasn't worked. "Then it's something else. If it were scabies, the cream would have worked."

I pull down the waistband of my jeans to show him my hip bones. "Doesn't this look like scabies to you?"

He barely glances at it. He turns his back to me and pulls a small wooden stick from a box on the counter. "Let me see your arm," he says, grabbing for it. He slides the pointy end of the stick across the palest part of my forearm, in a harsh, quick X.

"Ouch."

He steps back to admire the work as the X turns red and raised. "You see."

"What am I supposed to be seeing?"

"You have sensitive skin."

I wait for him to say more, but that seems to be the extent of his diagnosis.

"So this rash that I have pretty much everywhere is sensitive skin?"

"Maybe you're using a new detergent? You're allergic?"

"No, I'm not. And what about the fact that my husband also has a rash? And my father, too?"

"It must be something in the environment," he says, already starting to fill out my paperwork.

"But my dad lives in Minneapolis. That's where it started. My mother bought an infected pillow."

"If you're so convinced it's scabies, I'll prescribe you permethrin."

"Okay, if it's not scabies, what else could it be?"

"There is something called 'scabiophobia,' a fear of scabies. It's possible to convince yourself that you have it."

"Yes, but would that cause a person to break out in a rash? What about the fact that we're all covered in bites and itching like crazy?" I've raised my voice a bit; I need to calm down. The last thing I need is to have an argument with this man. He's the only dermatologist at the clinic my husband and I go to, and all the other ones covered by our insurance had at least a two-month wait for an appointment. "Could you at least do a skin scraping to check for scabies?"

He shakes his head. "Those tests are inaccurate. They're not worth doing."

I've read that, too, so I don't argue. "Maybe the scabies is resistant to permethrin? I read online that that can happen." He flinches as if I've just told him what a pompous ass he is, which is what I'd like to do.

"No. That is not possible."

I've read about two cures that seem to work even in the toughest cases.

"Can you prescribe me ivermectin pills?" I ask. Normally used for something called "river blindness," ivermectin is used off-label for scabies and is supposedly almost 100 percent effective.

"Ivermectin? No. There's no proof that it works."

"There is proof," I say. "There are all kinds of studies."

"I haven't seen any proof."

"Okay, what about a sulfur lotion? Could you prescribe that?"

Sulfur has been used since ancient Roman times to cure scabies and is still prescribed for pregnant women, since it's nontoxic. I've already tried calling pharmacies to see if I could get it over the counter, but in New York, at least, you need a prescription.

He laughs. He actually laughs at me, and I want to slap that smug smile off his face.

"No one uses sulfur anymore. It's messy."

"I don't care if it's messy. We've had these things for over a month. We'll try anything. We're desperate. Please."

He shakes his head and writes me a prescription for permethrin.

* * *

LATER THAT EVENING David and I are walking to a restaurant he's reviewing in the East Village when he says, "Goddammit . . ." I know what it means. He's found another bite.

"Where is it?" I ask.

"Here," he says, lifting up his shirt a little. On his stomach is an angry red welt. "I have to admit, I'm kind of pissed off at your mom about this."

"You have every right to be pissed off," I say. David and I both hate being late, so we're walking quickly. "I'm so infuriated I could—"

My cell phone rings. I pull it from my purse. A California number.

"The subletter," I say to David and press the button on my phone to answer.

"My friend said the apartment is funky," Carolyn says in a chipper voice. I've always hated the word "funky." I never know if it's supposed to be a good thing or a bad thing. "She said it's cute in a bohemian way."

"Okay, good."

"So I've thought about it and I definitely want it."

"Great. So it sounds like it'll work out, then." I give David the thumbs-up sign and he smiles a little. At least we have one less thing to stress out about.

"She did say it could use a good cleaning," Carolyn chirps.

I stop walking. "Excuse me?"

We're at a corner and we have the walk sign. David motions with his hand for me to continue, but I shake my head.

"It's just that Isabel said your apartment was a little dirty. So I had an idea: If you guys will spring for a cleaning person before I get there, it's not a problem."

"Our apartment is *not* dirty."

"Oh, sorry," Carolyn says. "It's really not a big deal."

"Actually, I don't think you're the right person for the apartment after all."

David raises his eyebrows.

I nod *yes*. He's left the decision-making process about the subletter up to me, so I know that if I veto Carolyn, he won't love it, but he won't stop me. The light turns red.

"But I'm ready to FedEx you the money tomorrow. A check for the whole six months and the deposit."

"I'm sorry," I say. "That's a big issue for me, and . . . well, now I just don't think it'll work."

"I don't understand." A whine is creeping into her voice. "Your apartment being dirty is a big issue?"

"I'm not going to get into it," I say. "Our apartment is clean. It's a nice apartment. And I'd like to have someone living there who appreciates it." I'm punishing her, but at the moment I don't care. There's probably no worse insult in the world to me than calling my apartment dirty.

David motions for me to follow him and we cross the street against the light.

"Listen, Jessie, please. I've already made so many plans. Can we forget what I said?"

But I'm on a roll. "By the way, your friend was really rude. I can't stand the idea of her being in our apartment while we're gone, judging us—"

"Isabel's hardly a friend! I promise I won't allow her inside, ever. Please, Jessie."

David looks at me, concerned. He can hear her begging tone even if he can't hear her words.

I feel myself caving. She wasn't *trying* to offend me. Maybe I've been too hard on her. David points to the restaurant's awning a few yards from us.

"Look, Carolyn. I need to get off the phone now, but can I

call you back tomorrow? I need to talk everything over with my husband. Let us sleep on it, okay?"

"Okay," she says, managing to sound both petulant and pathetic.

I already know we'll let her move in. I've never been good at saying no.

ONE OF MY greatest fears comes true a few days later, when I find out that Sandy's come down with the bugs, too. But at least Sandy agrees to go to an actual doctor. He tells her that it must be fleas from her two cats (even though neither of the cats has fleas). My husband sees a dermatologist—he got lucky on a cancellation list—who diagnoses him with body acne. David spends fifty dollars on a medicated body wash that does nothing. Every time one of us hears a new opinion, we want to believe. Anything would be easier than dealing with these permethrin-resistant scabies—assuming that's what this is.

And soon after Sandy comes down with them, my mother makes an announcement: She was wrong, she tells me, about being cured of the scabies when she was in the hospital. Apparently she has the bugs now, too.

Over the next few weeks she uses the most extreme methods to try to get rid of them. First, something called lindane, which is so toxic that it's banned in eighteen countries. You're supposed to use it once. Just one time. But she creates a ritual: She covers her body in lindane at night, and then in the morning she washes it off in a hot, hour-long tea tree oil infused bath. As soon as she gets out of the tub, she applies another coat of lindane.

I beg her to stop, telling her what a horrible idea that is, especially because she's recovering from cancer, especially because if she applies the lotion right after a hot bath her pores are still open and the chemicals can get directly into her bloodstream—but she won't stop. She's punishing herself.

I'm so afraid of giving these bugs to someone that I'm still holding my writing class in a bar rather than our apartment, turning down almost all offers of plans, and certainly not shaking anyone's hand. "I'm just getting over a cold," I'll say, when someone tries to shake my hand—which is exactly what I used to say when I had repetitive strain injury.

All the sympathy and goodwill my mother garnered from having cancer has been squandered. Taking care of my mother, and of cleaning her house, is once again all my responsibility. Which I should be used to, and can normally handle. But right now I'm so steeped in trying to rid us of these bugs (while keeping the whole embarrassing tale a secret), get things ready for Italy, and teach my classes, that I can barely take care of myself. In fact, I can't take care of myself. I'm drinking too much wine and not eating enough food. I'm losing weight; I can tell because I have to put a new hole in my belt to hold up my jeans, even though the only real exercise I get is hauling laundry back and forth from the Laundromat every day.

My mother calls me almost every night. She needs me. But if I can't take care of myself, how am I supposed to take care of her, too?

13

BUT THE WORST THING, THE VERY WORST THING, HAPpens one morning in early June. It begins with a phone call. It's Sandy. I know something's wrong because I just talked to her last night, and besides, she never calls me in the morning.

"What's wrong?" I ask immediately.

"Honey, I need to tell you something," she says, her voice fake-cheerful, "and I need you to hold it together."

"What is it?" I already have a feeling.

"Your dad had a heart attack."

The room is spinning. I burst into tears. I somehow manage to croak out the words to my husband, and it's just like when we found out about my mom's cancer—we sit on the couch and he tries to hold me and protect me while I hold the phone and all its bad news against my ear.

"He's going to be okay," she says. "I need you to keep it to-gether, Jessie!" Sandy hardly ever raises her voice and I'm snapped to attention.

I wipe my tears. I take a deep breath. "Okay. I'm here."

"They could tell from the blood test that it was a minor heart attack. He has to have angioplasty—it's very common," Sandy says, and the room rights itself and stops spinning.

"He's going to be okay," I tell David.

"We're at the hospital now. Oh, wait, they're taking him. I'll call you as soon as it's done."

WHEN DAVID AND I had known each other only a few days, we were exchanging stories about our families, the way couples do when they're just getting to know each other. I said offhandedly that if my dad ever died I'd have to be locked away in a mental institution. I wasn't being hyperbolic; it's just something I've thought for as long as I can remember. David and I were walk-ing through Old Town Square in Prague and he dropped my hand when I said it.

"You need to deal with that," he said, but not unkindly. "It's going to happen someday."

"No, it's not," I said, pretending I was joking and reaching for his hand again.

As we wait for Sandy to call back from the hospital, David keeps at least one of his hands on me—over my shoulders, on my knee, or holding my own hand—at all times. I have no idea how I managed to find such a wonderful husband and I want to tell him that, I should definitely tell him more often than I do, but all I can think about right now is my dad.

Finally Sandy calls. "You should probably sit down, honey," she says, and I immediately start crying again. "It's worse than they thought. Your dad's arteries are too blocked for the angio-plasty. He has to have a bypass, probably a quadruple bypass."

Not my dad.

Not my dad.

I can't say anything because I'm crying and Sandy's telling me that he's going to be okay, that Aunt Eve's dad had a bypass twenty years ago and is still doing great, and that maybe this is why my dad gets tired so easily and after this he'll be in better shape than ever—

"I can be there tonight," I tell Sandy, already making a mental list: find a substitute for my classes, get the plane ticket—where's my suitcase? That's right, up in the closet—

"Actually honey, what would be better is if you'd come here when he gets out of the hospital. I know I'll need help taking care of him when he first comes home. From what I've heard this surgery can be really taxing—they have to pry apart your ribs."

That image. The blood and organs and bones. I do not want to think about my dad's ribs split apart. "I could come now and stay after he gets out, too."

"It's okay. I know summer's busy for you, with the double load of classes. It's better this way."

"Are you sure? I'd really like to be there for the surgery."

"Jessie, he's going to be okay. He's going to be. And I'll need your help when he gets out of the hospital."

"All right. Whatever you think is best."

After we get off the phone I make the necessary arrangements to go back to Minneapolis.

I'll arrive to take care of my dad exactly seven weeks after I was there for my mom.

14

I TAKE THE NEW LIGHT RAIL SYSTEM FROM THE MINNEA-
polis airport to a stop that's half a mile from my dad and
Sandy's. She picks me up, warning me that since my dad
got back from the hospital yesterday, he's been really weak and
has hardly any energy. "But," Sandy says, "he's recovering and
he'll be fine. Okay, Jessie?"

"I'll keep it together, I promise. I just want to help you guys."
We're driving over the familiar streets of their neighborhood,
and the summer sidewalks are empty. The many gardens—
some filled with only wildflowers in the hippie houses, others
more sculpted, like Sandy's—are in full bloom.

"And some bad news," Sandy says. "We think Rick still has
the bugs. He discovered some new bites this morning."

"Dammit," I say. "That is *not* what he needs right now."

"I know," Sandy says, switching on her turn signal. "As far as I can tell I don't have them anymore. And you don't, right?"

"I don't know. It changes every day at this point. But at the moment I'm not itching, so maybe not. But I won't feel like they're really gone until I've had no itching or bites for at least a few weeks."

"I guess all we can do is keep trying different things and hope that one of them works. We've got all the furniture draped in sheets and I'm trying to change those every day but it's hard to keep up with all the laundry."

"I'll be in charge of the laundry and changing the sheets while I'm here," I say. "And I want to cook and clean, too."

"Thanks, sweetie," Sandy says. "We can really use the help right now. In fact I have a project for you today, if you don't mind—I need to run over to a client's house for an hour or so this afternoon." She explains that they need to rent a hospital bed for my dad. He had a hard time getting up the stairs to their bedroom last night and they've decided it'll be easier if he sleeps in the living room.

"I'll set everything up," I say, happy to have a task.

We pull into the alley, and Sandy presses the garage door opener tucked onto the back of her car's sun visor.

"Are you ready, Jessie? Because I want you to be prepared for how your dad looks . . ."

"I'm fine," I say, though my stomach is completely knotted and I can feel tears, lots of them, building behind my eyes. "The last thing I want to do is create more stress. I'll just pretend he looks the same as always."

When we walk in the back door and I see my dad sitting on one of the kitchen chairs, I let out a small gasp that I hope no one hears. My dad of seven weeks ago was sturdy, with strong arms, broad shoulders, and a thick head of dark brown hair. He could practically build a house with his bare hands. This father is frail; even his hair is thinner. My strong father looks weak and it scares me.

"Hi, Pop," I say, trying to keep the shock out of my voice.

"Hi, honey." For a second I think my dad is mad at me about something because he doesn't get up. Then I realize he's so weak he can't get out of his chair.

"Hi, Pop," I say again, as I walk toward him and open my arms.

"Careful about touching me," my dad says as I hug him, and I know he means about the bugs.

"I'm not worried," I say, and what I mean is, *I don't care: I'd be infested with the bugs for the rest of my life if it meant that you'd get better* but I don't say it because I don't say things like that, I can't, even though I wish I could. And when I lean back from hugging my dad I blink away my tears as best I can.

"So how does your old man look?" my dad asks.

"He looks good!" I lie and he laughs.

"Look a little closer," he says and smiles, and that's when I see the space in his gums, right in front, where a tooth should be.

I'd forgotten: His front tooth had died and he was going to have it replaced with an implant. The process involved pulling the dead tooth, waiting until the area healed, and then having the implantation surgery. My dad had the heart attack after the dead tooth had been pulled but before the implant procedure happened, hence his toothlessness. And because it's dangerous for a heart patient—Jesus, my dad is a *heart patient*—to be put under anesthesia, he may never be able to get the new tooth implanted.

"See," he says, opens his mouth, and puts in a retainer he'd had in his front shirt pocket. The retainer holds one fake front tooth. He smiles again.

"With that in, you no longer look like your name should be Cletus," I say.

"In that case," my dad says and pulls it out. "I'd better not use it, because I do like the name Cletus . . ."

Good. My dad still has his sense of humor.

Sandy comes back from her office where she was making a phone call.

"Will you two be okay for a few hours?" she asks.

"We'll be fine. Pop, do you want me to make you something to eat?"

"I'm trying to get him to eat yogurt, Jessie, maybe he'll listen to you," Sandy says, blows us kisses, and heads out the back door.

"So, how about some yogurt?" I ask.

"Um . . . no. I can't eat anything without getting queasy. It's a side effect from all the drugs they have me on. Did you see them?" He gestures with his head to the counter, where half a dozen prescription bottles are lined up in the space that used to hold vitamins. He yawns. "Actually, honey, do you think you could help me to the couch so I could lie down?"

"Of course." I walk over to him. "Let's see . . ."

I place my hands under his arms and start pulling upward. "Ouch!" my dad yells. "My chest is still really sore."

"Sorry. How about this way?" I put my shoulder against him and allow him to lean on me. Then I take a step forward, and another, and somehow we make it to the couch. He sits down, then leans back, holding his hand over his chest the whole time, as if he's afraid the stitches from his wound will come loose and his heart will fall out.

I don't blame him, considering the surgery he's just had: his ribs pried apart, his heart placed in a machine that kept it warm and beating while the doctors replaced his blocked arteries with veins from his leg. It's no wonder he feels fragile.

When he's settled on the couch, I pick up a *Natural Health* from the stack of magazines on the side table and take it over to one of the chairs. By the time I've read the table of contents, my dad is asleep.

That's when I hear a scraping sound at the front door. Maybe one of their cats is trying to get in. But that seems unlikely; there's a cat door at the back so they can come and go. I get up, go to the door, and look out the little window next to it.

It's my mother.

She's trying to shove a paper bag into their mailbox and it's not fitting. I watch as she kneels down on the stoop and methodically takes everything out of the paper bag—a giant bottle of Maalox, a loaf of bread wrapped in Saran wrap, and some kind of electronic device—and sets it down next to her. Then she puts everything back into the bag and again tries to force it into the metal mailbox.

I open the front door.

"Hi, Mom."

"Oh, hi, honey! Don't look at me, I'm too fat!" Her weight has always fluctuated—as does mine—and now her body looks like a blood-swollen tick on two toothpick legs.

"Shh, my dad's sleeping."

"Oh, okay, sorry," she whispers. "I was wondering if you were here yet, but I didn't want to disturb anyone so I thought I'd just drop this off and then wait for you to call me when you had a chance, I'm sure you're really busy with your dad right now . . ." she's talking so fast that she has to take gulps of air between her words to keep going. "He-ah, take this!" She thrusts the paper bag into my hands.

"Mom, I told you on the phone that he's not going to take Maalox." Sandy's against it because it can create a cycle of nausea. Since my dad got back from the hospital yesterday he's been trying natural remedies like ginger and charcoal.

"Just keep it in case he changes his mind."

"Okay," I say. It's not worth arguing with her about it. I can always just toss it. "What's the electronic thing in here?"

"It's a blood pressure checker. He needs to check it at least three times a day, but more like five times is better. Oh, and Jessie, I found something that works to get rid of the itching from the scabies," my mom says. I cringe at the word.

"We don't know for sure that's what they are," I say.

"Oh, yes we do . . ." she singsongs as she pulls back the cuff on her jersey. "See these burrows, these are a classic sign," and I know she's right because of everything I've read online. Her wrist and forearm are riddled with tiny bites, along with the telltale burrows, which are tracks the bugs leave in their wake. None of us has had burrows, until now. Seeing them is both depressing and somehow—in a very, very twisted way—affirming. At least it proves what these things are.

"I'm taking bleach baths," my mom says. "It totally helps the itching."

"Please tell me you didn't just say you're taking baths in bleach."

"I am," she says, nodding. "It's totally helping."

When did my mother start saying "totally"?

"Do you know how dangerous that is? Baths in bleach?"

She starts laughing. "Oh, I just pour a few capfuls into my hot baths. And I'm still doing the tea tree baths, too, so I just take two baths a day."

"And are you still doing the lindane?"

"Yup," she says, nodding proudly. She leans forward conspiratorially. "Sometimes I add a capful of that to the bath, too."

I am beyond horrified. "Mom, are you trying to kill yourself? I told you lindane can cause seizures. What if you had a seizure? How would you call for help?"

"Don't worry about it! It was prescribed by Dr. Paulsen, so it has to be okay," my mom says. "I'll figure out how to get rid of these bastards if it's the last thing I do. I'm going to be the guinea pig for all of us."

"Listen, I know you feel guilty about these bugs, but please stop what you're doing—you could be doing permanent damage to yourself! And you just had cancer."

"Jessie," my dad calls from inside. "Is everything okay?"

"Yeah, Dad, I'm just talking to my mom. I'll be right there."

"Hi, Helen," my dad calls out weakly.

"Oh, hi, Rick," my mom says.

I'm not about to invite her in. She'll stress him out too much, especially because she's in one of her hyper moods. She was finally able to go back on her antidepressants and they must be kicking in.

"Mom, please promise me you'll stop all this nonsense."

"Don't worry about me," she says. "Now just give your dad that Maalox. He should take it every hour. And remember to take his blood pressure. And the bread—oh, Jessie, I made that bread myself. I told you I've been making bread lately, right?" She doesn't give me a chance to answer. "You have to make sure Rick and Sandy try it and then you tell me what they think, okay? I don't want to bother them. So you'll tell me."

I take a closer look at the bread. "They won't eat this, Mom. It's made with white flour."

"But you said they wouldn't eat *oat* flour, so I specifically didn't use it."

"No, I said *white* flour. They won't eat *white* flour."

Her face falls. "Oh. I guess I'll have to eat it, then." She takes the bread back from me.

I feel bad for her. She's trying to be helpful. I take the loaf of bread from her hands and put it into the bag with the other things she's brought. "I'll eat it. I'll make toast with it in the mornings."

"Okay, honey, that's great!"

"I need to get back to my dad," I say. "But I'll call you later, okay?"

"Do you think I should come in and show Sandy how to use the blood pressure machine?"

"She's not home, but it looks pretty straightforward." It's a simple electronic device that has a cuff attached. I can't imagine getting confused by it.

"Okay. Bye, then," she says and turns and wobbles toward her car.

My God, what am I going to do about my mom? I ask myself as I head back to my dad, who needs me to help him up from the couch and into the bathroom.

I'M AWAKE, NOT sure why, and trying in vain to make out the time on the clock in my dad and Sandy's guest room. At the edge of the curtain I can see the orange beginnings of sunlight.

Someone calls my name.

But no, that can't be. It's way too early.

Only there it is again: "Jessie!"

I leap out of bed and run down the hallway. "Sandy?" I call out.

"We're in the kitchen!"

I sprint down the stairs. Sandy's standing behind my dad, who's seated at the kitchen table; she's holding him upright with her hands under his arms. His eyes are closed and his mouth hangs open.

"Dad!" I yell. He doesn't respond.

"We took his blood pressure and it was too high—" Sandy says.

"Have you called 911?"

"No, I gave him some nitroglycerin, like they told us to at the hospital, and his blood pressure was still too high, so I gave him another one—"

Right then my dad collapses forward, his head clunking onto the table. Sandy and I pull him back and he's not bleeding, thank God, but he's still unconscious.

"I'm calling 911," I say and snatch the phone off the counter. After a hundred years a 911 operator answers. "Hello? I need an ambulance right now!" I demand.

"Ma'am, you need to calm down. What is your emergency?"

"My emergency is that my dad is dying right in front of my eyes and I need an ambulance RIGHT NOW!"

"Okay, ma'am, you really do need to calm down. What is your emergency?"

"Are you serious? You're telling me to calm down right now?"

"Yes, I am. What is your emergency?"

"Let me talk to your supervisor!"

"Jessie, calm down," Sandy says and I do. I try, anyway.

"Okay, look, sorry," I say and explain as calmly as possible that my dad had a quadruple bypass a week ago, has been out of the hospital for only a few days, and now he's passed out and we don't know why. "So if you could please send an ambulance we'd really appreciate it."

"We'll get an ambulance to you right away," she says and confirms the address.

I set down the phone and the edges of the room start blurring. I know what's happening because it's happened before.

And then, sure enough, everything's black and I'm down.

When I open my eyes Sandy's above me, saying, "Jessie, Jessie, come on," and I feel bad for being such a drama queen and get to my feet.

My dad is still hunched over the table, but now his forehead is resting on his folded hands—did Sandy put them that way or did he regain consciousness and do it himself?

Before I can ask, Sandy says, "I'm calling Mark," and picks up the phone to call her cousin who's a cardiac nurse and lives in the neighborhood. I go over to my dad and I have no idea what to do to make him not die, I have never felt this helpless or useless in my entire life, so I drape myself over him, hugging him, thinking please please please don't die don't die don't die. His skin is clammy, even through his nightshirt. I stay like that maybe one or two minutes, until Sandy gets off the phone. Where is that goddamn ambulance?

"Honey, Mark says it was the nitroglycerin, we shouldn't have given him two. Rick's going to be okay, it just has to wear off."

"You're sure?"

"Yes. Mark knows what he's talking about. Now, how are you doing?"

"I'm fine. Sorry about fainting." The last thing Sandy needs is to have to worry about me, too.

She puts her hands on my dad's back. "Rick, we're right here. Can you hear us?"

"Pop?" I say.

He's still out cold.

"Jessie, he's going to be okay," Sandy says and I believe her because she's never lied to me before. I know she's watching him, so I tell Sandy I'll be right back and I go into the bathroom. I leave the door open so I can hear when the ambulance comes—what is taking them so long?—and turn on the water and splash some on my face. My heart is racing, my jaw is locked with tension, but I feel the teensiest bit reassured because of what Sandy's cousin said. Except then I step out of the bathroom and my dad's face from that angle looks completely gray and lifeless— Sandy lied to me, he's not going to be okay, he's already gone. I rush toward him as the edges of the room go blurry.

And I'm on the floor.

Again.

I'm just coming to when the paramedics arrive. The room seems so foggy that at first I mistake them for firemen, thinking we're in a burning house. I hear one of them say, "Who are we here for?" Meaning me or my dad and I roll onto my side, then get to all fours, and then somehow I'm standing. While the ambulance guys put an oxygen mask over my dad's face and lift him onto a stretcher Sandy explains what happened with the nitroglycerin and says we're pretty sure that's what it was.

"Was he sitting up when you gave him the nitro?" one of the ambulance guys says and Sandy nods yes; the guy says, "Well, that's a problem, too. The person should be lying down because what it does is make your blood pressure drop and if that happens too fast—"

My dad starts shaking his head a little from side to side, then his eyes open and he reaches for the mask. His color's already starting to return as he gets the mask off, and the first thing he says is to the paramedics: "I have to tell you that I think I have scabies, so if you touch me, use rubber gloves."

I feel like killing my mom for making my dad have to worry about something like that at a time like this. The ambulance guys start wheeling him on the stretcher toward the front door and one of them says, "It's okay, sir, let's just get you to the hospital so they can really check you out."

Ten or so people are already out there on the sidewalk—ambulance sirens are big action on a quiet Minneapolis street, and the neighbors all knew the sirens were for my dad, because everyone knows about the heart attack and the surgery. My uncle Darren, aunt Eve, and cousin Billy, who live next door, are among the crowd.

Now my dad is saying he doesn't need the ambulance. "It was just that damn nitro," he's saying, "I'm okay," but I'm sure he's just saying that about the ambulance because of how expensive they are.

"Rick," Sandy says, "we need to find out why your blood pressure was so high in the first place," and then I say he should definitely go, and then Eve says it, and Mark the cardiac nurse, who's just arrived, says it, too, and finally my dad says okay.

Only one of us, Sandy or me, can ride in the ambulance with my dad, so Uncle Darren volunteers to drive me to the hospital. Sandy's in the waiting area near the emergency entrance when I get there. She tells me my dad's being examined right now. Her eyes are red. The television mounted to the wall blares *The Price Is Right,* though the room is empty aside from us.

"I don't know how much more of this I can handle," Sandy says and starts crying. She puts her hands on my shoulders and I honestly think that my dog standing up on his hind legs and reciting the Gettysburg Address would be less bizarre to me than seeing Sandy like this. I hadn't realized, until that very moment, how dependent we all are on her. Our family might be splintered, but she holds the pieces together—my dad, me, my missing brother, my stepsister . . . even my mom. If Sandy loses it, there will be no core, no one to count on.

I can't let that happen.

"Sandy, he'll be all right, I know he'll be all right." What else is there to say?

She sniffles. "I know. He will be. He will be."

"He will be," I repeat.

Pretty soon, a nurse comes out to the waiting area and says my dad is being moved up to the cardiac floor and that we can meet him there.

The cardiac floor is where he was just a week ago, for the bypass, so Sandy knows it well. When we get to his room, my dad's sitting up in his bed, looking pretty much back to normal.

"Hi, guys," my dad says. He tells us that even though it's clear he passed out from the nitroglycerin, he'll probably have to stay overnight for tests to determine why his blood pressure was so high—it's still high now, but nothing like this morning.

"You're alive, Pop! It's so good to see you talking," I say, and Sandy leans over my dad's bed to hug him.

"And check out these digs," my dad says.

His room is more like a suite, with a hospital bed in one area and off to the side a generously sized love seat, a reclining chair, and a wide coffee table. I stretch out on the love seat.

"I could sleep here. Dad, do you want me to stay here with you?"

"Sure, honey, we could have a slumber party."

"And Sandy," I say, "we could ask for an extra bed for you, so you can sleep here, too."

"We'll see," Sandy says. "Maybe Rick won't really need to stay overnight."

We're all so relieved about my dad being back to normal that we barely notice as a nurse slaps a sign on my dad's door and then another above his bed: CONTAMINATED.

"Jesus Christ," I say.

"I had to tell them," my dad says.

How humiliating. I suppose it's necessary—none of us wants to spread this any more than the nurses want to catch it—but I just wish the signs didn't have to be so *big*.

Sandy has to deal with a bunch of real estate stuff, and by now it's about 8:00 and her day is just beginning. Her cell phone is ringing constantly, mostly about business, though friends and neighbors concerned about my dad keep calling, too.

There's a special room on the floor for making and taking cell phone calls and that's where Sandy is when the jauntiest looking fellow I've ever seen comes striding into my dad's room. Even though he's wearing the typical white coat of a doctor, he exudes the air of being swathed in tweed. He looks like he'd wear one of those flat hats my husband and I call "chappies"; he looks like he smokes expensive cigars and plays golf and has a perfectly gorgeous wife who has a perfectly gorgeous toddler and a perfect AKC-registered Cavalier King Charles spaniel. I'm guessing he's a little older than I am, maybe forty, but I get the feeling he's always looked and acted about forty, even when he was five or eleven or twenty.

The doctor picks up my dad's chart from the end of the bed, flips through it, and says, "I'm Dr. Nelson." He holds out his hand for my dad to shake.

"Uh, I'm not sure you should . . ." my dad says, gesturing with his head toward the "contaminated" sign.

"What's that about anyway?" Dr. Nelson asks.

"I've been exposed to scabies," my dad says, probably phrasing it that way because it sounds better than saying he "has" it.

The doctor immediately looks over at me as if I'm the one responsible, and I feel like yelling, "Hey, I didn't give it to him, my mom did!" only I'm not sure how much better that is.

"That's my daughter, Jessie," my dad says.

Dr. Nelson nods at me and then turns back to my dad. "Well, I'm not concerned about scabies," he says and shakes my dad's hand, which makes me like him.

He says he can get my dad's blood pressure and his pain down. "Way down," he says and grabs my dad's toe, which is sticking out from the sheet, and kind of wags it. "Though you may need to be here for a few days. I hope you didn't have any grand plans."

Once we're alone, my dad wants my opinion about asking Dr. Nelson to be his cardiologist—he needs to choose a regular one—and I say yes, that doctor really seems to know what he's talking about.

When Sandy comes back, we tell her about Dr. Nelson; it feels like something big has been accomplished.

Sandy says, "Wait a minute, Rick, you were talking to the doctor just now?"

"Yes. Why?"

"You don't have your tooth in."

In our rush this morning with the ambulance, no one thought to bring his tooth—we had more important things on our minds.

My dad says, "Geez, I didn't even think about that. I'm kind of embarrassed now."

I'm kind of embarrassed, too. But then again, my dad's conscious, he's talking, the color in his face is completely back. He's okay. That's what matters.

"You know what, you guys? Who cares if the cardiologist thinks we're Cletuses," I say.

My dad starts laughing. "I think at this point I'm beyond a Cletus: Not only am I missing a tooth but I have scabies!"

And then we're all laughing, and it's the best feeling in the world.

* * *

A FEW MINUTES later a nurse comes in and tells us she's going to treat my dad with permethrin. Of course it makes sense that they want to do this, but it'll be my dad's third treatment with it and none of us has high hopes—though we're not about to argue with the nurse. Sandy says she's going to use this opportunity to run home and deal with a few real estate things, and I decide to go into the room where you can make cell phone calls.

"There's a computer in there," Sandy says, as we say goodbye in the hallway. "In case you want to check your email."

I decide that after I call David, I'll use the computer to look up my dad's symptoms and make sure the theory about the nitroglycerin is correct. There's no harm in double-checking. As I walk down the hallway, I try to look only at the beige-carpeted floor and not into any of the rooms that have their doors open. But I can't help it. I find myself looking into all of them—and I'm relieved when everyone is old, way older than my dad. That means he's going to be okay.

When I reach David, I tell him about the horrible morning and that we'll probably be here at the hospital for a few days.

He says he'll call my dad later in his room to say hi. Then he tells me that he may have found an apartment for us in the Italian village. He's already received photos of two places from a guy there. David emails them to me as we're on the phone. No one else is in the room, so I go over to the computer and sign in to my account.

One of the options is inside the town's medieval walls and the other is adjacent to a parking lot, so we make the obvious choice. The photos are a little blurry, but from what I can tell, it looks like a small, rustic apartment at the top of a steep stone staircase. There are a few shots of the village, too, of the cobblestone streets and the tiny town square. I remember it from when we were there five years ago: When we lived in Rome for three months, we took a day trip to the village, and have been talking about going back ever since.

David's excitement about the trip is palpable and I don't blame him. After all, we've been planning this for almost a year. I was excited about the trip as well, until my mother's cancer and my dad's heart attack. Now the thought of leaving the country makes me nervous. What if something happens to one of them while I'm there? It's hard enough being 1,200 miles away from two parents in ill health, but I can't even imagine being 4,000 miles away, with an ocean between us. Of course, David can tell what I'm thinking because he always can.

"Magpie, your dad's going to be okay. That's what the doctor said, right?"

"Right."

"So you can stop worrying."

"I'll try."

"Remember, you're strong."

"Thanks," I say, thinking, Sometimes.

DR. NELSON DOES a bunch of tests on my dad that turn up nothing unusual. My dad's blood pressure is at an acceptable level, too. Each day Dr. Nelson comes in to my dad's room fewer times than the day before. On the third day, he says my dad's pain level is higher than some people's, but that doesn't necessarily mean anything's wrong. He's healing at a slower rate, but he *is* healing. Then on the fourth day, after not seeing the doctor at all, we're told that my dad's going home.

"Well, I guess that means I'm okay," my dad says, as if trying to convince himself.

On the way out, we make an appointment for my dad to see Dr. Nelson the following week, and as we're walking through the parking lot to the car I tell my dad and Sandy that I can change my plane ticket and stay for the appointment if they want.

"There's no need, honey," my dad says. "I'll be okay. I just need time. And I know you've got your classes and you're getting ready for your big Italy trip."

"We'll see," I say.

Over the next few days, I cook and do laundry, trying to make myself useful. My other task is taking my dad out for walks. He's supposed to go around the block, but the first day he's too tired to even try. The next day just getting from their house in the middle of the block to the next corner takes ten minutes, and immediately afterward he needs to lie down in his rented hospital bed.

But the day after that, he goes one and a half blocks, and the next day, when he goes all the way around, the three of us are as happy as if he's just won a gold medal in the Olympics.

He's definitely improving. But still, I don't like the idea of being so far away.

On my last day in Minneapolis, my dad, Sandy, and I are having our usual lunch of salads with something on top—this time it's grilled salmon—when I say, "Guys, I'm thinking about not going to Italy. Maybe I should stay with you instead, and help out around here. That way I could keep an eye on my mom, too."

"Jessie, that's a terrible idea," Sandy says.

"No way," my dad says. "You're not her mother. You don't have to *keep an eye on her*—and anyway, she's fine, the cancer's gone."

"But you're not fine. I could help out."

"For six months! No way. I don't want you changing your life for me."

"Dad, it's just a trip. I don't even have to be there. David's the one working on a book about the place, not me."

They both shake their heads and say *no way, uh-uh, absolutely not* and I know it's not worth trying to convince them.

"Okay," I say. "But remember, if you need me to come back at any point from Italy, I'll do it. Happily."

"Sweetie, we appreciate all your help, but that's not going to happen," Sandy says, popping a bite of romaine into her mouth.

15

WHEN I GET BACK TO NEW YORK, I IMMEDIATELY throw myself into getting the apartment ready for our subletter. David and I have decided we're going to repaint around the windows, recaulk the bathtub, get new curtains for the front room, and replace the toilet seat and some of the lighting fixtures. It's not entirely because of the bitchy friend's comments, but partially. Also, we figure, the nicer the apartment is when Carolyn arrives, the more careful she'll be with it.

Online, I order some thick velvet curtains for the front room, then David and I go to Bed Bath & Beyond to get the rest of the things we need. The Container Store is across the street; we stop in to buy some of those plastic bags that shrink down into flat pouches. We'll use those to store our clothes away. We want to clear out as many dresser drawers, shelves, and as much closet space as possible.

Every time I'm in The Container Store I'm amused and disgusted by the fact that there's an entire retail chain peddling ways to store possessions. The store must be a hoarder's paradise, since so many of them think their problem is not having enough space, or the proper arrangement of their space, rather than simply having too much stuff. That thinking applies to everyone, really, not just hoarders, and it's the reason The Container Store thrives. Instead of whittling down our belongings, we just look for better ways to stash them.

I wish we weren't always being urged to *buy, buy, buy, consume, consume, consume*. It's no wonder the United States has six million hoarders. That said, hoarding isn't exactly the sole province of Americans: It spans the globe, as well as the centuries. In Melbourne, Australia, one in four house fire deaths since the year 2000 has been attributable to hoarding. In Russia, hoarding is called "Plyushkin Syndrome" after the landowner of the same name—whose farm rots around him as he acquires more and more possessions—in Nikolai Gogol's nineteenth-century novel *Dead Souls*. And Dante reserved the fourth circle of hell for the hoarders and the wasters. Their punishment was to push massive boulders toward each other on a bright and barren plain, the hoarders yelling, "Why do you waste?" and the wasters yelling, "Why do you hoard?"

In fact, there have been cases of hoarding in almost every country, on every continent except Antarctica.

After David and I get home from our errands, we sort through our clothes and store away the winter things we won't need in Italy. We replace the caulk around the bathtub, install the new toilet seat, paint the windowsills in the front room, dust, vacuum, sweep, and mop. For me, behind each action is the thought of our subletter running a white-gloved hand over every surface, of her blond friend in the champagne-colored suit walking through the apartment and judging, judging, judging.

I TALK TO my dad on the phone at least once a day. We discuss the different medicines he's taking and their side effects (nausea, dizziness, headaches), his energy or lack of it, and the amount of pain he's in. I get into the habit of asking him what his pain level is on a scale of one to ten, just like my repetitive strain injury days. I'm concerned because his chest still really hurts, usually a five or six, and his doctors keep saying his pain level is abnormal.

I talk to my mother on the phone, too. She's completely fixated on the bugs. It's all she'll talk about—with a few minutes every other call or so dedicated to her lawsuit. I'm as determined to find a cure for the bugs as she is. But her incessant discussion of the minutiae, about every single doctor's appointment—and she's going two or three times a week now, showing up without appointments and demanding to see him—makes me not want to talk about it with her at all.

Whenever my dad is thinking about taking a new medication, I google it, trying to find out as much as I can for him. One day while I'm online researching a blood thinner, on a whim I type "hoarding" into the search engine, just to see what will come up. I've done it before, but it's been a while.

And this time, something new appears among the links: an online support group called Children of Hoarders.

"You're not going to believe what I just found," I call out to my husband, who's in the living room. I'm in the front room, where I usually work.

"What is it?"

"It's about hoarding," I say and get up so I can explain without yelling. It's not like I thought my mother was the only hoarder in the world, or that I was the only child of one, but I would never have guessed there were enough people like me to warrant an entire support group.

"You're going to join, right?" he asks.

"I'm not sure." The idea makes me nervous.

I sit down in front of my laptop again. To partake in the message boards, even just to read them, you must be approved by an administrator, which entails sending an email stating your relationship to the hoarder: son, daughter, son-in-law, etcetera. But if I were to send an email, *I'm the daughter of a hoarder,* there would be written proof of who my mother is, of who I am. I'm not sure I'm ready for that.

I jump up from my chair and start pacing the narrow hallway between the rooms.

"Join," my husband calls out. "It would be good for you."

"I don't really want my name out there like that," I say. "It's embarrassing."

"Then get a new email address and do it anonymously."

"Oh. Okay."

I sign up for another Gmail address, one that has no similarity to my name, and then I gather my courage and write the required email. I sign out only as "Jess." And I stare at the words for a full minute before I hit send.

Once I do, I'm so filled with nervous energy that again I can't sit still. I go to the gym across the street and run on the treadmill for half an hour. By the time I've come home and showered, there's already a response from the Children of Hoarders group—welcoming me and giving me the password so I can view all the pages.

And there are many pages. It's here I learn the term "Wonderful Stranger." And it's here I discover that many hoarders are, or were, nurses, like my mother. It turns out her habit of moving things from one pile into another—rather than actually organizing or getting rid of anything—is known as "churning."

It never occurred to me that a hoarder could have more than one packed property, but postings on the message boards reveal that many have storage spaces in addition to their cluttered homes. Or they'll inherit a house, but rather than moving in they'll simply fill it with junk. One poor woman has two parents who are hoarders: They have a hoarded house and *three* rented apartments. As I read these stories I'm almost glad my mother has hardly any money. She can't afford another place.

I get the impression that many people here, not just me, are reluctant to reveal their true identities—there are almost no real names on the message boards. Instead, it's full of nicknames like Near_Cat or Frosty999 or LaStraka, and there's one person who calls himself No Name Whatsoever. One of the most frequent posters appears to be Starlene, whose mother has Diogenes syndrome, which is characterized by severe self-neglect and is the most extreme type of hoarding. Starlene grew up among piles of dirty adult diapers and used maxipads and animal feces that covered the floors of every room. The house had no heat or running water. Starlene used buckets for toilets and took showers at her schools' gyms. She lives in another state from her mother now but has actually received angry calls from her mother's neighbors, chastising her for "letting" her mother live that way. They've called Starlene cruel and ungrateful. Reading that infuriates me. It reminds me of the guilt trip I received from Mean Lesbian Neighbor. If they only knew.

After years and years of pleading with her mother, and after countless unsuccessful cleanup attempts—each involving verbal abuse (and threats of physical abuse) by her mother—Starlene has finally given up. As difficult as it is, she knows that she has to detach emotionally. She has to give up the hope of saving her mother in order to save the one person she can: herself.

I admire her. And I'm tempted to respond to her post, to tell her that she's brave and to wish her good luck, but I'm too much of a coward to post anything.

When my husband comes into the room, I'm sitting slouched over the bookshelf we've turned into a desk, still reading through the message boards.

"I have to run over to the library for a book," David says. Our dressers are both in here because there's not enough room up in the sleeping loft; he begins rifling through his, pulls out a T-shirt, and looks over at me. "Are you okay?"

I nod.

"Have you been crying?"

"No," I say, and laugh a little. "Yes." I wipe the corners of my eyes with my fingers. "It's sort of overwhelming."

"Maybe you should just look at it in small doses at first," he says, peeling off his T-shirt and putting on a new one. He immediately puts the old one in the laundry bag and then goes into the bathroom to wash his hands. It's part of our new protocol, because of the bugs—changing clothes a few times a day, placing all worn clothes directly into the laundry bag, washing our hands in the hottest water possible after taking off the clothes or putting them into the washing machine. We're so used to these ridiculous measures that we don't even mention them anymore.

My husband leaves and I close the browser window. It's comforting to have found others like me, but also unsettling; cowardliness isn't the only thing that kept me from posting anything. I'm not ready to betray my mother like that.

When I think about how alone she is in that crumbling

house, surrounded by unfinished projects and undiscarded trash, I feel so sorry for her. And while I realize that the amount of energy I spend trying to change my mother is excessive— even if my dad and Sandy hadn't been telling me so for years I'd know it—I just don't think I'll ever be able to stop.

DAVID LEAVES FOR Italy on a Wednesday. The first thing I do is strip the mattress pad from the bed and carry it down the loft stairs to the living room. Then I go back up to the loft with the vacuum cleaner. When I'm done sucking up every bit of dust, I wrap the mattress with the most expensive allergen-and-bed-bug-protective cover I could find (shockingly, I couldn't find one that specifically protected against scabies), and put a clean sheet on top of that.

I won't sleep up there again. I'll sleep on the mattress pad on the living room floor and right before I leave for Italy, I'll scrub down every surface in the apartment and carry the mattress pad out to the garbage. That way, by the time the subletter gets here six weeks after we've gone, no one will have slept in the bed for nine weeks. Supposedly these things can't live on surfaces for longer than seventy-two hours, so maybe I'm being overly cautious, but I don't care. I would never forgive myself if someone got these things from me.

I'M LIVING A monastic and lonely life. My friends all know I'm leaving soon for six months and they want to see me to say goodbye, but I'm terrified of infecting people with the bugs and I'm too ashamed to tell anyone about them.

It's impossible to avoid everyone, though: I agree to meet an old friend and her fiancé at an outdoor bar in my neighborhood and I spend the entire time trying not to accidentally brush up against her or let any of my skin touch the bench's fabric. By now I'm a pro at this, always wearing long sleeves I can pull down over my wrists, always making sure my shirts don't ride up in the back and expose any skin that could then touch whatever chair or couch I'm sitting on. When I flew to and from Minneapolis last time I wore a hooded sweatshirt and put the hood up so my head wouldn't touch the seat. At the outdoor bar, my friend tries to hug me as we're parting and I say, "I've got a cold." If she wonders why I haven't been coughing or sneezing at all for the past two hours, she doesn't say anything.

After three years of working together, the students in my private writing class have become my friends and they want to have a good-bye party for me. We have it at the same bar we've been meeting in for the last three months (after the initial excuse of potential bedbugs, I continued to say we didn't know if our apartment was clear and no one pressed it). We're all squeezed into a small banquette area. I'm hardly present as I sip from my pint of Guinness, trying desperately, once again, to make sure I don't accidentally touch someone's bare skin. And while I laugh and joke with everyone, I'm actually focusing on not scratching. Because I itch all over: my scalp, my neck, my waist, my ankles. It's torture.

At the end of the night, after fending off a round of good-bye hugs, I walk home through the dark West Village streets, feeling lower than I've ever felt. I'm not sure how much longer I can take this. Between dealing with the bugs and worrying about my dad's heart and my mother's hoarding, I'm being crushed.

THERE'S A REASON I couldn't bring myself to tell anyone about the bugs. The shame and embarrassment of the bugs became entangled with the shame and embarrassment of my mother's hoarding, which runs deep. It runs back to before she was hoarding-hoarding, back to when I just knew there was something different about her—when I was ten years old and her house was the junk house that I didn't want to be associated with.

Though I'm not sure I knew the word "stigma" back then, I feared it, and in many ways still do. Because in spite of the many advances in understanding and treatment for mental illness, the stigma surrounding it remains. And as Susan Nathiel writes in *Daughters of Madness,* "The bond between a mother and her children is an idealized one in our culture, and that bond is assumed to be strongest and most mutual between mothers and daughters. Sons are expected to grow up and away from their mothers, but a daughter is expected to stay close, to learn from her mother [...]."

That's why telling someone that you have a family member who is mentally ill might attract curiosity, but admitting that you're the *daughter* of a mentally ill *mother* almost certainly earns a look of sympathy, then of suspicion. If my mother is mentally ill, then I must be, too.

If I forget this guilt by association, it's never long before I'm reminded. At a friend's party someone I didn't know well was describing someone I'd never met. "She's a little odd," the woman said. "She must be, because after her parents got divorced she lived with her *dad.* You have to wonder what was wrong with her mother."

I wish I'd said, "I lived with my dad, too. So what?" or "Even if her mother's a complete nutcase, that doesn't mean she is." But I was caught off guard. And the longer I waited to say something, the more impossible the task became.

Sometimes, without realizing it, I even act as if I have a

mental illness to mask: Recently I realized that before I leave the apartment I'll often ask my husband, "Does this outfit make me look like a crazy person?" the same way another woman might ask if an outfit made her look fat.

The stigma attached to being the daughter of a mentally ill mother is the reason I kept my mother's hoarding a secret, the reason I kept the bugs a secret, the reason that for as long as I can remember, I've felt like I had a secret.

MY LAST DAY in New York I'm busy cleaning, doing the requisite laundry, and in the evening, saying good-bye to both of my parents. I'm worried about my dad because the last couple days his pain has moved from a five or six to a seven and once even an eight. Thankfully, we'll be able to communicate by email: One of the villagers told David we could share his internet account as long as we split the monthly bill. Apparently he strung a cord out his window, along the walls of three connected houses, across a narrow alley, and into our apartment. I make my dad promise to email me every day, and he laughs.

"I really mean it, Dad."

"Okay, honey," he says. "I'll check in with you every day."

When I call my mother to say good-bye, she's in a good mood.

"Oh, Jessie, remember I told you about Marcy?"

"She's the career counselor, right?"

"She's helping me sue those motherfuckers, yes. Well, anyway, I went to see her today and I asked her if I looked shorter"—here she starts gasping for air, she's laughing so hard—"because, because, because I said, there are six inches less of me!"

"What are you talking about?"

Does she even remember that I'm leaving for Italy tomorrow? For a second I consider not telling her. Just running away.

"That's how much of my colon they removed! Six inches. So there are six inches less of me!"

After she's done laughing, I remind her that I'm leaving tomorrow.

"I know," she says.

"And we won't have a phone." My mom doesn't have email or a computer yet. "So I'll have to call you from pay phones. But I don't know how often I'll be able to."

"Jessie, that's fine. Just go, have an adventure, and please don't worry about me. I want you to enjoy yourself. I've got so much to keep me busy right now—getting rid of the you-know-whats, and my lawsuit, and the gators—"

"Here's an idea," I say, interrupting her. "Harness all that energy and use it toward cleaning your house."

"Ha!" she says, thinking I'm joking. "That's a good one!"

16

AS I MAKE MY WAY TOWARD MY SEAT AT THE BACK of the plane, carrying a small backpack and with Abraham Lincoln in his duffel-shaped carrier slung over my shoulder, I'm thinking about what I hope to accomplish over the next six months in Italy: I have a novel to finish, I'd like to improve my horrendous Italian, and I'll be teaching an online writing class. And of course, I'm determined to get rid of the bugs.

Last week I found a company online that sells natural remedies specifically for scabies. The owner struggled with them herself for more than a year, and when she finally found something that got rid of them—in her case it was the Indian plant, neem, which David and I tried in pill form but not externally— she formulated the products. I ordered neem soap, neem lotion, neem oil, neem shampoo, and neem conditioner.

Between all the extra loads of laundry and various natural "cures," not to mention the wasted time that can't be measured monetarily, I've spent hundreds of dollars on this entomological adventure. Stuffed inside my luggage in the belly of the plane are bottles of an enzyme cleanser that promises to "neutralize" scabies, giant bottles of tea tree oil shampoo and conditioner, glass vials of pure tea tree oil, and half a dozen neem products. For the entire six months in Italy, I'm bringing one medium-ish rolling suitcase, one large backpack, and my small carry-on backpack. The potions and lotions and poisons for the bugs take up a quarter of my luggage space.

And besides the actual products, I'm bringing the bugs. Which means that now, not only has my mother's hoarding managed to cross the country from Minneapolis to New York City, but it's about to cross the Atlantic Ocean and make it all the way to Europe.

Because I'm traveling with Abraham Lincoln, one of the people at the gate told me to go to the front of the line and board with those traveling with small children or needing assistance. So I'm already settled into my seat—annoyingly in the last row before the restrooms—as the other passengers walk down the aisles and try to find room for their bags in the overhead compartments.

I'm flying Air France, and even though I took French for three years in junior high, when one of the flight attendants comes by and begins speaking to me in French, I haven't the slightest idea what she's saying.

"Sorry?" I say.

"Oh! I thought you were French. I just wanted to ask if you would like a pillow?" She's holding out a small white rectangle that I somehow missed before.

"Thank you," I say, accepting it. I pull down my shirt to make sure my skin is covered before I put the pillow behind my lower back.

I'm flattered that the flight attendant thought I was French. I like the idea of being someone else, from someplace else. My Italian teacher last semester used to say that it's helpful, when learning a new language, to come up with a new "self" for that language, to think in terms of your "Italian self," when speaking Italian. When he said it I was intrigued: I liked the idea of having an Italian self. I liked it a lot. But I'd forgotten about it until now.

Perhaps in Italy I could be a new person—I could be less anxious, less shy. More outgoing. I could finally stop caring so much about other people's opinions of me. I could even be bug free.

The more I think about it, the more I like the idea of an Italian self.

My Italian self does not let her secrets eat at her. My Italian self doesn't even know what hoarding is. And why would she, when her life has never been touched by it? My Italian self had a lovely, idyllic childhood and as a result is bursting with self-esteem. Did my Italian self ride horses? She considers it . . . but no. My Italian self played tennis instead. Or maybe squash. My Italian self is never angry, nor is she self-pitying; she is totally unfamiliar with the concept of self-doubt and has never felt even vaguely ratty or ragged next to well-groomed, well-dressed strangers. Wherever she finds herself is exactly where she belongs and the people around her are lucky to have this Italian Jessie.

This Italian Jessie is downright high on herself.

Maybe, I think, I'll give it a try. I'll become another person once this plane lifts off. And because this new person is bug free, I get up and pull my backpack from the overhead bin. I slide open the front pocket and take out the small bottle of neem oil I've kept there, with the thought that I'd rub some onto the areas of my skin that might touch the plane's upholstery. I pour about a teaspoon into my palm, slide my backpack into place and sit down again, rubbing the oil into my hands.

I've grown so used to tea tree oil, garlic, and now neem, that I've lost any sense of how bad these things smell. The scent of neem oil conjures up rancid almonds, motor oil, and flea dip.

To me, it's fine. No big deal.

But soon the people around me are sniffing the air with suspicious looks on their faces. Some of them point toward the bathroom. They think the dreadful odor is coming from there. But it's coming from me.

Even though I shouldn't leave Abraham Lincoln alone under the seat in front of me—the zipper on his carrier has been broken since we bought it and he knows how to maneuver his way out if I don't grab it in time—I have to wash this stinking oil off my hands. At least six people are looking around, toward me and toward the bathrooms, with disgusted looks on their faces. Some are even pinching their noses closed.

I leave my seat as quietly as possible, trying not to rustle Abraham Lincoln's carrier in the hopes he won't realize I'm gone and panic. In the bathroom, I turn on the water, soap up my hands, and wash them as best I can, but even after I've dried them with a scratchy paper towel my hands still feel greasy. I press them to my nose and breathe in. This stuff is clearly impossible to get off. My hands still reek.

But I can't leave Abraham Lincoln alone for too long. I exit the bathroom and take my seat again, sitting on my hands and praying the smell has dissipated in the cabin.

It hasn't. The plane has filled to capacity, but rather than buckling themselves into their seats, the passengers are standing, some spilling out into the aisles, sniffing the air like truffle-hunting pigs. Two flight attendants have joined the search for the source of the stench and are going through the overhead compartments, pulling each piece of luggage to their faces and inhaling. One of them shakes her head and begins walking briskly to the front of the plane. Is she going to tell the pilot? Have I just caused the flight to be delayed or even cancelled? I have only a forty-five-minute layover between this flight and the one from Paris to Rome—I was already concerned about making my connection.

And David doesn't have a cell phone. If I miss my connecting flight I'll have no way to reach him other than email.

Jesus. All of this because of the neem. All of this because of the bugs. All of this because of my mother's hoarding.

"Excusez moi?" a flight attendant says to me as she pops open the bin directly overhead.

I'm too nervous to be flattered about being taken for a Frenchwoman again.

"Yes?" I ask, trying to find a facial expression that says *I have no idea where that putrid smell originated. I certainly had nothing to do with it.*

"Do you 'ave perfume in your bag, miss? Maybe some musk that broke?"

I shake my head vigorously. "No, I hate perfume," I say, and right then Abraham Lincoln pops his snout from the carrier.

"Down," I hiss at him and with my foot try to push the carrier farther back under the seat.

The flight attendant, in her smart blue skirt and jacket, reaches into the overhead bin and pulls my backpack toward her. "Maybe in 'ere?" she says and sniffs the outside of my bag.

Abraham Lincoln's whole head is out now.

"No," I say, both to her and to Abraham Lincoln.

"Okay," she says, and to my shock she slides my backpack inside again.

Abraham Lincoln, stuck half in, half out of his carrier, starts screeching. His smoke-detector-sounding screeches.

The flight attendant looks at me in horror as Abraham Lincoln breaks free from the carrier and leaps onto my lap, still screeching, his mouth pulled back in a wolflike grimace. His giant ears are pressed down close to his head. Poor thing. He's terrified. I wrap him inside my hooded sweatshirt in an attempt to soothe him. Normally when I fly with him, once the plane has lifted off I allow him out of the carrier and onto my lap, covering him with a blanket to keep him hidden. The few flight attendants who've ever noticed have smiled and said how cute he was. No one has ever reprimanded me.

Until this Air France flight attendant.

"Miss, she must be in this kennel!"

"Okay, sorry," I say, struggling to peel Abraham Lincoln off my lap.

My poor Italian self. I miss her already. Murdered through neem overdose, she lasted about two minutes.

I finally get Abraham Lincoln's claws out of my jeans and try to shove him back into his carrier.

The flight attendant, still standing in the aisle with her arms crossed and a frown on her face, repeats, "She must be in this kennel!"

"I'm trying," I snap. "This bag doesn't really close."

Everyone is watching at this point. At least it's taken their minds off the noxious neem.

"If she is not in the kennel—"

"He," I correct.

"—I will 'ave to tell the pilot."

Finally I smush his head down and manage to get the carrier

zipped. The flight attendant gives me a curt nod and walks past the bathrooms to the back of the plane where she disappears behind a curtain. I fear she's discussing me with the other flight attendants; maybe they know I'm the one who stank up the plane and they're plotting a way to get me off. Me and my screeching dog.

The rest of the passengers are seated, the overhead bins closed, and people seem to have forgotten—or are ignoring—the smell. Finally the announcement comes over the intercom, in French and English, that we should prepare for takeoff.

ROME IS MY favorite city, and not just because it's where David and I got married. I'm beyond relieved when Abraham Lincoln and I make it there without further incident. From the airport I take a train into the city; David and I have planned to meet in the station. He's there, waiting for me on the platform, smiling. As soon as I see him I know that coming here was the right decision. This is my life, my little family: my husband and our dog. And my dad and Sandy understand that, which is why they rejected my offer of skipping Italy and staying with them for the next six months. I'm filled with gratitude that they did. They're much smarter than I am.

We take a train, then a bus, to the village. As the bus turns a corner, our destination comes into view. I've been there before, but that doesn't make the sight any less breathtaking. The village sits like a floating island atop 450-foot cliffs that jut straight up from a lush valley. The jagged-roofed houses are made of the same sand-colored stone as the rock on which they sit, giving the whole place a dramatic, monochromatic eeriness. The village seems stolen from a fairy tale. Unreal.

The bus lets us off on the side of the road and we walk the rest of the way up the hill, across the parking lot and past the pay phone I'll use to call my mother and my dad and Sandy, through the narrow archway in the town walls (an opening too small for cars, rendering the village pedestrian only), and up the serpentine path to the marble bench–lined town square. I feel like I've stepped inside a sepia-toned photograph.

Only one hundred people live in the village, many of them artists and aging hippies from all over Italy. It's a day-trip and weekend destination, which is why there are so many shops and restaurants for a place no bigger than a football field. The chunky, uneven stones used to pave the narrow streets were taken from the riverbed in the valley below. As we walk through the square we pass a store that sells colorful, flowing skirts—the kind of shop you might see on a college campus. The proprietor, a thin, dark-haired man clad in gauzy white, is sitting on the steps, smoking a cigarette.

"Ciao, Dav-id-e," he calls out and waves.

"Ciao, Paolo," David says and introduces me.

"Wel-come," Paolo says.

"Thank you, I mean, *grazie*."

"He seems nice," I say to David as we continue crossing the square.

"Everyone here is really friendly so far," David says. "In fact, we've been invited to a dinner party tonight. I said I wasn't sure because I wanted to see how tired you were."

"That sounds fun. I'll take a nap and I'll be fine," I say.

We reach the steep stone staircase I recognize from the photo and David pulls a key from his pocket.

"I really hope you like it," he says.

"I'm sure I will," I say, following him up the stairs. All I want is a break from the drama of the last three months. That alone makes the place already seem like heaven.

The main room serves as both living area and kitchen and has a sleeping loft above it. A big open fireplace sits in one corner of the room and thick, dark wood beams stripe the ceiling. At the back of the apartment, right off the bathroom, there's an area the size of a large walk-in closet with a couch in it.

"I borrowed that couch from one of the villagers. I thought it could be your writing spot. I've been working there mostly," David says, pointing to the kitchen table.

"It'll be perfect," I say and stand on my tiptoes to kiss him.

EVERY OTHER DAY David gets a bus and then a train into Rome; the rest of the time he works at home, reading, translating articles, or writing in the main room. I plant myself on the couch to write, with Abraham Lincoln curled up next to me. I also register for an intensive Italian class in Rome, starting next month.

In the evenings we sit out on the square and talk to the locals, practicing our Italian as they practice their English. They show us around their art studios and invite us to join their impromptu potluck dinner parties outside one of their apartments or even right on the square. On the nights nothing is happening, David and I eat at one of the five restaurants, feasting on fat homemade pasta with rich, wild boar–inflected tomato sauce; a simple spaghetti sprinkled with pepper and sheep's cheese; or my favorite, *paglia e fieno* (straw and hay): thick fettuccine-type noodles with lots of grated Parmesan, juicy cherry tomatoes, fresh basil, and a dousing of olive oil. On the side we always order the ubiquitous garlic-intense broccoli rabe and carafes of the cheap and delicious house wine.

I feel spoiled and happy.

My dad's good about emailing me every day, and at first everything's fine. But then, after I've been in Italy about a week, with each email he begins to sound worse. His pain levels are really high and he hardly has any energy. The daily walks around the block have regressed to just one trip to the corner and back. He's got an appointment with Dr. Nelson coming up and the day of the appointment I check my email about a hundred times to see if there's news.

When it comes, it's bad.

One of my dad's new arteries has collapsed. He has to have a stent put in. It's not major surgery, but the worrisome part is that Dr. Nelson has no idea what the source of my dad's pain is—the collapsed artery wouldn't cause it. I fear that when the surgeons implant the stent they'll find the true reason for my dad's pain, and it will be unfixable.

I reply to my dad's email and ask if I should come back to Minneapolis to help out. I know Sandy's working constantly to make enough money for their high health-care costs; she's having a hard time doing that and taking care of my dad, too. I don't want to go, but if they need me, I'd be there as fast as I could get on a plane.

My dad writes back and says he'll let me know after the surgery. But maybe.

The day of his surgery I pace and pace. Finally, because I know it'll be a while before my dad's out, I ask David if he'll take a walk with me. We go down to the valley below the village, where sometimes at night we can hear wild boar snorting and carousing and doing whatever it is wild boar do. Instead of making me feel better, though, the walking makes me even tenser and more worried than when I was just pacing inside the apartment.

David says, "You're going to have a heart attack yourself if you don't calm down."

I feel blurry at the edges and I'm afraid I'm going to faint. I grab onto David's shirt and lean against his chest.

"Let's go back," David says, stroking my arm. "Maybe there will be an email."

There isn't an email when we get to the apartment, nor is there one an hour later, nor an hour after that. I try calling Sandy's cell phone from the pay phone in the parking lot and the voice mail comes on right away, which makes me think my dad must still be in surgery.

Finally I get an email, but it's not from Sandy or from my dad. It's from Aunt Eve. The subject line simply says: *your dad*.

Because we have a dial-up connection, the message takes forever to open after I click on it. "What the hell does *your dad* mean?" I yell, as I wait for the message to load. "That is not the kind of subject line I want to see. I want to see *your dad is fine,* or *no need to worry.* Not just *your dad.* Jesus Christ!"

After a hundred years, the message opens. *Your dad is okay. The surgery is done and he's resting but Sandy was too busy to email so she asked me to do it.*

And I can breathe again.

I get an email from my dad the next day. He wants to take me up on my offer to return to Minneapolis. They could really use the help, he says, though he hates to drag me away from Italy and David. I hate it, too. But they need me.

Because of the short notice, the plane ticket is outrageously expensive, but my dad and Sandy put it on their credit card. I'll be there for two weeks.

I'm getting whiplash from all the back and forth these last three months: New York City to Minneapolis to New York City to Minneapolis to New York City to Italy to Minneapolis. For a few devious seconds I consider not telling my mom I'm coming. But I do. I call her from the pay phone in the parking lot. Of course I tell her. She needs me, too.

17

THIS TIME WHEN I ARRIVE, MY DAD CAN GET OUT OF HIS chair to hug me, so at least he's better than right after the bypass. His main limitations are that he can't carry anything (including the laundry they still need to do each day because of the bugs), he can't walk very far, and he doesn't feel comfortable driving. I don't drive at all—officially I have my license, but I've never owned a car, nor driven one since I was twenty. Since the whole reason I'm here is to take some of the load off Sandy, having to ask her for rides to the grocery store sort of defeats the purpose. But I have no choice. I offer to re-learn how to drive, but Sandy says since I'm only here for two weeks, it's not worth it.

When I mention this to my mother the second night I'm in Minneapolis, she volunteers to drive me anywhere I want and take my dad to his appointments. It's a sweet offer, and I feel bad when I tell her that driving with her would probably give my dad another heart attack—and definitely induce panic attacks in me. But I have to tell her the truth or she'll keep asking and asking and asking. And she's not offended, anyway. She just laughs.

The driving situation notwithstanding, I'm able to make myself useful at my dad and Sandy's. I do the daily laundry, assorted cleaning tasks, and around noon I make lunch. Usually we have a salad, but sometimes soup or something frozen from the co-op. Because he's so nauseated from his medications, my dad isn't eating much. Since the first surgery he's lost thirty pounds. I always set some of the lunch aside for Sandy and if she has time she'll sit down with us. In the late afternoon, I start figuring out what to make for dinner.

I'M TRYING TO keep one foot in David's world by listening to the two Italian instruction CDs I loaded onto my iPod. When Sandy's home and I know my dad has company, I duck out for a walk along River Road, listening to the Italian lessons and whispering along.

When David calls, the third day I'm in Minneapolis, I'm thrilled to hear his voice.

But he doesn't sound happy. Last night he found out that some of the villagers have come up with nicknames for us.

"What are they?" All day I've been itching like crazy; even though I know it's a bad idea, I take a paper clip from the dispenser on my dad's desk and scratch my ankle with it.

"You're *bruschettini*."

"Little bruschetta? What does that even mean?"

"I'm not sure," he says, "but I don't think it's insulting, like mine."

"What's yours?"

"*Aglio* kid!"

"Garlic kid? Why?"

"Because I smell like garlic all the time! Because of the fucking bugs!"

"Oh, Jesus. I'm sorry." I toss the paper clip into the garbage.

"These things are affecting my life now," David says. "I want the villagers to like me. I want them to talk to me."

"I understand. Look, I'll find something to get rid of these things, I promise." I feel so guilty that David has to pay the consequences of my mother's hoarding. He probably wishes he had a normal mother-in-law, a wife with a normal family.

"I'm sorry," I say again.

"I know," he says, sighing.

It doesn't matter how many times I apologize. The only thing that will make things better is getting rid of these fucking bugs.

MY MOTHER HAS a telephone phobia, she freely admits it, and whenever she answers the phone her voice has a tentative tone. But tonight she sounds even more fearful than usual.

"He-llo?"

"Hi Mom, it's me. How's it going?"

"Oh, fine," she says, but her voice sounds flat. "How's your dad?"

"The same. He's in a lot of pain and he's exhausted."

She asks what medications he's on, and I tell her even though we've already covered this.

"Maybe you should start looking for a new job, Mom, to give you something to do."

She loved her job. I know that's why she's obsessed with suing them. She wants to punish her former employers for hurting her feelings. They rejected her, they abandoned her, and that is unacceptable, especially because the nursing home was her sanctuary after Roger died. She had friends there. It was her social life, and now that it's over I don't know how she'll find human connection. Our phone calls are definitely not enough.

"The problem is that if I work, it might affect my lawsuit."

I'll let that slide. Even though I don't see how she could possibly believe she has a chance of winning her lawsuit when she had so many warnings, there's no point in trying to talk her out of it.

I look at the clock. It's 8:00, when my dad needs to take his nighttime pills. I need to go remind him because Sandy's still out at an appointment. I should have waited until afterward to call my mom.

"What about some kind of cancer survivors' support group? You could meet people and learn how to stay healthy at the same time."

"I don't know," she says.

"What about one of those walking groups for seniors? You love to walk."

"I just wish I was good at something," she says. "I wish I had a talent."

"You like knitting."

"I know, but to be honest with you, Jessie . . . I'm not very good." The flatness in her voice now has an undercurrent of whine.

"What do you think I should try?" my mom asks. "You always give me the best advice."

I look at the clock again. I really need to get out to the living room, where my dad is. The phone I'm on has a cord, so I'm tethered at the other end of the house from him. Tethered by my mother's demand for my attention, too.

"Just tell me what I should do, Jessie."

"Mom, please," I groan. "Stop."

"What?" She sounds alarmed.

"I'm here to take care of my dad. You had your turn with the cancer. Let me take care of my dad now."

"Okay," she says, and I can almost hear her sitting up straight. "I don't want to add to your stress. That's the last thing I want to do."

I feel crushed and terrible. She has no one else. "I'm sorry. I don't mean to be a bitch."

"Oh, no, it's okay," she says, and that's the problem: It really is okay with her. She has the lowest self-esteem of anyone I know. And when I think about that, I feel even worse.

"Listen, my dad has a doctor's appointment tomorrow afternoon and Sandy's taking him. We could get together then if you want."

"That would be fantastic. What should we do?"

Normally when I'm here with David, we borrow my dad or Sandy's car and David drives. We'll pick up my mom and go out to lunch or a café or a museum, and then always a used bookstore afterward.

There's a park that's two blocks from her house and about ten from my dad and Sandy's. I suggest that we meet there.

"That sounds great. Call me in the morning, okay?" my mom says, sounding about a hundred times more chipper than she did thirty seconds ago. "And I've got something to show you . . ."

"What?"

"It's a surprise!"

BEFORE MY DAD and Sandy leave for his appointment, I ask them to see if the doctor will prescribe the sulfur lotion that my dermatologist wouldn't because of its alleged messiness.

"It's worth a shot," my dad says. He pulls me to him sideways and kisses me on the head. "Bye, honey."

As they walk out the back door and toward the garage, Sandy's strides are purposeful, her back straight, while behind her my dad moves hunched and slow, his hand over his chest as if he's about to pledge his allegiance to the flag.

I grab my purse and make sure I have my keys and sunglasses. There's no reason to rush, though, because my mother's always late.

Except this time, she's not. As I walk up, she's sitting on a bench digging through a wrinkled paper bag.

"Hi, honey!" She's wearing black leggings and a blousy turquoise shirt, with her keys on the orange plastic coil around her neck. She sees me looking at the plastic coil, removes it, then shoves it into the black fanny pack she sometimes slings purse-style over her shoulder.

I sit down next to her and she asks how my dad is.

"The same, basically. And he's tired because he's not sleeping well."

"Tell him to take an antihistamine about half an hour before bed. Twenty-five milligrams. We gave it to patients at the nursing home all the time." She slips a thin cardboard box from the paper bag she'd been digging through. "And now, I have some things to show you." The box is about the size of a deck of cards, and from it, she slides out a foil sheet and hands it to me. "It's ivermectin."

The river blindness cure that's used off-label for scabies. The foil sheet is separated into squares, with perforated edges between them. Each square holds something about the size of half an aspirin. "Where'd you get this?"

"From Dr. Paulsen. I remembered that your doctor wouldn't give it to you. Well, now I have some for all of us."

"That's great, thank you." Why didn't I think to ask her? It didn't even occur to me.

"I told him I needed it for you and Dave and your dad and Sandy. But what I'm really going to do is test it out on myself first. If it works, then I'll give it to everyone. Although I decided that since you and Dave will be in Italy, I should give it to you now. I'll give you enough for three doses each."

"But you're only supposed to take it once."

She giggles. "I've been taking it every day for the last five days."

"Mom . . ."

"It's okay. I know it's safe. Now, let's figure out how many of these pills I have to give you. The dosage depends on how much the person weighs, but it's in kilograms. Dave is easy—he should take the same number of pills I take, which is twelve."

"Why should he take the same amount as you?"

"Because, I hate to tell you this, but I think we weigh about the same amount."

She does look at about her plumpest point. But still. "He's six feet tall. You're not even five feet. How could you weigh the same amount?"

"Believe me, we do," she says. "Now how much do you weigh?"

I tell her and from her fanny pack she pulls out a pencil, the tiny kind you get at IKEA or a miniature golf course. Using her thigh as a writing surface, she starts jotting something on the paper bag. Before I can see what it is, she crosses it out. "Okay, okay, let me think . . ."

"How many pounds are in a kilogram? That's all you need to know."

"Two something, I think, but wait, just let me think here . . . let's see, let's see, if I take twelve pills"—she writes the numer-

als one, two, three, four, all the way up to twelve, then methodically circles each number a few times—"Let's see, twelve pills,
then eleven pills, then ten pills . . ." She starts mumbling and
I can't make out what she's saying. She crosses the numbers
out, making big Xs through each of them, then lifts her pencil
and freezes. Only her lips are moving. I feel like I'm watching a
movie where a mad scientist scribbles a million different formu-
las on a chalkboard and at the end, proves something that will
save the world.

She's still mumbling, but now it's loud enough that I can
hear: ". . . twelve pills, ten pills, no *eleven* pills or wait, no, twelve
pills for two and seven, no, eight for—"

"Mom!" I grab her wrist. I'm honestly a little frightened.

Because of the bugs and my dad's medical problems, I've
hardly been thinking about my mother's hoarding. But I know
that these scrambled thoughts are part of it. Hoarding is partly
an information processing problem—the inability to make a
decision, convoluted categorization, and memory deficits that
hoarders contend with all fall under that umbrella—and what
I've just witnessed is an example of seriously flawed information processing. I feel like I crawled inside my mother's brain for
a second and came upon a terrifying place. No wonder she can't
keep her house organized.

"Mom," I say, softer this time. "Come back to earth, okay?"

"Okay, honey, sorry." She sounds embarrassed and dis-
tracted. She looks up at the tree above us, then puts the pencil
against the paper again and writes the number eight. "Jessie,
you need to take eight pills."

"All right." When she leaned forward I caught a glimpse
of something on her chest, up near the front of her shoulder.
"What was that thing I saw on your . . ." I tap the upper front part
of my shoulder to show her. "I thought I saw something there."

My mom pulls out her shirt, looks down. "Oh, that? That's just a chemical burn."

"A *what* kind of burn?"

She tugs it down to show me: It looks like old, mangled skin, like my dad's wrecked fingernail from the car accident.

"I just put a little too much bleach in the bath one time," she says.

"You're still taking baths in bleach? I thought you stopped doing that."

"Well, I need to get rid of these things, don't I?"

I put my head in my hands and let out a small groan. I can't believe this is my life. If someone had told me six months ago that soon I'd be sitting on a park bench arguing with my mother about bleach baths while she doled out off-label drugs for a parasite, I never would have believed it. This whole thing is completely absurd.

"I know you feel guilty about the bugs, Mom, but *please* stop punishing yourself."

"I'll be okay. Now listen. I'm giving you twenty-four pills for you, and thirty-six pills for Dave. That's three doses each."

She starts struggling to separate the pills—she can't seem to tear the perforated edges of the blister pack apart. Finally she gets one. "Here, Jessie, one . . ." she says and hands it to me. She starts tearing off another.

"Wait a minute." I take one of the sheets and count the pills on it. "There are twelve pills on each of these. So if David needs thirty-six pills, give me three sheets for him. And two sheets for me."

"Okay," she says and reaches into the paper bag, presumably for another box of the pills. "Oh! I want you to look at this." She gives me a handwritten letter. No, it's a copy of a handwritten letter. "It's the letter I wrote to the judge who dismissed my law-suit. I'm appealing his decision."

"Please tell me you didn't send a handwritten letter to the judge."

"Why shouldn't I?"

"Um, because it makes you look like a crazy person?"

"Ha!" she laughs. "Just read it and tell me if I get my point across. I spent a lot of time on that letter."

I can tell she did because there are words crossed out and then rewritten in the margins—whole sentences even. But all in all, it's a pretty good letter. And I tell her that.

"Thank you," she says.

I'm starting to feel antsy just sitting here on this bench. It's not even facing the park, but a busyish street. "Do you feel like walking through the park, Mom?"

"Sure, honey. I could use the exercise," she says and scram-bles to her feet. "I haven't been able to go to the Y at all be-cause it would ruin my experiment with the baths and the lindane."

We walk over the winding cement path through the park. My mom has her fanny pack strung diagonally across her chest and the paper sack clutched under her arm like an evening bag. But after just a few minutes, she grabs my arm and leans all of her weight on me.

"What is it? Are you okay?"

She's huffing and puffing. "I just need a minute."

"I'm sorry," I say. "Maybe it's too hot out for a walk. Come over here, Mom." I pull her a few feet off the path, into the shade underneath a big oak tree. It's a sunny day, at least eighty de-grees, and of course we're both wearing long sleeves and long pants because of the bugs. No wonder she's overheated.

We stand there while she catches her breath. She cools herself by pulling her shirt forward and away from her chest, in a fanning motion.

I catch another glimpse of her bleach burn. It looks like molted snakeskin. A shudder ripples through me. Just imagining one of those creatures is enough to send me into a panic.

"Can I ask you something, Mom?"

"You can ask me anything."

"Why have you always teased me about snakes?"

"What . . . what are you talking about?"

"You know. The rubber ones you put in my Christmas stockings, the plastic ones you leave lying around for me to find. The basement? Mom. Come on."

A bicyclist goes by on the path, his spokes glinting in the bright sun. My mother follows him with her gaze.

"Mom?"

"I don't know what you mean," she says.

I step directly in front of her so we're facing each other. "You don't remember saying, 'Don't go down to the basement. There are snakes this big'"—I hold up my hands in a big circle—"'that will bite you.'"

"I . . . I can't believe I did that," she says, almost in a whisper.

"Well, believe it, because you did. And now I'm terrified of them."

I feel a little sorry for her because she was just so winded and now she looks genuinely distressed, but there's no way I'm going to tell her that her snake-teasing was no big deal. *Hey, no problem, it's all good!*

Ever since Roger died, about once a year she'll say, "I really regret the way I was to you kids. I wasn't the best mother and I'm sorry." I always tell her that she was a better mother (we both use the past tense) than her mother was, and how could she know any better when she had such a terrible childhood, she didn't have a good example, blah, blah, blah—all the things she's told me many times. In other words, I let her off the hook immediately.

This time, I'm not going to do that.

"It's the weirdest thing," she says, staring off into the distance as if she's reading from a faraway screen.

"What is?"

"My mother did the same thing to me. About dogs. She used to say, 'Don't go across the street; there are dogs over there that will bite you.'"

I've never thought about why my mom was so afraid of dogs. Why haven't I ever asked?

My mom looks guilty, ashamed. "My mother did it so I wouldn't cross the street and get hit by a car . . ." She trails off. Half a second later it's like a switch has gone off inside her: "Oh, Jessie! That must be why I did it! I told you there were snakes in the basement so you wouldn't try to go down the stairs and fall down. I was protecting you!"

"There's one problem," I say. "I'm almost forty years old. I'm not in danger of falling down your basement stairs."

"Well. I guess it's just something I picked up from my mother, then," she says, as if declaring the conversation over. But I don't want it to be.

"You see how it affected me, though, right? The same way you're afraid of dogs is how I feel about snakes. That's why I've asked you so many times to stop."

"I guess I didn't remember."

I don't see how that could be true, but I'll let it go.

"You'll remember now, though, right, Mom?"

"Yes. I will."

After all these years I've succeeded in getting her to stop hoarding something: She's finally willing to discard the idea that the snake-teasing was funny. And to me, that feels like a major accomplishment.

MY DAD AND Sandy return from the doctor's appointment with reassuring news: Despite his pain, everything looks good and my dad is on track for a full recovery. They've procured a prescription for the sulfur lotion, too. The only place that can prepare it is something called a "compound pharmacy" and there's just one in the Minneapolis area. It's in a distant suburb and closes at 4:00. And it's 4:15.

"I'm going to try calling, in case," I say, snatching the prescription from my dad's hand and running back to his office where the phone number of the pharmacy is still up on his computer. After five long rings, an answering machine picks up. Closed.

"So how did it go with your mom today?" my dad asks when I come back into the kitchen.

I decide not to mention the snake-teasing conversation. I'm pretty sure it would upset him.

"It was good. She says taking an antihistamine before bed will help you sleep. Twenty-five milligrams. That's what she did for patients at the nursing home."

"Really? Like Benadryl?" my dad says. "I think we might have some. Can you go check on that shelf in the closet next to my office?"

I go look and sure enough, there's an unopened box.

"I might try that tonight," my dad says.

"I might, too," I say.

THE NEXT DAY Sandy gets the sulfur lotion. I'm so excited to try it that I go to bed early that night, so I can put it on as soon as possible. It's not really that messy; it's lotion after all, not Vaseline—though it does smell pretty rotten egg-ish.

Immediately, the itching lessens. And by the morning, it's almost gone. No new bites either. My dad and Sandy both feel better, too.

Finally, a glimmer of hope.

After the second night of the sulfur lotion, I'm convinced that it's going to cure us. Not only have I had no new bites and almost no itching, but the sulfur seems to have a healing effect on my skin; the red marks I've had for months around my hip bones and on my chest are starting to clear up already.

When I call my mom, I tell her to stop all the nonsense and to get some of this lotion instead. "I don't think so, honey," she says. "I feel like my experiment is paying off. Little by little these bastards are dying. I can tell."

"But why do it little by little? I promise you, this sulfur is working."

"We'll see."

Meanwhile, my dad, Sandy, and I are ecstatic. And each day my dad seems to have more energy. He begins taking one nap a day instead of two, and suddenly he's eating more. One afternoon when I ask my dad how he's feeling, he says, "I actually forgot about my chest pain for a while, which is pretty good, for me."

We're going to do the lotion for seven nights, but decide to continue covering the furniture and changing bedding and towels every day until I leave, just to be sure. It doesn't feel as burdensome now that I know the bugs are on their way out.

I've already told David all about it over email, but when he calls and I say that for the first time in four months I am 100 percent certain that there are no parasitic mites living under my skin, I actually start crying.

"I can't wait until you come back so I can be finished with these things, too!" he says and I haven't heard him sound this cheerful in months.

"But I have to warn you," I say, "the sulfur smells a little strong."

"I don't even care. I'll just stay inside the apartment and get reading done that week."

I need to find a way to get more lotion so I can bring it back to Italy. I could ask my dad to call his doctor for a refill, but I need to call my mom anyway. I have to convince her to give up her "experiment" and try the lotion. I'm sure she can get her doctor to prescribe it for her since he seems willing to give her anything she wants.

Again, she balks.

"But we already know what you're doing isn't working. You're still itching and getting bites. Right?"

"Well, yes."

"Then for fuck's sake, why won't you try the sulfur lotion?"

She doesn't say anything.

"Sorry," I say. "I'm just really frustrated with you."

"I know."

"You know, but you're still not going to change your mind, right?"

"Right."

"Okay, fine. Listen, Mom. Maybe you don't want to try the lotion, but I need more of it to bring back to Italy. Could you get Dr. Paulsen to prescribe you some?"

"Of course, honey. I'll go today. In fact, I'll go right now."

"Thank you. Could you get a lot? I want a big supply."

"Sure," she says. "It's the least I can do. And when I get the prescription, I'll bring it to the Target pharmacy—they know me there, and I won't leave until it's filled."

"The only place you can get it is this compound pharmacy in Richfield."

"We'll see about that!" she says.

By dinnertime, she's dropped off four big bottles. I can't depend on her, I can't get her to clean her house, I can't even always trust that she's telling me the truth. But once in a while, my mother has the ability to make me really happy.

MAYBE IT'S JUST chance, maybe it's a combination of time passing and the bugs vanishing; but for whatever reason, at the end of my two weeks in Minneapolis, my dad is doing much better. He can even drive himself to and from his appointments now. He still can't carry full laundry baskets down to the basement, but Sandy can handle the back-to-normal amounts of laundry they'll have now that we're free—finally, finally, finally, free—of the bugs.

There's just one more thing I need to take care of. The day before I fly back to Italy, I meet my mom in the park to say goodbye.

"You know I'm going to ask you again to try the lotion, right?" I say, sitting down next to her. Like last time, she was already here when I arrived.

She laughs. "Yes, honey, I know you are. But I'm determined to continue my experiment."

"You know what? I almost, *almost,* admire your stubbornness. But where is that tenacity when it comes to cleaning your house?"

"The house still looks marvelous from the last time you cleaned," she says. "Do you want to come see it?" She points in the house's direction.

"No," I say quickly. It's a visceral reaction. "I'm cured of the bugs now"—I can't say or even think those words without a wave of euphoria washing over me, and that feeling will last for months—"and until I know that you're cured, too, and that your house is bug free, I can't go in there."

She looks confused, as if she's trying to work out a complex equation. "So you're saying you won't go into the house unless I do the sulfur?"

That's not what I meant. I hadn't thought of using the sulfur lotion as leverage. I consider it. And then I consider something else: all the hell that house has put me through. The nightmares—yes, I've had nightmares in which I'm trapped there with all the windows and doors bolted shut, and others where I'm trapped under piles of junk; the actual hours spent and muscles used cleaning and cleaning and organizing; all of the stress and the arguments and the mini breakdowns; the sheer weight of the responsibility; the sheer weight of the secret. Maybe it's time for me to walk away.

Walk away.

It's not my house. It's not my problem.

"I'm emancipating myself from your house," I say.

"Emancipating yourself? So you think you're a slave to the house?"

"Or think of it as a divorce," I say. "Whatever. It doesn't matter. I'm done. I'm never setting foot in your house again."

"That's fine, you won't need to," she says. "I plan to keep it looking marvelous."

"I hope you do, Mom. I really hope you do."

And the next day I fly back to Italy, armed with the proper poisons to finally break what I think is the last link in the chain between me and my mother's hoarding.

18

LIFE BACK IN ITALY SEEMS PRETTY MUCH IDEAL AT FIRST. David is cured of the bugs within a week and we toss out the remaining bottles of tea tree oil, hoping to never smell it again. The marble benches on the square soak up the sun all day and stay warm long after dark; we linger there late into the night, chatting with our new Italian friends. David and I even host a dinner party, making nachos with strips of *piadina* bread because we can't find tortilla chips. A youngish mother named Daniela wants to practice her English, and she and I begin doing a twice-weekly language exchange. One hour we speak only Italian, and the next hour we speak only English.

I begin the intensive Italian class, and for the last three weeks of September and the first week of October I take the bus, then a train to Rome each weekday for three hours of instruction. If David has to go to Rome for research he'll meet me when my class is finished, always taking Abraham Lincoln in his shoulder bag, and we'll go out to lunch or to a museum, or if it's late enough, a wine bar.

I keep in touch with my dad and Sandy through email, and with my mom through weekly calls from the pay phone. My dad's health continues to improve. He and Sandy even install a makeshift gym in their basement, with a treadmill and a stationary bike, so my dad can get a cardio workout each day.

After I've been back in Italy about a month, my mother tells me that she's finally cured of the bugs, too. She went to the emergency room because the itching was driving her insane. After he heard all the medicines she'd used, the doctor there told her she was cured a long time ago, and the itching she was experiencing now was from overtreating herself. As soon as he told her that, the itching stopped.

My mother is excited because she has a new friend, Tina, a former coworker who "is just wonderful." My mom can't wait for David and me to meet Tina the next time we visit. I'm happy to hear that my mom has someone to make plans with and I hope the friendship lasts.

I should be ecstatic: My parents are both healthy, we're all bug free, and David and I are living in a stunning Italian village.

But something's wrong. As October passes and the warm weather fades and the days get shorter and colder, melancholy comes for me. The stone of the square—and of the apartments, everything in the village is made of stone—that once held the warmth from the sun, now holds cold. I'm freezing all the time, and it's a damp chill that settles into my bones and stays. It's the same weather as San Francisco's, which I hated. It's not just the weather, though. I feel as if someone has snuck up behind me and draped me with one of those protective lead aprons you have to wear at the dentist during x-rays. I'm weighted down, each step heavier than the last.

I start staying in our apartment more, even though the only heat source is the fireplace that neither David nor I can keep going for more than twenty minutes. I don't want to be around people. I stop meeting Daniela for our language exchange. I'm cranky, snappish. I'm tired all the time, yet I can't sleep at night.

One evening David convinces me to go to a dinner party at a local artist's apartment. He thinks it would be good for me to get out and socialize, practice my Italian. So I go. The apartment is right at the edge of the cliff, directly overlooking the valley below. I feel a little vertiginous as I walk in. There's a huge spread of food on a long table: three pasta dishes, salad, broccoli rabe, bread, tangerines for dessert, and lots of wine. The walls are covered with the artist's paintings: jewel-toned women and girls. At one point I'm talking to another guest, struggling in my still-not-great Italian to explain that in the United States, it's normal not to live with, or even near, your parents. For some reason the whole room of fifteen or so people decides to stop speaking right then and listen as I fight my way through this foreign language, backing myself into a verbal corner as I attempt to make my now pointless-seeming point. Finally I reach the end of my sentence, exhale, and take a sip of wine.

As I'm holding the glass to my lips, one of the other English speakers there says, "Wow, Jessie, who's your Italian teacher?"

At first I'm confused, but then the people in the room who understand English start laughing—not in a raucous or mean-spirited way, but still, it's clear that I'm the object of the laughter. And I don't like it.

After that, I let David go to dinner parties by himself. One of the villagers has lent us a television, and I huddle under blankets on the couch watching it with Abraham Lincoln at my side. And while there's really nothing wrong with the village itself, I can't wait to get the fuck out.

In November I start counting the weeks until we leave. In December, I switch to days. I can't wait to get out because I know that the heaviness that has settled over me, the lack of energy, my loss of interest in anything pleasurable (except over-eating and overdrinking enough to regain all the weight I'd lost and then some) is just temporary. I'll come back to life again once we return to New York.

WHEN WE DO return, it's to a few hassles from the subletter. She couldn't figure out how to turn on the shower, so instead of emailing me to ask—which she didn't have a hard time doing when she needed to find the nearest bank—she called the building's super and had him replace the faucet. The new one is both more complicated and uglier than the last. But worse than that, she had the locks on the door changed, claiming that the keys I'd FedExed to her didn't work. Immediately upon our arrival home, she begins demanding that we reimburse her for the three-hundred dollar cost. At first we refuse (I tested those keys at least half a dozen times before I sent them to her), but her constant emails—*Do the right thing, Jessie, come on, I know you're an honorable person!*—wear me down. Eventually David and I decide that though it's unlikely, maybe somehow I'd sent her the wrong set. We give in and pay her.

Those small things aside, I should be happy to be back in New York; after all, it's what I'd desired for months. I try to act cheerful, but there's a cold and aching stone inside me, and I fear that's the real me, the pessimistic, sad, cranky core of me. I fake it. I meet friends for dinner or drinks or coffee, and I try to listen to what they're saying and understand what they're talking about, but it's as if I'm swathed in cotton, mummified, and that extra layer keeps me from feeling connected to anyone.

February, March, and April pass and I keep waiting to feel happy, or even just not unhappy, but nothing changes. I know something is wrong with me, but I figure it will go away. And just like when I had the bugs and couldn't bring myself to tell anyone, I tell no one besides David how I feel.

ON MAY FIRST, David leaves to go back to the village for a month to do more research. Without him, I feel myself sinking even more. I'm endlessly walking through wet concrete trying not to get sucked down, and it's not working.

When I finally comprehend that what I'm experiencing is depression—most likely clinical depression—I feel like an idiot for not realizing it sooner. And what's really embarrassing is that the only reason I do realize it is because of a television commercial for an antidepressant. It's one of those woman-walking-alone-and-moping-type commercials. Superimposed over the woman is a list of symptoms, beginning with the obvious ones: Lack of energy? Yes. Trouble sleeping? Yes. Chronic feelings of sadness? Yes. Then some symptoms I hadn't expected: Irritability? "Yes," I say out loud to no one. A hard time making decisions? "God, yes."

I had no idea that irritability or indecisiveness were aspects of depression. For the last six months, I've been so irritable it's as if I've had constant PMS. And though indecisiveness has always been a problem for me, since last fall, I've been even worse. Ordering in restaurants has become a nightmare: After taking five minutes to decide, as the waiter stands there tapping his pen on his pad, I'll likely hunt him down a few minutes later because I've changed my mind for the gazillionth time.

I've always taken a perverted pride in the fact that I'm the one person in my immediate family who hasn't been medicated for depression. I've also always been skeptical of antidepressants' efficacy. But I need to do something. When David calls from Italy, I ask him what he thinks about me getting a prescription for one. "Do it," he says.

Even though my mother has battled black moods for most of her life, I don't even consider asking her for advice. I plan to never mention it to her.

IT FEELS A little like a defeat when I make an appointment to see my doctor. At the same time, it's exhilarating to be taking action.

A few days later, in her office, I list some of my symptoms and my doctor says it definitely sounds like depression. She asks if something in particular caused it and the only thing I can think of is that maybe it's some kind of delayed reaction to all the stress of last year. I tell her about my mother's cancer and my dad's heart attack. I leave out the hoarding and the bugs. Chronic stress can certainly trigger depression, she says, and writes me a prescription for Wellbutrin. She also says that my first few days on it I might feel a little anxious, and she gives me a prescription for Xanax, too.

She's right about the anxiety: I spend much of the first day staring out the window, terrified that I'm going to fling it open and throw myself out. It's not that I want to jump—I don't—it's that I'm not convinced that I won't. I actually have to press my palms against the window frame to reassure myself. Yet for some reason I can't go stand anywhere else, or sit down.

I've never taken Xanax before, and maybe because the pill's so small, especially after I break it in half as my doctor instructed,

I'm not expecting it to work. But it does, pretty quickly. I'm still wired and panicky, but calm enough to take Abraham Lincoln out for a long walk.

The second and third days are still tense; I feel dizzy, my heart pounds, and I've slept for only eight or nine hours total in the last two nights.

The fourth day is better. Much less panic. By the fifth day I feel fine: no racing pulse, just my usual amount of anxiety, and I slept well the night before. I still feel depressed, which disappoints me, even though I know these drugs take weeks to kick in. David comes home at the end of May and says I seem happier, though I don't feel any different.

IN JUNE, I'M walking along the Hudson River as I sometimes do, when I notice that my iPod is sounding utterly fantastic. Because of the times I helped my dad test out his new audio gear, I can easily tell the difference between a crap stereo and a good one. And suddenly my iPod sounds as good as one of my dad's best systems.

I take out my earbuds. Did I buy new ones and not remember? They look the same. Besides, I would remember. And my iPod certainly hasn't changed. I put the earbuds back in and switch from the Lemonheads to Outkast. Again, the music sounds excellent. I try Radiohead, the Rolling Stones, PJ Harvey. I'm hearing individual parts to the songs that I haven't noticed, or at least appreciated, before. And these parts are coming together to create a vastly wider spectrum of sound. I continue walking, blown away by what I'm hearing, still baffled as to why. And then I realize: It's the Wellbutrin. I'd become so depressed that everything had gone flat, including music. Now it's round again.

19

I CONTINUE TO FEEL BETTER AND BETTER OVER THE course of the summer, and in August, exactly a year after my dad, Sandy, David, and I were cured of the bugs, my mom tells me over the phone that maybe they were a good thing.

"The scabies might be the stress that pushed your dad over the edge into having a heart attack, and the good thing, Jessie, is that he had the heart attack before it was a massive one—so he could have the surgery and be okay. If he hadn't been under so much stress he may not have had a heart attack for a long time, and that one could have been a lot worse."

"Sure, Mom," I say. If she wants to make herself feel better about the bugs it doesn't hurt anything. Besides, she might have a point.

"Oh, Jessie, I need your address."

"Why? I've told you before how small our apartment is. I don't want anything."

"It's just a book. Please, Jessie, I know you'll really love it."

"What's the book?"

"It's a surprise."

I give her my address, then forget about it.

About a week later the buzzer rings, sending Abraham Lincoln into a barking frenzy. It's UPS, a package, and I have to go down and sign for it. The box is heavy for a book. She probably included more than one.

When I get inside the apartment, I grab the scissors from the drawer where we keep them and sit on the floor to open the box. It's wrapped tightly in tape. I can just picture my mom squinting in concentration as her tiny fingers hold down the edges of the box, while with her other hand she unpeels the tape, being sure to wrap the box up so carefully; it's a cute image and I smile at the thought.

I snip the tape away and get the box open. Inside is some kind of new-agey book, one of those One Rule a Day for a Happy Life–type books, which is a little surprising because my mother doesn't usually go for that kind of thing. Whatever was making the box so heavy is underneath a layer of newspaper. I lift that off and find something wrapped in tissue paper. I try to pull it out of the box, but it's jammed in there. The object is soft, so it's not another book. Maybe it's some kind of pillow? But why would it be so heavy?

Finally I get the thing out of the box and cut away some of the tissue paper. I can see parts of it: forest green, with patches of a silky lighter green material in some spots, and a netted material in others. The netting is stretched tightly across the fabric, it almost looks like—I tear away the rest of the paper—scales. I scream.

It's a stuffed snake.

About four feet long and surprisingly lifelike.

I go into the kitchen, get a garbage bag, and throw it over the snake. Then I scoop the whole thing up, flip over the bag, and tie the top in a tight knot.

I'm stunned. How could my mother not remember our talk? I can't think of any reason for her to do this. Her motives are so incomprehensible that I'm more confused than angry. I thought she'd finally understood the effect her behavior has had on me. I thought she even felt bad about it. I was wrong.

The stuffed snake looks handmade. I wonder how much of her dwindling savings she wasted on it. I pick up the garbage bag with the snake inside, walk down the stairs with it, and put it directly into the garbage.

WHEN SHE CALLS a few days later, I'm prepared.

"Hi, honey, how're you?" she asks, her voice bright with al-most-laughter.

"Fine, Mom," I say. "You?"

"I'm good." She pauses. "So, have you gotten any *interesting* gifts in the mail?"

"Oh, right," I say. "Thanks for the book."

"And?"

"And what?"

"Wasn't there something else in the box, too?"

"No, just the book," I say, trying to sound confused. "Why?"

"There was something else in the box, besides the book." She sounds nervous.

"Really? What?"

"Something I thought you might find amusing."

She thinks it's funny. Incredible.

"That's weird," I say. "You know, come to think of it, David opened the box. I wasn't home when it came."

"Can you ask him if there was something else in the box?"

"He's not here. He's teaching tonight and won't be back until late."

"When he gets home, ask him if there was something else in the box, because I know I put it in there."

She sounds panicked now. I don't feel the slightest bit sorry for her—though I'm not enjoying it either.

"Mom, you shouldn't be buying me things; you don't have the money. What was it?"

"It was a stuffed snake."

"Excuse me?" I feign surprise.

"A stuffed snake."

"Why would you send me that?"

"I thought you would think it was funny."

"I certainly wouldn't think it was funny. I'd probably think it was terrifying. I bet David saw it and threw it out. He was probably protecting me because he knows how afraid of snakes I am. Don't you remember the conversation we had about this last summer?"

"I guess so," she says, sounding close to tears. One mention of the Bird Man or John Lennon and she'd be over the edge. I'm not that cruel, though it's tempting.

"Mom, how could you think I'd find a stuffed snake amusing?"

"I got it at the Renaissance Festival."

It must be the antidepressants that keep me from going ballistic on her. Instead, I just say, "Well, I'm glad David kept me from seeing it." Then I can't help but add, "It's a good thing someone cares about my happiness, because my mother certainly doesn't."

"Oh," she says. That's it. *Oh.*

* * *

LONG BEFORE I ever heard the word "hoarding," I knew there was something different about my mother. That's why I always get uncomfortable in groups of people if the talk turns to childhood stories. I either change the subject or clam up, hoping no one asks anything about my childhood and specifically my mother. In the rare case that someone does ask, I just say "She's eccentric," or "She's hard to describe."

I was so nervous the first time David met her. We'd been together about six months; I'd moved from New York to San Francisco to be with him and we were in Minneapolis for a visit. Before David, my mother had met only one other boyfriend, and that was eleven years earlier. She was on miraculously good behavior that night, and afterward the guy said she was "nice," but I hadn't had as much invested in him. I was only nineteen.

David's opinion of my mother mattered to me. She was a reflection of what I might become. I feared that he would see something in her that would turn him off to me, maybe even make him rethink our plans for the future.

Some hoarders have extremely neat appearances, which is part of how they're able to hide their behavior, but my mother isn't one of them. She's always been sort of rumpled looking. And the older she gets, the more she chooses comfort, both physical and mental, over style. The keys on the plastic coil around her neck give her mental comfort and are a vivid example of how little she trusts her memory. She's so afraid of forgetting where she put them that she'd rather treat herself like a seven-year-old and wear her keys around her neck.

The day David met her, we went to a Chinese restaurant where my mother drank cups of tea as if she were a frat boy and they were tequila shots. Each time the waitress passed, my mother would flag her down: "Say! Could I have some mo-ah tea!"

When my mother found out that David had gone to college in Santa Cruz, she peppered him with questions about the charming beach town she'd visited once when she and my dad were living in Berkeley. She was sweet and curious and funny.

Still, even though she'd behaved reasonably well, I was nervous. Afterward, we dropped her off at her house and as soon as she was out of the car, I turned to David and said, "Do you still love me?"

"Of course." He laughed. "Your mom's cute. She's adorable, actually."

And after all these years and the various hells she's put us through, he always treats her with respect. Which I appreciate immensely. Because no matter how loony or misguided or even occasionally cruel my mother may be, I still feel protective of her. I always have, and I always will.

BUT PROTECTIVENESS ASIDE, after the stuffed snake incident, I'm more determined than ever to not end up like my mother. Given the strong genetic component to hoarding, sometimes I worry that the proclivity is within me, lying dormant, waiting for a catastrophe to set it in motion. I begin to mentally sift through my behavior, hoping that self-awareness will be the inoculation I need.

I'm definitely not a hoarder in terms of possessions, and it's not hard for me to keep things organized in our apartment. But I am really indecisive. It's gotten a little better now that I'm no longer depressed, but I still take too long to make decisions, and often when I do, I second-guess myself endlessly.

Then there's my ridiculously bad sense of direction. Even

after living in New York for ten years, I have to consult a map before setting off to *any* destination—new or not. When I was in graduate school, there was one class that met in a different building from all the others, and every week when class ended, I'd walk outside and head the wrong way down the sidewalk. Every class, for the whole semester. I was living in student housing, and each week after I'd taken a few steps, I'd hear my name from a classmate who lived in my building; I'd turn around and he'd be pointing in the opposite direction. Could this geographical dyslexia mean that my brain also has lower activity levels in the area of spatial orientation, like a hoarder's? It seems possible.

I'm shy and prone to isolation the way my mother is, and I often have to force myself to make plans with people or go to a party. When I do, I'm always glad I did, but I have to remind myself to make the effort. My natural tendency is to stay inside and nest.

And I'm a perfectionist, there's no question. But my mother is responsible for only half my genes, which means I have a fifty-fifty chance of ending up like my dad, whose perfectionism forces him to continue working and working to the point where he endangers his own heart, rather than my mother's style, which shuts her down before she's even started.

I suppose the best inoculation is to try to be as self-aware as possible—and to trust that even though the propensity for hoarding may lie somewhere in my genetic code, that doesn't mean I'm doomed.

20

I'VE ALWAYS BEEN INTERESTED IN HEALTH AND HAVE wanted to write about it, so when one of my former students emails to tell me that she's been hired as an editor at a health website and asks if I'd like to write for her, I jump at the chance. Soon I'm writing articles about Alzheimer's disease, heart disease, and epilepsy. I write a series of five-hundred-word articles on psoriasis, then fibromyalgia. The more uncommon the condition, the more interested in it I find myself. I love the research, the interviews with all types of doctors and experts, and the writing itself.

It's been a few months since the stuffed snake incident and I'm feeling good. I feel freer of my mother and her house than I ever have, and I'm proud of myself. I'm also surprised at how easy it was.

I do feel a little wobbly when a student in one of my classes turns in a story about a woman with thirty-three cats, permanently drawn drapes, and towers of newspapers and mail on her front porch. In the story, she's referred to only as "the crazy cat lady."

My classes are workshops—the students hand out their stories one week and the following week listen and take notes while the rest of us critique the story. As I'm preparing for class and reading the story for the first time, I feel my face and neck flush when I get to the crazy cat lady. My hands shake. My skin prickles. I don't know how I'll be able to discuss this story without betraying my secret. And it's not just that. I'm a little disappointed in my student; he's sensitive and bright, not someone I'd expect to employ such an easy stereotype.

I always start the workshop by asking what a story's strengths are, and with this one everyone is impressed by the humor. They find the cat lady and her garbage-strewn, feline-filled lawn hysterical.

"Okay, but what else is there about this woman?" I ask the students. "Does she feel like a well-rounded character, or does she feel like a—"

"She's a crazy cat lady," one of them blurts out. "What else is there to know?"

"What kind of history does she have? How did she get to this point?"

Silence.

I find the whole thing sad. And I'm offended on my mother's behalf.

But just like when I couldn't get upset with our subletter over the "dirty" apartment accusation, I can't get upset now. They don't know any better. Many, if not most, people don't. So many people have no concept of hoarders as real human beings. So many people have no idea that hoarding is a mental illness, and that those suffering from it have feelings, pasts, and sometimes even children.

I START WONDERING if there's a story about hoarding I could write for the health website, something that could help humanize the disorder (this is still a few years before the reality shows about hoarding debut). I begin doing preliminary research. Much has been written about the Collyer brothers, but I didn't know that the term "Collyer's mansion," is used by rescue personnel all along the East Coast to refer to a clutter-packed home, where rescue workers may have a hard time getting through. Similarly, in the Midwest, a hoarded home is labeled a "packer house," and on the West Coast it's called a "Habitrail house."

When I read these epithets, I picture my mother's house in flames, with three or four firemen stopped at the doorway, surveying the obstacle-crammed interior as one of them radios in, "We've got a packer house here. Send more guys."

The thought brings tears to my eyes. I so desperately want her to change, want her house to change. But, I remind myself, I'm done taking care of her. I walked away.

Still, I want to understand. So I read articles, studies, interviews with specialists in the field, and books about hoarding. I'm fascinated by a 2005 study of people who suddenly began to hoard after traumatic brain injuries. One subject was a twenty-seven-year-old man, who after undergoing surgery for a brain aneurysm, began to accumulate tools that were nearly the same (and sometimes exactly the same) as tools he already had. After he bought the items, he completely lost interest; many times he didn't even bother to take them out of the bags.

Just like my mother and her unopened Savers bags clogging up the hallway. It's as if having the possession isn't important. It's the acquisition, and the high that accompanies it, that matters—which is one reason some specialists are looking into the possibility that hoarding is an impulse control disorder, like compulsive gambling or kleptomania.

The more I research the topic, though, the more I begin to question my idea of writing an article about it. For one thing, so far my articles have all been five-hundred words long. It would be impossible to sum up hoarding in that short a space. And more important, it wouldn't be like the Children of Hoarders message boards where I got an anonymous email account so no one could trace the words *my mother is a hoarder* back to me. I'm a terrible liar. If my editor or someone else asked why I wanted to write an article about hoarding, what would I say?

THE REST OF that fall, things are okay between my mother and me. She knows she screwed up by sending that stupid stuffed snake and she's on good behavior. When I talk to her on the phone she's more subdued, but not in a depressed-sounding way, just in a controlled way.

In November, she asks if David and I are coming to Minneapolis that Christmas and I say yes.

"Good, because I might need you guys to move a shelf for me."

"I told you, I'm not setting foot inside your house again."

"But the bugs are gone!" she says. "My house is safe, I promise!"

"It's not about the bugs, Mom. I just don't want to go into your house. I can't be responsible for it anymore."

"Fine. I'll just hire someone to do it, then," she says, as snappish toward me as I've heard in years.

"Good idea," I say.

* * *

WHEN DAVID AND I get to Minneapolis that December, we bring my mother to a new Vietnamese restaurant in St. Paul for lunch. It's two days before Christmas; yesterday Sandy suggested I invite my mom to their house on Christmas Eve. They've never done that before.

"Are you sure?" my mom says when I tell her. Her eyes are wide.

"I'm sure. It would be nice, wouldn't it?" I tell her my stepsister is inviting her dad and her high school boyfriend so it'll be a small group of Christmas orphans and not just her.

"You should come, Helen," David says. "It'll be fun. We'll play Trivial Pursuit."

"Oh, I love Trivial Pursuit!" my mom says. "But are you sure it's okay?"

"Yes, Mom. That's why they invited you."

"Well, okay then! Why not?" She picks up her teacup and takes a big swig.

I'm happy to be able to give my mom a place to go on Christmas Eve. Even though she never celebrates holidays and claims not to care about them (and as a kid her family never celebrated Hanukkah or even the kids' birthdays), I always feel sad on holidays because I know my mother is alone. No matter how much fun I'm having there's always a little part of me thinking of her.

The food arrives then and my husband, being the adventurous eater he is, has ordered frog legs. I can't help but think of Abraham Lincoln's bad back leg when I see the withered, breaded stalks.

My mom picks up an egg roll and takes a bite. "These are absolutely delicious!"

"These aren't," David says, pushing his plate away.

My mom dumps soy sauce on the other dish she's ordered, fried shrimp, which glisten under the restaurant's fluorescent lights.

"You shouldn't be eating greasy food, Mom." I know I'm nagging, but it's frustrating that she hasn't changed her diet at all since the cancer. And now that I've already started, I might as well continue: "And be careful about using too much salt. Soy sauce has a ton of sodium in it."

"I hardly ever use salt." She spears a shrimp. "Oh, I have to ask you two something. See, I've got this shelf in my kitchen, and I want to paint the wall that it's covering, but it's too heavy for me to move. Could you two do it when you drop me off?"

"Is this that same shelf you asked about before?" I say.

"Yup." She takes a gulp of her tea.

"I thought you were going to hire someone to do it."

She shrugs. "I didn't know how to find someone."

"You could have called my dad and Sandy—they would have given you Joe's phone number."

"I didn't want to bother them."

David looks at me and cocks his head, as if to say, *Why not?*

And I'm thinking the same thing. Oh, why not.

Maybe it'll even be a good challenge, a test of my willpower to see if I can go into her house and resist the urge to clean.

I think I can. And I have to admit, I'm curious about the way her house looks. I'm more than curious: I'm excited. I try to tamp down that feeling. It's just a house, a house I'm no longer responsible for. Just a house.

"Should we?" I ask David.

"Yeah," he says and I get even more excited, though I'm not about to let my mother know that.

* * *

AFTER LUNCH, ON the way to my mom's house, I ask David to stop by dad and Sandy's. David and my mom wait in the car while I run inside and grab two pairs of rubber gloves from a box under the sink.

"Don't take this the wrong way, Mom," I say when I get back into the car with the gloves. "But after what we went through, I'm not taking any chances."

"It's okay," she says. "I understand."

My stomach does a nervous flip-flop when we get to my mother's house, even though I saw the exterior when we picked her up. Her house always looks better in the winter because you can't tell the state of the lawn when it's covered by snow. The sidewalk isn't shoveled, though, which is a problem. In Minneapolis you can be fined for not keeping your sidewalk clear. I don't remember her telling me about a falling out with Mean Lesbian Neighbor, but I'll need to ask her about it. My mom is walking ahead of David and me up the icy, snow-packed path to her front door. I grab his arm and lean close: "Don't touch anything besides the shelf. And don't touch anything at all without these gloves."

He nods.

When my mother pulls open the door to the front porch and we step inside, I shouldn't be surprised to see stacks of boxes, full garbage bags, and a mound of mail that—judging by its size—is at least a month old. I shouldn't be surprised, yet I am. I take a deep breath and tell myself to stay calm. It's not my problem.

She fumbles to get her plastic coil of keys out of her fanny pack/purse, and I feel a cold dread in my rib cage. I'm beginning to wonder if coming here was such a good idea. But it's just a shelf. We'll be here five minutes. Finally she unlocks the house's heavy front door. I motion to David and we both put on our rubber gloves and step inside.

The hallway isn't as crowded as I feared. The china cabinet is in clear view, not buried by clutter. Some of the coats are actually on hangers on the freestanding clothing rack. Some, though, are piled underneath—I have to pin my arms to my sides to keep from picking them up and properly hanging them. In the corner sits a stack of three boxes with a bunch of mittens and scarves and hats piled on top. All in all, it's not that bad.

Then we walk into the kitchen.

"There's the shelf," my mom says. "See, wouldn't that wall look good if it were blue?"

"The shelf" is one of those giant metal shelving units that normally go in a garage for tools. This one appears to hold pots, pans, pasta strainers, and other cooking supplies. Each of the three shelves on it is fully packed, but at least they're halfway neat.

I wish I could say the same for the rest of the room.

Her kitchen is total chaos.

Empty paper grocery bags lie like rejected kites all over the dingy linoleum floor. The counter is crowded with cereal boxes and stacks of paper plates and glossy black rolls of garbage bags and cans of soup and at least three toasters. The kitchen table is equally cluttered, if not more so, and the new stove and refrigerator are covered in grime.

And that damn dishwasher is still here.

"Is that thing working yet?" I ask, pointing at it.

"Almost," my mom says, and I feel my jaw tighten.

"Mom, why? This kitchen looked so good. What happened?"

"What do you mean?"

David's looking around in amazement. He hasn't been inside since the first cleanout, which was almost five years ago. He's probably forgotten how bad her house can get and how overwhelming it can feel to be inside it.

"Tell me," I say, "what's the point of painting that wall when the whole room is such a mess?"

"Oh, it's not bad," she says.

I realize that one of the hallmarks of hoarding is lack of insight into the problem, and I've witnessed my mother's blindness to hers more than once. But I'm still shocked. How can she not see it? I feel like shaking her until she wakes up.

Instead, I snatch the roll of garbage bags from the counter, tear one off, and start tossing in trash from her kitchen table.

"Jessie! I need some of those things," my mother says.

I pause. I look down at the garbage bag, open in my hands. What am I doing? But then again, dumping a few things doesn't count as cleaning. "You need an empty Styrofoam coffee cup? Or dried-up, moldy lemons? Do you really need filled-in crossword puzzles?" I look at the dates on the edges of the puzzles. "From seven months ago!"

"I guess not."

David has already started taking the pots and pans off the metal shelving unit, stacking them on one of the kitchen chairs. "Helen, where do you want us to move this? There's not really another wall that's big enough for it."

"I just want the shelf moved temporarily. Just move it forward a few feet so I can paint behind it, and then I'll get someone to move it back."

"Hang on a minute," I say. "No. You'll never move it back and it'll end up staying in the middle of the room just like this dishwasher."

"So I shouldn't bother taking the stuff off?" David asks me.

"No, I don't think so."

"But how will I paint that wall, then?" my mom asks.

"I thought you weren't going to Savers anymore?" I ask her,

holding up two muffin tins I've just discovered that both bear bright pink Savers price tags.

"I'm not."

"Then what's this?" I point to one of the tags.

"Hey," David says, "there are four more of those, right here." He's holding a stack of muffin tins from the metal shelves. Two are still in boxes.

"Really?" my mom asks. She goes over to take a look.

"Oh, I see," my mother says, studying the items in David's arms. "One is for little muffins, no, *two* are for little muffins, the really tiny ones that are so cute, and see, this one is stainless steel and here, this one is ceramic." She turns to me, holding up a grimy box with a black-and-white illustration on the side. "Isn't that fantastic, Jessie? A ceramic muffin pan!"

"Do you make muffins, Helen?" David asks. If I'd asked the question I wouldn't have been able to keep the sarcasm out of my voice, but David sounds sincerely curious, and maybe he is. My mom does have manic baking marathons occasionally, like when she was making bread after my dad's heart attack.

"I haven't yet," she says. "But I'm going to. I'm going to *very* soon!"

I'm tempted to try to convince her to let me get rid of three of the muffin tins, but David's stacking everything neatly back on the shelf and they don't take up too much room. I'll save the conniving/begging/bribing for something bigger.

I've filled the garbage bag with stuff from the table and milk cartons and coffee cans from the floor, so I tie it up and carry it to the back door. "I'll be right back," I say, and duck outside. I don't have a coat on so I run across her snowy backyard as fast as I can to the trash can in the alley.

When I come back in, David's standing by the back door.

"Magpie," he whispers. "What are you doing? Remember,

you decided that cleaning isn't your responsibility anymore. *Remember*?"

"It's okay. I mean, we're already here. Do you mind if we stay and clean just a little?"

"I guess not," he says. "But only if it's not going to upset you too much."

"I'm fine," I say. "Really. Completely fine."

Actually I'm better than fine.

I feel absolutely exhilarated. Alive.

"Okay, if you're sure," he says as we walk back into the kitchen.

I hear the staticky sounds of a radio and peek into the living room where my mom is trying to find a station on her clunky '80s-era stereo. The living room is cluttered to a medium-pack rat degree, but the kitchen is clearly the epicenter of the hoarding and where I need to focus my attention. At least for today.

"What should I do?" David asks.

"Maybe clear off the counter? Throw out the empty boxes and anything else that should be tossed?"

"Sure," he says.

"Thanks, that'll be really helpful because I'm going to scour that table as soon as I find some sponges, and if you can get the counter cleared off, I'll be able to get that scrubbed down, too. After that I'll sweep and mop. And then I can clean the stove and refrigerator—"

"Don't forget, we need to get your dad's car back to him."

"Right. Do you know what time it is?" There are no clocks in my mom's kitchen.

David gets his phone out of his jeans pocket—awkwardly because of the rubber gloves—and tells me.

"That gives us an hour," I say, and just as I'm about to add, *not nearly enough time,* David says, "That's plenty of time."

Shoved at the back of the cabinet under the kitchen sink is a cellophane-wrapped four-pack of sponges. Actually there are a lot of cleaning supplies under here: bleach, dish soap, scouring pads, glass cleaner, and shiny green cylinders of Comet. I grab the sponges and one of the Comets and get to work on the table's stickiest spots.

Suddenly the radio comes on, the local NPR station, loud. Disturbingly loud. My mother appears in the doorway. "I just love this Ira Glass. Don't you just love Ira Glass, Dave?"

"Sure, Helen," he says, as he tosses the carcasses of cereal boxes into a garbage bag.

"Do you like him, too, Jessie?"

"Mom, don't you think that's a little loud?"

I have to scream in order for her to hear me. She disappears into the living room. I'm instantly brought back to a day in my late teens when I was riding in my mom's car with her. She'd recently decided that she liked heavy metal music and insisted on blasting it as we drove; for a few minutes I felt like I had a cool mom, one of those moms who was more like a friend. One of those moms you could tell anything to. But then the song changed to something really grating and she refused to turn it down.

This time she's more amenable. She turns down the radio and comes back into the kitchen.

"I wish you and Dave could meet my friend Tina," she says. "She's just incredible. Do you think after this we could go over to Tina's house? Just for a few minutes? She only lives about ten minutes away."

"We need to get my dad's car back to him. He has to pick up some real estate signs for Sandy."

On the other hand, maybe I could call my dad and ask him if it's okay for us to be late with the car, so we can clean longer.

Or maybe David could drive the car back and return in a cab. Or it might be better for David to drive the car back, then have my dad drop him off here, and then when we're finished cleaning David and I could take a cab to my dad and Sandy's—

"Was there a fire here, Helen?" David says, and when I look over, he's pointing to the decades-old microwave on the counter.

"What?" I say, walking closer to it. The yellow Formica underneath the microwave is brown—I thought it was dirt or coffee grounds, but now I can see that the counter has been scorched.

"Just a little one," she says.

"Are you serious?" I ask. "You had a fire?"

We've got a packer house here. Send more guys.

"It was nothing. It didn't get farther than the counter."

I pull out one of the kitchen chairs and collapse onto it. I feel hollowed out, all my energy sapped. "Do you know how scary that is, Mom?"

"Helen, is it okay if I use your bathroom?" David asks, already walking out of the room. He probably senses an argument and wants to flee the scene before it happens.

"Of course, Dave. You know where it is."

"This is serious," I say to my mom. She's leaning against the refrigerator with her arms crossed over her chest. "If you had a fire here, no one could get in. You could die. It's happened before, in houses like this."

"But look," she says, pointing to the hall. "They could get in. The hallway is clear."

"It is now. But what about six months from now, or a year, or two years? How long will it stay clear?"

"Forever," she says.

I can't let my mom die in this house.

"We need to get you some help. Would you please consider seeing a therapist who specializes in hoarding?"

"Oh, no. I don't need that."

"What about hiring a cleaning person? I could do the initial cleanout and then we'll have someone come in once or twice a week for maintenance."

I've said these things before, but I'm desperate.

"A cleaning person isn't necessary," my mom says. "And it's too expensive."

David comes back into the kitchen, wiping his hands on his jeans. He's no longer wearing his gloves, but I guess it doesn't really matter. He's clearly trying to stay out of our conversation because he walks right past us to the counter, where he continues picking up and shaking cereal boxes and cracker containers, trying to figure out which ones are full and which are empty.

"Besides," my mom says, "you don't need to worry about fires. I've got smoke detectors. See?" She points to a spot above the door to the basement, where a tiny red dot is blinking on a white plastic device. Okay. That makes me feel a little better. "And there's another one," she says and points above the refrigerator, where high up on the wall there is indeed another smoke detector.

"What about in the other rooms?" I ask.

"Oh, yeah, I've got one in every room. I've even got one on the front porch. I put them up about six months ago."

That's why I didn't see them last time I was here. They're a huge relief. For once my mother's partial paranoia is a good thing.

"Listen, Jessie," my mom says, lifting a frying pan from the stack of dirty ones on the stove. "I want to show you this new cleaning method I've got." She carries the pan over to the sink, where she fills it with water and dish soap. Then she walks back to the stove with it—carefully so none of the soapy water spills—sets it down on one of the burners, and turns on the flame. "See, what I do is boil the soap in the pan. That way I know it's clean."

"Oh, Mom."

DAVID AND I get as much done as we can before my dad needs his car back, and when we leave and the fresh cold air hits my face, the embarrassment and anger at myself sets in. I failed in my vow not to enter her house.

Worse, I failed at my vow not to clean.

I thought I was better, I thought I'd successfully separated myself from my mother's compulsive hoarding, but I hadn't. My obsession with cleaning her house hadn't ended. I should have known it was too easy. The first chance I had, I caved—all it took was walking through the front door. I have no control when it comes to my mother's house. None.

But then again, maybe it's not such a bad thing. Maybe I can clean a few hours each time I visit. A semiannual maintenance. After all, who could it hurt?

21

MY FRIEND JULIA AND I ARE FANATICAL ABOUT THE HBO show *The Wire*—we can talk about it for most of a cocktail or dinner party, much to the annoyance of those around us—and for months we've been waiting for the season premiere in the first week of January. I've invited her over to watch it and for the occasion, I buy a nice bottle of red wine and make a special trip to Sahadi's for hummus, baba ganoush, olives, and little spinach pies.

There's just one small problem. A few days after David and I were in my mom's house cleaning, I started itching again, all over. But I know it's a coincidence. It has to be. I don't want to say anything to David because it will just freak him out unnecessarily. The air was so dry at my dad and Sandy's, and it is in our apartment, too. That must be it.

When my friend comes over she's wearing ballet flats without socks, even though it's winter. Although it's impossible that we have the bugs again, I'm still relieved when she doesn't take off her shoes and walk barefoot through our place. We have a pleasant evening, and when Julia leaves I go out with her so I can walk Abraham Lincoln.

As soon as I come back into the apartment, David says, "Magpie," in that tone and I know what he's going to say. Actually after that he doesn't say anything, he just holds his forearm out toward me, where there's a big red welt.

"A mosquito bite?" I say hopefully, even though it's not mosquito season.

He shakes his head and lifts his shirt. Two more welts. "To be honest I've thought they were back for a few days but I didn't say anything because I wanted to be sure."

"Fucking hell," I say. "I thought the same thing."

David drops down to the couch, shaking his head.

Abraham Lincoln is standing in the doorway between the living room and the kitchen, staring at David and wagging his tail. He's waiting for his postwalk treat, which David always doles out.

I march up the stairs to the sleeping loft. In the bottom drawer of the nightstand I kept a bottle of the sulfur lotion and it's still there at the back of the drawer. Somehow I must have known we'd have the bugs again.

When I come back down to the living room, David is frowning, petting Abraham Lincoln distractedly.

I start to pace. I pass the open bathroom door and have an urge to tear off my clothes and turn the shower on as hot as possible, then curl up on the floor of the tub, letting the water beat down on me until every fucking bug is drowned and dead. If I thought it might work, I'd do it.

"If she doesn't have the bugs," David says, "how could we

have gotten them from being in her house? Wouldn't she have them, too?"

"I would think. But with these things, who the hell knows?"

"Could we have worn something that was still infected?" David asks. "Maybe something we forgot to wash?"

"From a year and a half ago? I don't know, maybe my mom never got rid of hers." I sit down next to David and put my head in my hands.

"But how could that be? And besides, we've seen her twice since we were cured and we didn't get them."

"True." And for the last few years, whenever we walk anywhere she insists on holding on to my arm, so we've even had skin-to-skin contact. My bloodstream is coursing with adrenaline, every muscle tight. "I'm going to call her right now." I jump to my feet, but David grabs my hand and pulls me back.

"Let's do the medicine tonight and see what happens—maybe we don't really have them. We don't know for sure."

It's after midnight anyway, and though my mother often stays up until 4:00 or 5:00 in the morning knitting or reading, she wouldn't answer her phone now. I never call this late and she doesn't pick up for anyone else.

I grab the three wineglasses from the table, carrying them by their stems into the kitchen.

Oh, no. Julia.

I step back into the living room. "I'm going to have to tell Julia. What if she gets them? I should email her right now."

"You should. I mean, you have to."

"But what'll I say? Oh, hey thanks for coming over and, by the way, you now have scabies!"

"What about keeping it vague? Maybe say we were exposed to something . . . maybe something from your cousin Billy . . . don't little kids always get rashes and infections? Ask her if she's noticed any itching and tell her to keep an eye out for it. Then, if she writes back and says yes, that she's itching, you are definitely going to have to tell her."

"That's what I'll do."

These bugs have done the impossible: They've turned back time. I'm right back in that awful, awful summer. The memory of those four months remains in my muscles and I feel myself hunching my shoulders, trying to make myself disappear.

"Why did I go back in there!" I scream. Abraham Lincoln jumps down from the couch and dashes into the front room.

"It's my fault," David says.

"How could it be your fault?"

"I took off my gloves." He shakes his head. "I never should have taken off those fucking gloves."

WE START THE sulfur lotion that night and spend most of the next day cleaning and doing laundry. David's winter coat is washable, but mine is a vintage orange wool pea coat. I put on the warmest washable coat I have, a jean jacket, over a thick sweatshirt and walk to Old Navy, where I buy a cheap puffy black coat. It's so shapeless that I feel like I'm walking around in a sleeping bag, but it can go in the dryer.

I wrap my wool coat in a garbage bag and stash it in the back of the closet, knowing I won't wear it again until next winter, if then. Throughout the day I grow angrier and angrier, at myself and at my mother, especially as I see the mental toll this is taking on David. He's trying to stay positive, but his brows are permanently furrowed and he hardly says anything. He opens a beer at 5:00, which he rarely does, and drinks it in about ten minutes. After that, I open one, too.

We were both holding out hope that this was a false alarm,

but by the time we decide what to have for dinner—takeout Korean because neither of us wants to cook—it's obvious that we have the bugs again. We're both itching severely and getting bites.

After dinner I call my mom. At first she thinks I'm joking.

"I wouldn't joke about that," I say. "Believe me."

"But how, Jessie, how?"

"You tell me."

"Oh my God. Let me think here . . . let me think . . . I just don't know how it could have happened . . ." She sounds so genuinely concerned that it catches me off guard. "I don't have them anymore," she says. "I think I don't. No, I really don't think I do. Are you sure you have them?"

"I'm sure."

"And Dave, too?"

"Yes. Thankfully, we still have some of the lotion."

She's silent for a few seconds. Then she bursts out: "Oh, no, Jessie!"

"What?"

"I was at your dad and Sandy's on Christmas Eve. What if I gave it to the people there? Oh, and I had such a nice time, too, with that delicious meal and the Trivial Pursuit."

She'd been cute and fun that night. I was on her team and she got every question right, answering the other team's under her breath. "You didn't give it to them. They didn't come into your house."

"If they get it, too . . . I just don't know what I'll do if I gave these things to them. And you and Dave, when you were so nice to clean my kitchen that day . . ." She sounds choked up, as if she might cry, and I can't help but soften toward her.

"Mom, you need to do the medicine. The sulfur lotion this time," I say gently. "Either they're still in your house or maybe you have the bugs without having symptoms. Do you have any of the lotion left?"

"I'm not sure. I think so. Maybe. Oh, Jessie, I'm so sorry. I just . . . I just can't believe it. Please tell Dave how sorry I am." She's actually moaning.

"It'll be all right. At least this time we know what it is and how to get rid of it. We'll be fine, Mom, don't worry."

And just like that, I'm comforting my mother for giving us the bugs again. That makes a lot of sense.

OVER THE NEXT week, I keep trying to reach my mom, but she's not answering her phone. I'm worried because she sounded so out of sorts when I talked to her—and sometimes when I worry I fall into an ugly downward spiral of "what ifs." Everywhere I am: the grocery store, the library, the ATM, the Laundromat, the gym, walking with Abraham Lincoln, wherever I am, I imagine my husband coming through the door or down the street, searching for me with a scared look on his face; I imagine him approaching as if I'm very fragile and saying, "Something happened. It's your mom."

And then he'll tell me that she's killed herself. She's never threatened suicide, but between her history of serious depression, how guilty she feels, and the fact that last time she was pretty much committing slow suicide with the bleach baths and the lindane, who's to say what she's capable of?

I call and call but she doesn't answer and I can't leave a message because her voice mail is full. Not that she ever checks it anyway. So typical. So maddening, especially because I have another pressing reason I need to reach her: We're running out of the sulfur lotion and I need her to get more from her doctor. It's not working as quickly as it did last time. And this time

David's even getting bites on his face. He's puffy and uncomfortable and he's really pissed off. I feel like crying whenever I look at him. The only good news is that my friend Julia assures me she has no itchiness whatsoever.

I begin calling my mother every hour. Then I remember a signal we used years ago and decide to try it. I call and let the phone ring once, hang up, wait a minute, and call back. She picks up.

"Mom, are you okay?"

"Oh, hi, honey!" She doesn't sound depressed. She doesn't sound distraught.

"I've been worried about you," I say.

"About me? I'm fine. How're you?"

"Not well," I say. "Pretty terrible, actually. We're running out of the sulfur lotion and I need you to get us some more."

My mother says nothing.

"Mom? Are you there?"

"So what's the weather like in New York?"

"What?"

"I'm asking you what the weather is like there."

"What's going on? Aren't you going to say anything about getting us more lotion?"

"I've thought about it since we talked and I'm convinced you must have gotten it another way. I just don't see how you could have gotten them from my house when I don't have them."

The hairs on the back of my neck bristle. "Maybe when we were there we touched something you haven't touched in a while—like your broom or your mop."

"Ha, ha," she says. "Look, I'm sorry you two are going through this."

"You're sorry we're *going through this*? It's your fault we're going through this."

"I don't know what to tell you, Jessie." Her voice is cold. Distant. Controlled.

"What you're going to tell me is that tomorrow morning you're going to see Dr. Paulsen to get a prescription for more sulfur lotion. I can't get it here—I tried last time, remember?"

"Dr. Paulsen hates me now. I asked for too many prescriptions and now whenever I go there the nurses tell me he's busy and to make an appointment."

"Then call and make an appointment," I say. "Look, I don't care how you do it, but you need to get us some of that lotion. David has bites all over his face."

"Really?" I hear laughter in her voice. I'm sure it's nervousness, but even that's unacceptable. All week I was worried about her and this is how she treats me. How she treats David.

"Don't you fucking dare laugh about this, Mom."

"Jessie, I'm sorry, but I can't go back to Dr. Paulsen. I can't help you."

I can't help you.

As if she ever could.

My chest goes tight. I'm hot, light-headed—not as if I might faint, but as if I might lift off, blasting out the window and into the sky. I don't think I've ever been this angry.

"Listen, Mom. If you don't do this for me, this one thing I'm asking—"

"But I can't!"

"If you don't do this for me," I say and now I've moved beyond anger, beyond rage. "If you don't do this for me, Mom, then we're done."

As I say the words, I know it's already happened. We *are* done with the way things were. Even after I told myself I'd walked away, I still clung to a shred of hope that I could change her, that I could unclutter her mind so she could be a normal mother. I did. That's why I had that most recent cleaning frenzy. Somewhere inside me, hope remained. Now that hope is gone. I'm done for real this time. I'm done cleaning her house, I'm done feeling responsible for her, I'm done feeling guilty that I can't fix her.

There's a line I read somewhere about the climax scene in a story: Something must die, so something else might live. I must kill my obsession with cleaning my mother's house.

It's dying.

There.

Now it's dead.

And what will live? My sanity, my marriage, my skin. Me.

"Okay, fine," my mother says. "Fine. I'll go see Dr. Paulsen."

THREE DAYS LATER a box arrives from my mother and I ask David to open it in case of snakes. Other than five big bottles of the lotion, the box is empty.

I call my mom to thank her, but she doesn't pick up the phone, and I don't try again.

Instead, I find the online Children of Hoarders group again. This time I introduce myself to the group and post some of my story, mostly about the last year and a half. I write that at this point I can't even muster anger at my mother; I'm just profoundly disappointed and sad. I feel heartbroken, like I'm grieving. In a way, I guess I am.

Right away I get responses: *Welcome, Jess,* and *We're happy to have you here,* and *I hear you,* and over the next few hours, as I read their stories and respond to some posts, I begin to feel something I rarely have: a sense of belonging. It's intoxicating to feel understood. The empathy among members works like an antidote, neutralizing the poison of my secret, of all of our secrets.

Someone's posted a link to a site about adult children of alcoholics, because there are so many shared characteristics between them and children of hoarders. It makes sense: Both are shame-soaked atmospheres, in which the child is almost always parentified, or made to feel like the adult in the situation. Both circumstances can rob children of their childhoods. Because my parents went through rehab and got sober when I was a kid, as a teenager I was given a few books about codependency and about being the adult child of an alcoholic. I even attended some Alateen meetings back when my mom was hanging out at The Club. I still remember the advice I heard there: You can't change anyone else. You can only change yourself. It was something I'd known once, but had forgotten.

IT'S A FEW more weeks before David and I really feel like the bugs are gone. During that time, one of my best friends has a baby. She wants David and me to visit her in the hospital after the baby's born, and we would love to, but we can't. We can't risk giving the bugs to a newborn, or to a new mother. No way. When I talk to my friend on the phone I plan to lie and say I have a cold, but I'm sick of lying, *so* sick of lying.

I say, "My mom is a pack rat, and when David and I were in Minneapolis at Christmas we cleaned her house and now we both have a skin condition that's contagious."

"Poor thing, that sounds terrible," she says. "It's okay. You'll meet the baby another time."

My friend seems not at all concerned by my admission about the "skin condition" and more important, that my mother is a pack rat (that label doesn't give a full picture of the disorder, but sounds so much better than "hoarder," such an ugly word).

I'm surprised by how good it feels to tell my friend the truth.

It's not unlike the thrill I get when I throw things out. Afterward I feel lighter. And in the coming weeks I begin to think about picking up that article idea I'd abandoned—the one about compulsive hoarding that I'd been too much of a coward to pitch. Maybe I'll end up doing it after all.

SHORTLY AFTER DAVID and I are cured, my mother calls me in a panic. "Oh, Jessie," she says. "I really screwed up. I think I have the bugs, too. Maybe I had them all along and I didn't know!"

Anger rushes hotly through me, then drains away. I'm so tired of being angry at my mother. I don't have the energy for it anymore. I don't have the desire.

"Do the sulfur lotion, Mom. That's all I'm going to tell you. The lotion. That's it."

"Yes, honey. I'll do it."

She does the lotion for weeks, and finally that's the true end of the bugs. Later she assures me that she's thrown out anything that could possibly be contaminated (I'm not sure I believe her but I'm not about to go and check). Did she really have them the whole time and not know? Highly unlikely. It's equally absurd that something in her house was still infested. We'll probably never have a conclusive answer.

Regardless, knowing she's free of them, that her house is free of them, doesn't change a thing.

I'm still done.

22

SIX MONTHS AFTER OUR SECOND BUG ENCOUNTER, MY husband and I are spending Fourth of July weekend in Minneapolis. We're meeting my mom at an Indian restaurant she's been wanting to try that has an all-you-can-eat buffet. This will be the first time we've seen her since the day we cleaned her kitchen. Things have changed since then. A lot. As crazy as it sounds, I'm glad we got the bugs a second time: They snapped me back to reality.

And the reality is that I cannot stop my mother's hoarding. Only she can do that. The reality is that I am not responsible for her house. She is.

David and I get to the restaurant before she does. I'm not feeling great; I've got a cold and am congested and tired. I lean against the brick of the building as we wait for her to arrive.

Finally we see her rusty boat drive past us on its way into the parking lot.

A minute later she walks up. She's her typical rumpled-looking self, with a moth-eaten sweater jacket and her keys jangling on a plastic neon-orange coil around her neck. She's also wearing a tiny backpack over her shoulders and carrying her giant travel mug.

"Hi, Helen," David says.

"Hi, Dave. Hi, Jessie." She's blinking too much. She's nervous. "How are you two?"

"Good," David says, at the same time I say, "Sick."

"How are you, Mom?" I ask.

"I'm starving!" she says as David pulls open the restaurant's thick glass door.

I stop at the bathroom to blow my nose. When I join David and my mom at the booth, the waiter is standing there and we all order the lunch buffet. My mom also asks for coffee, holding up her travel mug for him to see.

Though it's prime lunchtime, there's no one else in the restaurant. The buffet table is draped in white cloth, with six different dishes lined up, three on each side, flanked by two big bowls of rice at one end and naan bread and chutneys at the other. While David and I make one trip around the buffet, taking portions of a few different things, my mom is zigzagging all over the place, and managing to move pretty swiftly, for her. Even after her plate is crowded, she keeps heaping on more, her lips pursed in concentration as she ladles on another scoop of *saag paneer* and chicken *tikka masala*.

David and I sit down and she yells over to us, "Don't wait for me. Eat while it's still hot."

By the time she slides clumsily into the booth David and I are both halfway finished. Her entire plate is covered. Because it's Indian and most dishes are stewy, the food can't exactly tower, but she has managed to make it into a mountainous mass, with three pieces of naan sticking out like footholds.

"Helen," David says, "don't you know that you can go back? It's all-you-can-eat."

"I know, but I couldn't decide what to try first."

I sneeze into my napkin and my husband smiles and nods his head as I sneeze a second time, then a third—for some reason I always sneeze in threes.

"Bless you," David says. My mother takes a bite of *saag paneer*.

"Thanks," I say and get up. "Be right back."

I go into the bathroom to wash my hands.

"You're okay?" David says when I return.

I nod. "Thanks for asking."

"I'm going for seconds," David says, and I slide out of the booth so he can get past me.

"Isn't this food fantastic, Jessie?" my mother asks as I sit down again.

"I wouldn't know," I say. "I can't taste very well right now, because I've got a cold." I realize that I'm being juvenile, bitchy, but it irks me that my mother never seems to notice or care when I'm sick.

And like clockwork, my mom changes the subject. "So what are you reading, Jessie?"

A tiny bomb goes off in my head. "Mom, can I ask you something?"

"Of course, honey. You can ask me anything."

"Why don't you ever care when I'm sick?"

"Oh," my mother says and looks down at her plate, her fork frozen in the air.

"I really want to know," I say. "It's something I've always wondered."

My mom sets down her fork. She looks up and meets my eyes. She's not smiling. "I know you're angry with me and I understand your anger," she says. "Please know that for as much anger as you have, I have that much regret."

I wait for her to laugh.

I count to ten, then twenty. Still, no laughter.

My mother's hands are on the table, one on each side of her plate. Her weird little thumbs with the crescent-shaped sliver of a nail. She's doing this thing where she rubs the side of her thumb along the pad of her index finger. I look down at my own hands and I'm doing the exact same thing.

I have a choice.

I make it.

"What are *you* reading, Mom?" I ask.

"Oh, Jessie, didn't I tell you? I'm reading all of Proust and it is ab-so-lute-ly incredible. Have you ever read him?"

"Only snippets for a class once," I say.

And just like that things are back to normal. Well, normal for us. Which is not normal, nor is it even consistent in its abnormality, but somehow my mother and I have found a way to navigate.

"My God, how that man could write," my mom says. David comes back then and sits down next to me. "What about you, Dave, what are you reading right now?"

While they talk, I find myself imagining that I've shrunk myself down, so tiny that I'm microscopic. As this microscopic being I'm able to enter my mother's mind. Once I'm in, I try to look around. It's dark, too dark to see. But I can feel what's in there. And there's so much. It's filled with isolation and disregard and abuse. It's filled with uncertainty and self-doubt. It's filled with laughter, too. It's filled with friendless winters. It's filled with salty breezes and ten happy years with a man who truly loved her. It's filled with chaos and emptiness when that man was gone. It's filled with ideas for flexible knitting needles and new ways to hold paintbrushes and keep notes tidy and protect one's knees and clip dollar bills and warm a neck; it's filled with information from newspapers, books, magazines; it's filled with rejections and preemptive rejections and self-loathing. It's filled with confusion. And fear. More than anything, it's filled with fear. It's a frightening vantage point from which to view the world and just as that microscopic being feels herself suffocating, my mother calls my name.

"Jessie, right? Don't you think?" my mom is asking.

"Sorry, what?" I say, coming back to the real world.

"Don't you think that show about the little people is just hysterical? I could watch that show all day long. They're just such a wonderful family. Such wonderful people . . ."

David and I look at each other and we both can't help but laugh.

"What?" my mom asks.

"Nothing. Sorry," I say, and my mom smiles.

"You two are funny," she says, looking from David to me. She wraps her fingers around her travel mug and picks it up in both hands to take a sip. It's empty. "Say," my mom calls out to the waiter. "Could I have some mo-ah coffee?"

AFTER LUNCH, MY mom gets into her car, and David and I get into the one we borrowed from my dad. When we drive away, for a split second I consider asking my husband to go past my mom's house so I can see how it looks. But I don't. I don't need to know.

Every so often I feel those papers at the lawyer's office beating like a telltale heart, my burden. They don't really matter, though. I'm her daughter, so with or without the papers, chances are someday—far, far off into the future, I hope—that house will become mine.

Someday, that mess of a house will be mine to deal with.

Probably.

But not today.

EPILOGUE

IT'S BEEN ALMOST THREE YEARS SINCE THAT DAY AT THE Indian restaurant. My mother's health is fine, in spite of the lack of green vegetables in her diet. My dad's health is fine, too. I haven't been inside my mother's house since the kitchen-cleaning-frenzy day. And I won't, until I absolutely must. My mother understands this, and other than claiming her house is "like a gazillion times better," she hardly mentions it anymore. And I never ask.

A few days ago my mother called me, breathless with excitement. "Oh, Jessie, I just bought the most beautiful new car!"

"Did your car break down?" I asked. This happens with some regularity, as she always buys clunkers.

"No, no, it's fine, but now I have a spare. Anyway, Jessie, I can't tell you how beautiful this car is! And the best part is, it's a station wagon, so it's big enough for when I go—"

She cut herself off. I knew we hadn't been disconnected, because I could hear her breathing.

"Shopping," I said. "You were going to say it's big enough for when you go shopping."

"It's true." She laughed. "I was going to say shopping."

I could have launched into a lecture; I could have gotten frustrated. But what would be the point? I'm no longer that ten-year-old girl trying desperately to fix her so she'll become the mother I want her to be. She is who she is. I can accept it.

And I can admit it.

For so many years I was tormented by the idea of my mother's hoarding—her secret, which became *my* secret—becoming known, but once I began writing this book, I had no choice. When someone asked what I was working on, I couldn't lie. In the beginning, every time I said the words: "I'm writing a memoir about being the daughter of a compulsive hoarder," I'd set my jaw and feel my shoulders rise defiantly; I'd lock eyes with the person, scrutinizing for even the slightest flicker of judgment. I steeled myself for it. I expected it.

But no judgment came. Instead, people were curious and compassionate and empathetic: "My sister is the same way," or "My grandfather was like that," or "There was a guy like that in our neighborhood when I was a kid." Those who didn't have a personal connection to hoarding asked questions; nearly everyone wanted to understand it better. One day a friend emailed to tell me that *her* mother is a hoarder, too. A few days later another friend told me the same thing.

And an extraordinary thing happened: The more I talked about my mother's compulsive hoarding—and the more people who told me about their mothers, fathers, brothers, cousins, sisters, aunts—the weaker my secret became. Until it was gone.

ACKNOWLEDGMENTS

I owe enormous thanks to my diligent and dedicated agent, Melissa Sarver, who worked with me on this project from its inception, reading draft after draft and talking me through (and down when necessary) the entire process. It's a privilege to have you in my corner. I'm also very grateful to my exceptionally talented editor, Megan McKeever, whose enthusiasm for the project and shrewd editing skills made this a much better book and working on it a pleasure. Thank you to everyone at Gallery Books.

I'm forever indebted to my fabulous writing group, especially those who went way above and beyond: Paul Bravmann, Sandra Newman, and Michelle Herrera Mulligan. Huge thanks also to my brilliant friends who read drafts of this book: Anita Faranda, Lorna Graham, and Abbie Kozolchyk, as well as friends who've been supportive in ways too numerous to list: Erica Ackerberg, Alice Bradley, Mo Coslett, Catherine Coy, Nichole DiBenedetto, Elisabeth Eaves, Lauren Fox, Stephanie Elizondo Griest, Tania Grossinger, Melissa Ewey Johnson, Sol Kjok, Kate Lacey, Jana Larson, and Chloe Wing.

I would also like to thank my caring and kind in-law family, especially Cathy and Tom Kelly, who gave me the use of their bonus room at a crucial time. For the luxury of space and time to write, I'm also grateful to Wellspring House and the Writers' Colony at Dairy Hollow.

It's truly an honor to teach writing, and I'd like to thank everyone in The New School writing department for providing me with a place to do what I love. I'm constantly learning from my students, and I'd also like to thank all of them, past and present.

For her wisdom and counsel, I'm extremely grateful to Dr. Elizabeth Friedman.

To the founders of the Children of Hoarders message boards, and all the members: thank you, thank you, thank you. And thanks also to the many friends and acquaintances who've shared their own hoarding stories with me. Being able to talk openly about what was once an entirely hidden part of my life means the world to me.

It's to my father and stepmother that I owe everything. With the deepest gratitude I thank you both for your unconditional love, unceasing support, and for showing me, through example, the kind of lives and the kind of love that is possible. Thank you also for understanding my need to tell this story.

My sweet, smart, hilariously funny, and adorable husband, David Farley, has been encouraging me for years to write about my "dirty secret." This book would not exist without him. I'm utterly appreciative of his love, loyalty, spot-on editorial input, and wholehearted acceptance of me and all my weirdnesses. I still have no idea how I found such a wonderful husband, but every minute of every day I am grateful that I did.

And, of course, thank you to my mother, for allowing me to tell her story. Our story.

BIBLIOGRAPHY

ARTICLES

An, S. K., D. Mataix-Cox, N. S. Lawrence, S. Wooderson, V. Giampietro, A. Speckens, M. J. Brammer, and M. L. Phillips. "To Discard or Not to Discard: The Neural Basis of Hoarding and Symptoms in Obsessive-Compulsive Disorder." *Molecular Psychiatry*, 14 (2009): 318–331.

Anderson, Steven W., Hanna Damasio, and Antonio R. Damasio. "A Neural Basis for Collecting Behaviour in Humans." *Brain*, 128 (2005): 201–212.

Cermele, Jill A., Laura Melendez-Pallitto, and Gahan J. Pandina. "Intervention in Compulsive Hoarding: A Case Study." *Behavior Modification*, 25:2 (2001): 214–232.

Duenwald, Mary. "The Psychology of Hoarding: What Lies Beneath the Pathological Desire to Stockpile Tons of Stuff?" www.discovermagazine.com (October 1, 2004).

Frost, Randy O., and Rachel C. Gross. "The Hoarding of Possessions." *Behaviour Research and Therapy,* 31:4 (1993): 367–381.

Frost, Randy O., and Tamara L. Hartl. "A Cognitive-Behavioral Model of Compulsive Hoarding." *Behaviour Research and Therapy,* 34:4 (1996): 341–350.

Frost, Randy O., and Gail Steketee. "Hoarding: Clinical Aspects and Treatment Strategies." In *Obsessive-Compulsive Disorders: Practical Management,* eds. Jenike, Michael A., Lee Baer, and William E. Minichiello. St. Louis: Mosby, 1998.

Frost, Randy O., David F. Tolin, Gail Steketee, Kristin E. Fitch, and Alexandra Selbo-Bruns. "Excessive Acquisition in Hoarding." *Journal of Anxiety Disorders,* 23 (2009): 632–639.

Grisham, Jessica R., Randy O. Frost, Gail Steketee, Hyo-Jin Kim, Anna Tarkoff, and Sarah Hood. "Formation of Attachment to Possessions in Compulsive Hoarding." *Journal of Anxiety Disorders,* 23 (2009): 357–361.

Grisham, Jessica R., Gail Steketee, and Randy O. Frost. "Interpersonal Problems and Emotional Intelligence in Compulsive Hoarding." *Depression and Anxiety,* 25 (2008): 63–71.

Hartl, Tamara L., Shannon R. Duffany, George J. Allen, Gail Steketee, and Randy O. Frost. "Relationships Among Compulsive Hoarding, Trauma, and Attention-Deficit/Hyperactivity Disorder." *Behaviour Research and Therapy,* 43 (2005): 269–276.

Hartl, Tamara L., Randy O. Frost, George J. Allen, Thilo Deckersbach, Gail Steketee, Shannon R. Duffany, and Cary R. Savage. "Actual and Perceived Memory Deficits in

Individuals with Compulsive Hoarding." *Depression and Anxiety,* 20 (2004): 59–69.

Iervolino, Alessandra C., Nader Perroud, Miguel Angel Fullana, Michel Guipponi, Lynn Cherkas, David A. Collier, and David Mataix-Cols. "Prevalence and Heritability of Compulsive Hoarding: A Twin Study." *American Journal of Psychiatry,* 166:10 (October 2009): 1156–1161.

Kellett, Stephen, Rebecca Greenhalgh, Nigel Beail, and Nicola Ridgway. "Compulsive Hoarding: An Interpretive Phenomenological Analysis." *Behavioural and Cognitive Psychotherapy,* 38 (2010) 141–155.

Leckman, James F., and Michael H. Bloch. "A Developmental and Evolutionary Perspective on Obsessive-Compulsive Disorder: Whence and Whither Compulsive Hoarding?" *American Journal of Psychiatry,* 165:10 (October 2008): 1229–1233.

Lee, Royce. "Childhood Trauma and Personality Disorder: Toward a Biological Model." *Current Psychiatry Reports,* 8 (2006): 43–52.

Mueller, Astrid, James E. Mitchell, Ross D. Crosby, Heide Glaesmer, and Martina de Zwaan. "The Prevalence of Compulsive Hoarding and its Association with Compulsive Buying in a German Population-Based Sample." *Behaviour Research and Therapy,* 47 (2009): 705–709.

Muroff, Jordana, Gail Steketee, Jessica Rasmussen, Amanda Gibson, Christiana Bratiotis, and Cristina Sorrentino. "Group Cognitive and Behavioral Treatment for Compulsive Hoarding: A Preliminary Trial." *Depression and Anxiety,* 26 (2009): 634–640.

O'Connor, Anahad. "A Clue to the Hoarder's Compulsion for Clutter." *New York Times,* June 1, 2004.

Parker-Pope, Tara. "A Clutter Too Deep for Mere Bins and Shelves." www.nytimes.com, January 1, 2008.

Patronek, Gary J., and Jane N. Nathanson. "A Theoretical Perspective to Inform Assessment and Treatment Strategies for Animal Hoarders." *Clinical Psychology Review,* 29 (2009): 274–281.

Pollak, Seth D., and Pawan Sinha. "Effects of Early Experience on Children's Recognition of Facial Displays of Emotion." *Developmental Psychology,* 38:5 (2002): 784–791.

Preston, Stephanie D., Jordana R. Muroff, and Steven M. Wengrovitz. "Investigating the Mechanisms of Hoarding from an Experimental Perspective." *Depression and Anxiety,* 26 (2009): 425–437.

Samuels, Jack F., et al. "Sex-Specific Clinical Correlates of Hoarding in Obsessive-Compulsive Disorder." *Behaviour Research and Therapy,* 46 (2008): 1040–1046.

Saxena, Sanjaya, Arthur L. Brody, Karron M. Maidment, Erlyn C. Smith, Narineh Zohrabi, Elyse Katz, Stephanie K. Baker, and Lewis R. Baxter, Jr. "Cerebral Glucose Metabolism in Obsessive-Compulsive Hoarding." *American Journal of Psychiatry,* 161:6 (June 2004): 1038–1048.

Saxena, Sanjaya. "Is Compulsive Hoarding a Genetically and Neurobiologically Discrete Syndrome? Implications for Diagnostic Classification." *American Journal of Psychiatry,* 164:3 (March 2007): 380–384.

Saxena, Sanjaya. "Recent Advances in Compulsive Hoarding." *Current Psychiatry Reports,* 10 (2008): 297–303.

Steketee, Gail, and Randy Frost. "Compulsive Hoarding: Current Status of the Research." *Clinical Psychology Review,* 23 (2003): 905–927.

Timpano, Kiara R., Julia D. Buckner, J. Anthony Richey, Dennis L. Murphy, and Norman B. Schmidt. "Exploration of

Anxiety Sensitivity and Distress Tolerance as Vulnerability Factors for Hoarding Behaviors." *Depression and Anxiety,* 26 (2009): 343–353.

Tolin, David F, Kristen E. Fitch, Randy O. Frost, and Gail Steketee. "Family Informants' Perceptions of Insight in Compulsive Hoarding." *Cognitive Therapy and Research,* 34 (2010): 69–81.

Tolin, David F., Randy O. Frost, and Gail Steketee. "An Open Trial of Cognitive-Behavioral Therapy for Compulsive Hoarding." *Behaviour Research and Therapy,* 45:7 (July 2007): 1461–1470.

Turton, Shaun. "Melbourne Firefighters Call for Action on Hoarding." *Moreland Leader,* October 2, 2009.

Wincze, Jeffrey P., Gail Steketee, and Randy O. Frost. "Categorization in Compulsive Hoarding." *Behaviour Research and Therapy,* 45 (2007): 63–72.

BOOKS

Arluke, Arnold, and Celeste Killeen. *Inside Animal Hoarding: The Case of Barbara Erickson and her 552 Dogs.* West Lafayette, Ind.: Purdue University Press, 2009.

Frost, Randy O., and Gail Steketee. *Stuff: Compulsive Hoarding and the Meaning of Things.* New York: Houghton Mifflin Harcourt Publishing Company, 2010.

Kant, Jared, Martin Franklin, and Linda Wasmer Andrews. *The Thought That Counts: A Firsthand Account of One Teenager's Experience with Obsessive-Compulsive Disorder.* New York: Oxford University Press, 2008.

King, William Davies. *Collections of Nothing.* Chicago: University Of Chicago Press, 2009.

Kreger, Randi. *The Essential Family Guide to Borderline Personality Disorder: New Tools and Techniques to Stop Walking on Eggshells.* Center City, Minn.: Hazelden, 2008.

Lawson, Christine Ann. *Understanding the Borderline Mother: Helping Her Children Transcend the Intense, Unpredictable, and Volatile Relationship.* Lanham, Md.: Rowman & Littlefield, 2004.

Lehrer, Jonah. *How We Decide.* New York: Houghton Mifflin Harcourt Publishing Company, 2009.

Muensterberger, Werner. *Collecting: An Unruly Passion.* New York: Houghton Mifflin Harcourt Publishing Company, 1995.

Nathiel, Susan. *Daughters of Madness: Growing Up and Older with a Mentally Ill Mother.* Santa Barbara, Calif.: Praeger, 2007.

Neziroglu, Fugen, Jerome Bubrick, and Jose Yaryura-Tobias. *Overcoming Compulsive Hoarding: Why You Save and How You Can Stop.* Oakland, Calif.: New Harbinger Publications, 2004.

Osborn, Ian. *Tormenting Thoughts and Secret Rituals: The Hidden Epidemic of Obsessive-Compulsive Disorder.* New York: Dell Publishing Company, 1999.

Pascoe, Judith. *The Hummingbird Cabinet: A Rare and Curious History of Romantic Collectors.* Ithaca, New York: Cornell University Press, 2006.

Rapoport, Judith. *The Boy Who Couldn't Stop Washing: The Experience and Treatment of Obsessive-Compulsive Disorder.* New York: Penguin, 1991.

Solomon, Andrew. *The Noonday Demon: An Atlas of Depression.* New York: Simon & Schuster, 2001.

Tolin, David F., Randy O. Frost, and Gail Steketee. *Buried in Treasures: Help for Compulsive Acquiring, Saving, and Hoarding.* New York: Oxford University Press, 2007.

Dirty Secret

Jessie Sholl

INTRODUCTION

In *Dirty Secret: A Daughter Comes Clean About Her Mother's Compulsive Hoarding*, Jessie Sholl offers her readers a vivid look into the life of a hoarder's family. Her mother's curious disease, said to affect millions of Americans, causes Jessie to feel shame, embarrassment, and an unending desire to "cure" something she cannot fix. Through her mother's battles with compulsive hoarding and colon cancer, her father's serious heart attack, and a particularly stubborn scabies infestation, Jessie Sholl weaves together a new picture of a previously misunderstood disorder.

DISCUSSION QUESTIONS

1. "Maybe this time it'll work. Maybe this time it'll stay clean" (page 10). Throughout the memoir, Jessie's hopes are repeatedly raised and dashed as she tries to "fix" her mother's illness. Find a moment in the book in which Jessie is particularly hopeful, and one in which she is plagued by hopelessness. What feelings does Jessie associate with each instance?

2. Though Helen and Jessie have always had a tumultuous relationship, Jessie quickly makes her way to Minneapolis when she finds out about her mother's cancer. What does this say about their mother/daughter relationship? How does it relate to any mother/daughter relationships you've been personally involved in?

3. "Clearly, Roger's death had triggered my mother's true hoarding. And what disturbed me most was that she couldn't even tell" (page 16). Helen acknowledges that she is a hoarder, yet Jessie suspects she does not see the full extent of her disorder. Do you think there are moments when Helen feels remorse for her actions? If so, cite specific examples and discuss what may have triggered Helen's awareness.

4. "Also, like many hoarders, my mother reports feeling safer when she's surrounded by her possessions . . ." (page 27). Has there ever been a material object that you felt close to, one that made you feel safe? Discuss your feelings with the group. Why do you think this particular object drew so much of your attention? Can you imagine feeling that way about *all* of your material possessions, the way Helen does in the book?

5. What does each person in *Dirty Secret* fear the most? How do these fears affect his or her life, and do you think anyone has overcome his or her fear by the end of the book? If so, how?

6. One of the symptoms of compulsive hoarding is extreme indecision, a symptom Helen suffers from continuously throughout the book. How do you make difficult decisions? Discuss your decision-making tactics with the group. Has there ever been a time when you had difficulty making an important decision? How did you feel?

7. Sandy and Helen have some obvious differences, but are there any ways in which they are similar? Discuss with your group to see if you can find any hidden similarities.

8. "I liked having rules. I liked knowing that someone was aware of my whereabouts, that an adult was paying attention" (page 42). Teenage rebelliousness is common in our society, yet Jessie admits to craving structure. How do you reconcile her simultaneous desires to rebel as well as to adhere to a set of rules?

9. According to Jessie, she first became rebellious when she turned thirteen. To what extent do you think her rebellion was a reaction to her mother's disorder? To what extent do you think it was natural teenage inclination?

10. "There's no demonstrable link between hoarding and early material deprivation. But there is a link between hoarding and *emotional* deprivation. . . . Her cold and chaotic childhood home was the perfect breeding ground for the mental illness that would end up affecting us all" (page 81). Look back on the passages in which Helen's childhood is depicted. Did they change the way you felt about Helen? If so, how?

11. "I get a thrill each time I discard something. Getting rid of things is liberating. It's invigorating. It's easy" (page 150). Do you think that Jessie's need to throw things away is a reaction to her

mother's disorder? Discuss how your parents' actions when you were a child affected your behavior today; in what way does your behavior mirror or reject your parents' behaviors?

12. When Jessie and David's potential subletter calls their apartment "dirty," Jessie has a very strong reaction. Why do you think this was the case?

13. "I thought she'd finally understood the effect her behavior has had on me. I thought she even felt bad about it. I was wrong" (page 270). To what extent do you think Helen is aware of the pain she causes others, particularly Jessie? Are there moments in the book in which Helen is more acutely aware of her actions and their repercussions?

14. "And then I recognize it: Like stumbling upon the remains of a village buried by lava, the evidence of my last cleanup attempt lives on underneath. . . ." (pages 13–14). Why do you think Jessie continues to clean her mother's house after numerous failed attempts? In the end, what is it that finally causes Jessie to separate herself from the house for good . . . at least, for now?

15. Toward the end of the book, Jessie remembers old advice she picked up during her mother's time at The Club: "You can't change anyone else. You can only change yourself" (page 299). After numerous attempts, do you think Jessie is successful in any way in changing her mother? Similarly, what changes do you see in Jessie over the course of the book?

16. While hoarding is a specific disease, does it remind you of other illnesses such as alcoholism or drug addiction? Do Helen and Jessie's struggles seem similar to those in a parent-child relationship when the parent has an alcohol or drug problem? In what ways are their struggles unique because of Helen's hoarding?

READING GROUP ENHANCERS

1. As a group, watch some of the popular television shows that focus on hoarding. Then, re-read the generally accepted definition of hoarding found on page 21. Discuss: In what ways do you think hoarding is depicted accurately in pop culture? In which ways to do you feel it is falsified, or sensationalized?

2. Split your discussion group into two sections. Have one section make a timeline of the major turning points in Jessie's life and the other make a timeline of the major turning points in Helen's. After both timelines are completed, look for the major similarities and differences between the two. Then, discuss: Did the timelines add to your understanding of Jessie and Helen's relationship? Of Helen's disorder? If so, how?

3. If you're feeling particularly brave, do a Google search for "scabies," like Jessie did. Warning: The results are not pretty. However, they may add to your understanding of the family's bout with the disease.

4. On page 239, Jessie offers a beautiful description of the village where she and David lived outside Rome. Try to find more information about and pictures of other villages that surround the city of Rome. If you were to create an "Italian self," like Jessie does on the plane, what would your "Italian self" be like?

5. To learn more about author Jessie Sholl and read her blog, visit her website at www.jessie-sholl.com.

AUTHOR QUESTIONS

Q: In her review of *Dirty Secret*, author Stephanie Elizondo Griest applauds you for your "ceaseless courage." Where did you find the courage to begin writing such a personal book? Did the project become emotionally overwhelming at any point?

A: First of all, I don't feel particularly brave, and I'm very flattered by the idea that I had ceaseless courage. I wish it were true! The book began—in my head, anyway—about six or seven years ago; one day I happened to tell my husband about how I used to stare out the windows of my elementary school when I was ten and gaze back and forth between my mother's house and my dad and my stepmom's, and about the very different visceral reactions I had when I looked at each house. It was just a short anecdote, but as soon as I was done he said, "You know you need to write about this, right?" which of course I laughed off. But it ended up being the first scene I wrote for *Dirty Secret*.

It wasn't until I started writing health articles that I began to really think seriously about working on a book about hoarding. Especially after I joined the Children of Hoarders support group, because the shame and embarrassment that we all carry/carried around is just so ridiculous and unnecessary. Also, what helped while I wrote *Dirty Secret* was to push aside the thought that anyone was ever going to read it. Anytime I've written about myself I do that. I find it freeing and extremely helpful.

In terms of the project becoming emotionally overwhelming, it did, but only after I turned it in to my editor. The next day a serious exhaustion hit me and all I wanted to do was sleep for weeks.

Q: Were you concerned at all about how your mom would react to the book?

A: I wasn't concerned because I asked her permission before I wrote a word of it—if she'd objected at all, I wouldn't have written it. Thankfully, she was absolutely supportive of the idea. She read most of the book before it was published and loved it.

Q: *Dirty Secret* is the first memoir to be written by the child of a compulsive hoarder. How do you feel about breaking into uncharted territory?

A: I'm proud to be the first person to write a memoir about it, but I don't feel particularly groundbreaking—I'm sure that if I hadn't done it, someone else would have sooner rather than later. I'm just happy to get people talking about how hoarding affects families, and I'll be thrilled if my book allows others to feel freer about exposing their secrets.

Q: In recent years, the concept of "hoarding" has gone mainstream; people have familiarized themselves with the term through popular television shows like *Hoarders, Clean House,* and *Clean Sweep.* What are your feelings about the presence of compulsive hoarding in national media and pop culture? Do you think it is accurately depicted?

A: Overall, I think the television shows about hoarding are a good thing. Occasionally they can feel exploitative, but I like the fact that now when I say "my mother is a compulsive hoarder," almost everyone understands what I'm talking about. Before *Dirty Secret* was published and when the television shows were just beginning, I'd have people who didn't know what hoarding was—they'd never heard of it. After a while of me trying to explain they'd say something like, "Oh, right, a crazy cat lady!" Now people are beginning to understand that hoarding is a mental illness, just like schizophrenia or bipolar disorder.

In general, I think the shows accurately depict hoarded homes, although it's important to remember that they usually show the most egregious cases. Hoarding itself is a difficult disorder to accurately depict in a one-hour show because, in my opinion, it's very rare to find a person who is *just* a hoarder. There are so many mental illnesses that go along with it—and each individual is unique in their afflictions and levels of the afflictions—so to really delve into the psychology of each hoarder on the show would require a mini-series at the least.

Q: At the end of the book, you mention that other people reacted positively when you told them about your mother's disorder; many of them said they had a personal connection to hoarding as well. Did this surprise you?

A: This absolutely shocked me. I would say that the most rewarding part of writing the book so far has been those moments when someone tells me about their mother, brother, cousin being a hoarder; every time I hear it I feel less freakish, and it seems the person does as well. I also really appreciate the fact that no one has ever judged me harshly for being the daughter of a hoarder. No one. Maybe that expression is true: all our secrets are the same. I only wish I'd known it earlier, because I spent way too long being ashamed of something that didn't warrant it.

Q: On page 225, you describe your feelings of hesitation as you considered joining the Children of Hoarders online support group. What advice would you give to someone who was experiencing similar hesitations?

A: I would say that I understand the hesitation, but to go for it. You can always join under a pseudonym and lurk until you feel comfortable posting. There's so much to learn and it's just an incredible feeling to find people who understand *exactly* how you feel. It changed everything for me.

Q: Did you have to do a lot of research for this book, or did most of your knowledge of the disorder come from years of having been in such close proximity to it?

A: I did a lot of research for the book. I read everything I could get my hands on: books, academic articles and studies, interviews with experts; I also interviewed one of the most renowned specialists in the field. I enjoy the research process, so it didn't feel like work at all. I think having been in such close proximity to hoarding helped in terms of recognizing parts of it—for example, the information-processing deficits that most hoarders have—but otherwise, before I began the writing and the research I really didn't know much more about the disorder itself than, say, a viewer of *Hoarders* or *Hoarding: Buried Alive*.

Q: You've written numerous articles about health-related issues. Do you find that your research process is different for an article about an issue that hasn't affected you personally? Similarly, which did you find easier to write—a work you could distance yourself from or one that was so inevitably tied to your own life like *Dirty Secret*?

A: That's a good question. The process of writing *Dirty Secret* compared to an article (besides the obvious fact that my health articles are not book-length), was different in that I had to think of it in terms of scenes, with information about hoarding worked in throughout. I started out as a fiction writer, so I'm used to thinking in terms of arc and story, and I think (I hope!) that helped in terms of the narrative structure. And being part of the story, rather than writing as an outsider looking at a disease I'd never encountered, probably made it a little easier overall. But in terms of the research, it was pretty much the same: search for articles and studies, contact experts for interviews, hope they'll get back to you, and so on.

Q: Could you recommend some books or websites for people who want to learn more about compulsive hoarding?

A: I highly recommend a fascinating documentary about a daughter dealing with her mother's hoarding called *My Mother's Garden,* by Cynthia Lester. There's also a wonderful young adult novel called *Dirty Little Secrets* by Cynthia Omololu— the hoarding details are spot-on, plus it's suspenseful and well written. The book *Stuff: Compulsive Hoarding and the Meaning of Things* by Drs. Randy O. Frost and Gail Steketee uses case studies to explain hoarding in easily understandable terms.

As for websites, I would recommend starting with Children of Hoarders (www.childrenofhoarders.com). Even if you aren't the child of a hoarder you can look at the main page where they have an extremely thorough list of links and lots of information that's fitting, no matter where you fall on the spectrum—a child of a hoarder, a sibling, or maybe someone who's just curious about it and wants to know more. If you are the child of a hoarder I also strongly encourage you to look at websites for adult children of alcoholics. In terms of aftereffects, the overlap between children of hoarders and children of alcoholics is huge.

Q: What project are you currently working on?

A: I've just begun working on a literary thriller-type novel about two sisters. I'm also really fascinated by phobias—their history and potential cures—and hope to write about them someday.